FINISHED 50 POWERFUL SHORT STORIES FOR PROFICIENT ENGLISH LEARNERS (C2 ENGLISH)

Master Advanced English with Engaging Tales: Expand Vocabulary, Enhance Comprehension, and Sharpen Your Skills

Elizabeth Snow

Dear Readers,

Thank you for choosing Master Advanced English with Engaging Tales: Expand Vocabulary, Enhance Comprehension, and Sharpen Your Skills. This book was created with you in mind—curious learners eager to improve, storytellers looking for inspiration, and passionate individuals striving for mastery.

Each story in these pages was carefully crafted to not only entertain but also to challenge and expand your understanding of advanced English. As you journey through these tales, I hope you find moments of growth, discovery, and joy in learning.

Your feedback means the world to me. If this book has helped you on your language journey or sparked new ideas, I'd be deeply grateful if you could leave a review. Your thoughts and suggestions inspire improvement and help others discover the value of these stories.

Thank you for being part of this adventure. Keep reading, learning, and striving for excellence!

Warm regards,
Elizabeth Snow

CONTENTS

Title Page

Dedication

1. The Reverse Witness   1
2. The Night Without Stars   8
3. The Thoughts of Paintings   15
4. The Memory-Swappers   22
5. The Silence of Sound   28
6. The Last Breath   34
7. The Colorless World   40
8. The Eternal Echo   47
9. The Whispering Earth   54
10. The End of Shadows   61
11. The Body Clock   68
12. The Factory of Dreams   75
13. The Garden of Broken Thoughts   82
14. The Soundless World   89
15. The Clockwork Sun   95
16. The Paper God   101
17. The Dream Catcher's Curse   107
18. The Breath of Time   114

19. The Unseen Path   120
20. The Gravity of Memory   126
21. The Paper Thin Soul   133
22. The Eyes of Silence   140
23. The Wanderer Who Forgot   148
24. The Breathe of the Forest   155
25. The Last Dreamer's Ghost   162
26. The Sky Above the Stars   169
27. The Grief Collector   176
28. The Ink That Moves   184
29. The Cell of Time   191
30. The Smell of Memory   198
31. The Heartless Dream   205
32. The Forgotten Ocean   213
33. The Mapmaker's Curse   220
34. The Weight of Sound   227
35. The Mirror of Yesterday   234
36. The Taste of Stars   242
37. The Clock that Stopped   249
38. The Smoldering Sky   257
39. The Forest of Stolen Voices   265
40. The God Who Forgot   273
41. The Candle's Secret   281
42. The One Who Painted the World   288
43. The Invisible Thread   296
44. The Seed of Silence   304
45. The Breathing Book   312
46. The Falling Star Society   320

47. The Room Without Time	328
48. The Lighthouse Keeper's Secret	334
49. The Stolen Seasons	341
50. The Library of Souls	348
About The Author	355
	357

1. THE REVERSE WITNESS

The café was bustling with the typical hum of clinking mugs, low chatter, and the occasional hiss of the espresso machine. Seated in the corner, Jonah looked out of place. His fingers drummed an uneven rhythm on the wooden table, his eyes flitting toward the entrance every few seconds. A faint sheen of perspiration glistened on his forehead despite the chill in the air.

Opposite him sat Lydia, her expression caught somewhere between **incredulity** and curiosity. She sipped her cappuccino, watching Jonah as though he might disappear if she blinked.

"So," she began cautiously, placing her cup back on its saucer, "you see the future?"

Jonah nodded curtly, his jaw tightening.

"Not all of it," he clarified, his voice tinged with frustration. "Just specific events. Think of it as... snapshots. A mosaic of what's to come."

Lydia leaned back in her chair, her brow furrowing. "And you can't do anything about it?"

"No," he said, almost snapping. "That's the crux of it. No matter how hard I try, the events happen exactly as I see them. It's **immutable**. Unchangeable."

For a moment, Lydia said nothing. Then, with a quirk of her lips, she asked, "How does that even work? I mean, if you know something's going to happen, surely you can—"

"Stop it? Divert it?" Jonah interjected, his voice bitter. "That's what I thought at first. But every time I've tried, things end up worse."

Lydia frowned, folding her arms. "Worse how?"

Jonah exhaled sharply, his gaze dropping to his hands. "A car accident. Three years ago. I saw it—two cars colliding at the intersection near my apartment. I ran out, screaming, waving my arms to stop them. They swerved, trying to avoid me, and ended up hitting a pedestrian on the sidewalk instead."

Lydia's eyes widened. "Did the pedestrian…?"

Jonah nodded grimly. "She didn't make it. And the drivers? They survived. Minor injuries. But the guilt? That's on me."

A tense silence settled between them, punctuated only by the distant clatter of dishes. Jonah's shoulders slumped under the weight of his confession. Lydia, however, seemed **galvanized**.

"That doesn't mean you should stop trying," she said, her tone resolute.

Jonah looked up, his eyes **haunted**. "You don't understand. I can't save anyone. I'm a reverse witness, Lydia. I see, I know, but I can't intervene. It's like standing in the middle of a storm, watching the lightning strike, knowing it's coming, but being unable to warn the tree that it's about to be split in half."

The analogy hung in the air, heavy and vivid. Lydia pressed her lips together, her mind racing.

"What was the last thing you saw?" she asked finally, her voice softer now.

Jonah hesitated, his fingers curling into fists. "You don't want to know."

"Jonah," Lydia insisted, leaning forward. "Tell me."

He looked at her then, really looked, as though weighing whether to burden her with the knowledge. But in the end, the words tumbled out.

"A fire. Tonight. An apartment building downtown. I saw the flames consuming it, heard the screams. It'll be all over the news tomorrow morning."

Lydia paled. "And you're just going to… let it happen?"

Jonah flinched as though struck. "What do you want me to

do?" he shot back. "Call the fire department? Tell them what? That a building that hasn't even caught fire yet is about to go up in flames?"

"Yes!" Lydia exclaimed. "If there's even a chance—"

"And then what?" Jonah interrupted, his voice rising. "What if the fire doesn't happen because of a freak accident but because someone panics and causes it? What if my warning becomes the **catalyst**? This isn't a game, Lydia!"

The intensity of his words left her momentarily stunned. Jonah leaned back, running a hand through his hair. "I've learned the hard way that knowing the future doesn't mean I can rewrite it. It's like trying to outrun your own shadow."

Lydia studied him, her expression softening. "But isn't there any part of you that believes... maybe... just maybe... you could make a difference?"

Jonah laughed hollowly, the sound devoid of mirth. "Do you know how exhausting it is to carry that hope, only to see it dashed every single time?"

Before Lydia could respond, Jonah's phone buzzed on the table. He glanced at the screen, his face draining of color.

"What is it?" Lydia asked, alarmed.

Jonah's voice was barely a whisper. "The fire."

Lydia frowned. "What about it?"

"It's started."

She grabbed her own phone, quickly pulling up a news app. Sure enough, there it was—a breaking news alert about a fire raging through an apartment building downtown.

"Jonah..." she began, but he was already rising from his seat, grabbing his coat.

"I have to go," he said, his voice tight.

"Go where?" Lydia demanded, following him.

"To watch," he replied bitterly.

"To watch?" she repeated, incredulous. "Are you serious?"

"You think I enjoy this?" he snapped, spinning around to face her. "I hate it, Lydia. But being there... seeing it **unfold**... it's the only way I can make sense of this curse. Maybe one day, I'll find a clue, something I've missed before. Until then, I have to bear witness."

Lydia stared at him, torn between anger and pity. "You're not cursed," she said softly.

Jonah barked out a laugh. "Tell that to the people in that building."

And with that, he was gone, leaving Lydia standing in the middle of the café, the weight of his words pressing down on her like an unbearable truth.

Outside, the night air was **frigid**, but Jonah barely noticed. He walked briskly, his mind a storm of guilt and helplessness. As he approached the scene, the flames illuminated the sky, an eerie **juxtaposition** of beauty and destruction.

Jonah stood among the growing crowd of **onlookers**, the heat of the fire licking at his face. Sirens wailed in the distance, a **symphony** of urgency and despair.

For a brief moment, Jonah's eyes locked onto a woman on the third-floor balcony, her figure **silhouetted** against the inferno. She was holding a child, her face **contorted** in fear. Jonah's chest tightened.

"Jump!" someone in the crowd yelled.

And then, as if in slow motion, the woman leapt, clutching the child to her chest. Firefighters scrambled to catch them, their safety net barely in place.

Jonah exhaled shakily, a **flicker** of relief piercing his despair. But even as the woman and child were pulled to safety, he knew the rest wouldn't be so fortunate.

The future had **unfolded** exactly as he had seen it. Once again, Jonah was powerless to change it. And yet, he couldn't look away.

Comprehension Questions:

1. *Why does Jonah call himself a "reverse witness," and*

how does this affect his perspective on his abilities?
Jonah calls himself a "reverse witness" because he can see specific future events but cannot prevent them from happening. This ability causes him immense frustration and guilt, as his attempts to change the future often lead to worse outcomes. He feels powerless and trapped, likening his experience to standing in the middle of a storm and being unable to stop the inevitable.

2. **How does Lydia challenge Jonah's approach to his visions, and what is her perspective on hope?**
Lydia challenges Jonah by encouraging him to take action, even if it seems futile, believing there's always a chance to make a difference. She represents hope and determination, contrasting Jonah's despair and resignation. Lydia argues that carrying the possibility of change, even if it's uncertain, is worth the effort, and she questions Jonah's decision to simply watch events unfold.

Vocabulary List (C2 Level):

1. **Immutable** - Unable to be changed or altered.
   Jonah believed the future was immutable, no matter what actions he took.
2. **Incredulity** - The state of being unwilling or unable to believe something.
   Lydia's face was a picture of incredulity as Jonah explained his abilities.
3. **Catalyst** - Something that causes or accelerates change or events.
   Jonah feared his warning could become the catalyst for the fire.
4. **Symphony** - A complex and harmonious arrangement of sounds or elements.
   The sirens created a symphony of urgency and despair

during the fire.

5. **Juxtaposition** - The act of placing two contrasting things side by side.
   The flames created a haunting juxtaposition of beauty and destruction.
6. **Galvanized** - Shocked or motivated into action.
   Lydia was galvanized by Jonah's story, determined to convince him to act.
7. **Silhouetted** - Outlined against a lighter background.
   The woman holding the child was silhouetted against the blazing fire.
8. **Resignation** - Acceptance of something undesirable but inevitable.
   Jonah's voice was filled with resignation as he described his visions.
9. **Contorted** - Twisted or bent out of shape.
   The woman's face was contorted with fear as she stood on the balcony.
10. **Inferno** - A large, uncontrollable fire.
    The apartment building was consumed by a raging inferno.
11. **Flicker** - A brief or small movement or feeling.
    Jonah felt a flicker of relief when the woman and child were saved.
12. **Onlooker** - A person who watches an event without participating.
    Jonah stood among the onlookers as the fire blazed before him.
13. **Haunted** - Preoccupied with or troubled by guilt or worry.
    Jonah's eyes were haunted as he recounted the car accident he had witnessed.
14. **Unfolded** - Happened or became clear over time.
    The events of the fire unfolded exactly as Jonah had foreseen.
15. **Frigid** - Extremely cold.

The frigid air outside did little to cool the heat radiating from the fire.

2. THE NIGHT WITHOUT STARS

"Look up, Liora. What do you see?" Aron's voice echoed in the **cavernous** space, his lantern casting flickering shadows against the jagged walls.

Liora tilted her head, her dark eyes reflecting the dim light. Above them stretched an endless expanse of black rock, a far cry from the shimmering night skies of old. "I see emptiness," she replied, her voice laced with **melancholy**. "And silence."

Aron sighed, adjusting the straps of his pack. "That's all anyone sees now. Emptiness and silence. Do you ever wonder if the stories were true? That there were once lights in the sky, each one burning with its own fire?"

"They're not just stories," Liora said sharply. "My grandmother told me about them—how the stars used to guide travelers and make the oceans glimmer like liquid silver." She paused, her expression hardening. "And how greed stole them away."

Aron nodded, his gaze dropping. "The Elders said humanity dug too deep, searching for treasures they had no right to claim. They disturbed the balance, and the stars fell, burying themselves in the heart of the earth. A punishment, they called it."

Liora tightened her grip on her lantern. "Punishment or not, we're here to fix it."

"Fix it?" Aron let out a **mirthless** laugh. "We're just two people, Liora. Two people against an entire world that's forgotten what it means to hope."

"Then let's remind them," Liora said fiercely, her determination cutting through the gloom.

The two of them trudged deeper into the **labyrinthine** tunnels, the **oppressive** darkness pressing in on all sides. The air grew colder, heavier, as though the weight of the missing stars bore down on them.

"Do you think we'll find it?" Aron asked after a while, his voice softer now, almost childlike.

Liora glanced at him. Despite his bravado, Aron's face betrayed his **trepidation**. "We have to," she said simply. "Without the stars, the world is dying. Crops are failing. Rivers are drying up. People are losing their will to live."

Aron didn't reply, but his silence spoke volumes.

After hours of navigating the twisting passages, they reached a cavern unlike any they'd seen before. The walls glimmered faintly, as though imbued with a memory of light. At the center of the chamber lay a pool of liquid that **shimmered** like molten gold.

Liora stepped closer, her breath catching in her throat. "Aron," she whispered. "This… this is it. This is where the stars fell."

Aron approached cautiously, his lantern casting long shadows across the **shimmering** surface. "It looks... alive," he murmured.

"It is alive," came a voice, startling them both.

They spun around to see a figure emerging from the shadows—a woman draped in robes that seemed woven from the night itself. Her eyes glowed faintly, like embers in the dark.

"Who are you?" Liora demanded, instinctively stepping in front of Aron.

The woman tilted her head, a faint smile playing on her lips. "I am the Keeper," she said. "Guardian of the fallen stars."

"The Keeper?" Aron echoed, his voice trembling. "You're real?"

"As real as the stars you seek to reclaim," the woman replied. "But tell me, why have you come?"

Liora squared her shoulders. "To restore the balance. The world is dying without the stars, and we—"

"—think you can retrieve them and fix everything," the Keeper interrupted, her tone laced with **skepticism**. "Do you have any idea what you're asking for?"

"We're asking for hope," Liora shot back. "For light. For life."

The Keeper regarded them for a long moment, her glowing eyes **unblinking**. "And what makes you think humanity deserves the stars again? They were cast down for a reason, buried to protect the very balance you speak of."

Aron stepped forward hesitantly. "Maybe humanity doesn't deserve them," he admitted. "But without them, there won't be a humanity left to argue over who's deserving."

The Keeper's gaze softened, and for the first time, her **ethereal** composure seemed to falter. "The stars are not mere trinkets to be unearthed," she said. "They are fragments of the universe's soul. To retrieve them is to awaken forces you cannot comprehend."

"Then help us comprehend," Liora urged. "Teach us what we need to know. Guide us."

The Keeper hesitated, her luminous eyes flickering like a dying flame. "Very well," she said at last. "But know this: the path to reclaiming the stars is **fraught** with peril. It will demand everything of you."

"We're ready," Liora said without hesitation.

Aron glanced at her, doubt **flickering** in his eyes, but he nodded nonetheless.

The Keeper extended her hand, and as Liora took it, the cavern around them seemed to dissolve, replaced by a vast expanse of **shimmering** light. Stars floated in the void, their brilliance both beautiful and overwhelming.

"This," the Keeper said, her voice **reverberating** through the infinite space, "is what you seek to restore. But to do so, you must prove your worth. Each star is bound by a trial—an echo of the very forces that hold the universe together: courage, compassion, sacrifice, and wisdom. Only by mastering these can you reclaim the stars."

"What happens if we fail?" Aron asked, his voice barely above a whisper.

The Keeper's expression darkened. "Then the stars will remain where they are, and the world will fade into eternal darkness."

A heavy silence followed her words, the weight of their task settling over them like a shroud.

"Where do we begin?" Liora asked finally.

The Keeper gestured, and one of the stars drifted closer, its light pulsating rhythmically. "Begin with courage," she said.

The star's light enveloped them, and suddenly they were no longer in the void. They stood in a dense forest, the air thick with the scent of earth and decay. Shadows moved between the trees, and a low growl echoed in the distance.

"What now?" Aron asked, his voice shaking.

"Now," Liora said, gripping his arm tightly, "we find the courage to face whatever comes."

The growl grew louder, and from the shadows emerged a creature unlike anything they'd ever seen—a monstrous **amalgamation** of claws, teeth, and fury.

Aron froze, his breath coming in shallow gasps. Liora, however, stepped forward, her voice steady despite the fear in her eyes. "We're not here to fight," she said firmly. "We're here to prove ourselves."

The creature paused, its eyes narrowing. For a moment, it seemed as though it might attack. But then, slowly, it stepped aside, revealing a path bathed in starlight.

Liora turned to Aron, a small smile playing on her lips. "Courage," she said simply.

Aron managed a shaky laugh, following her down the path. "One trial down," he muttered. "Three to go."

As they disappeared into the light, the Keeper watched from afar, her expression unreadable. "May you succeed where others have failed," she whispered.

Comprehension Questions:

1. **What motivates Liora and Aron to seek the fallen stars, and how do they justify their mission to the Keeper?**
   Liora and Aron are motivated by the dire state of the world—crops failing, rivers drying up, and people losing hope. They justify their mission by arguing that humanity needs the stars not out of entitlement but as a means to survive and restore balance. Aron admits humanity might not deserve the stars but insists that without them, humanity won't survive to earn redemption.
2. **What does the first trial, courage, reveal about Liora and Aron's characters, and how does it reflect the Keeper's warning?**
   The trial of courage reveals Liora's bravery and determination to confront challenges head-on, while Aron's hesitation underscores his doubts but also his willingness to follow. The encounter with the creature emphasizes the Keeper's warning that reclaiming the stars requires facing peril and proving worth through actions, not mere intent.

Vocabulary List (C2 Level):

1. **Cavernous** - Vast, hollow, and deep, resembling a large cave.
   The cavernous space echoed with Aron's voice, amplifying its sound.
2. **Melancholy** - A deep, pensive sadness.
   Liora's voice was laced with melancholy as she described

the empty sky.

3. **Mirthless** - Lacking genuine joy or happiness.
   Aron let out a mirthless laugh, his tone filled with bitterness.
4. **Labyrinthine** - Complicated and maze-like.
   The labyrinthine tunnels stretched endlessly into the darkness.
5. **Shimmer** - To shine with a soft, flickering light.
   The pool at the cavern's center shimmered like molten gold.
6. **Ethereal** - Delicate and otherworldly, almost too perfect for this world.
   The Keeper's robes had an ethereal quality, as if woven from starlight.
7. **Trepidation** - A feeling of fear or anxiety about something that may happen.
   Aron's face betrayed his trepidation as he questioned their mission.
8. **Skepticism** - Doubt about the truth or authenticity of something.
   The Keeper's tone was laced with skepticism as she questioned their resolve.
9. **Reverberating** - Echoing repeatedly as a sound or effect.
   The Keeper's voice reverberated through the infinite space of the void.
10. **Amalgamation** - A mixture or combination of different elements.
    The creature was a monstrous amalgamation of claws, teeth, and fury.
11. **Oppressive** - Overwhelming and heavy, often causing discomfort.
    The oppressive darkness of the tunnels made it hard to breathe.
12. **Prove** - To demonstrate the truth or worth of something through action.

Liora stepped forward to prove their courage to the monstrous creature.

13. **Unblinking** - Steady and unwavering, often referring to a gaze or focus.

    The Keeper's glowing eyes remained unblinking as she judged their intentions.

14. **Fraught** - Filled with or destined to result in something undesirable.

    The Keeper warned them that the path to reclaiming the stars was fraught with peril.

3. THE THOUGHTS OF PAINTINGS

The gallery was quiet, save for the soft murmur of distant footsteps and the occasional shuffle of someone shifting their weight. Ezra stood before his latest work, a sprawling canvas drenched in shadows and whispers of light, the paint still faintly glistening in places. He clasped his hands behind his back, tilting his head as though **scrutinizing** his own creation.
"Masterpiece," murmured a voice to his left. He turned to find Marianne, the gallery curator, her dark curls framing a face that was always half-amused, half-skeptical. "The way you capture expression is **uncanny**, Ezra. Almost… too real."
He allowed himself a tight smile. "The goal of art is to provoke, isn't it? To make the observer feel."
Marianne stepped closer, her gaze fixed on the painting. It depicted a woman seated by a window, her hands clasped delicately in her lap, sunlight streaming through the glass and pooling around her feet. Her eyes were wide, her lips parted as though she were on the cusp of speaking.
"She looks like she's about to say something," Marianne said, almost to herself.
Ezra hesitated. "Perhaps she is."
Marianne frowned, glancing at him. "What do you mean by that?"
He waved her off. "Nothing. Just an artist's musings."
But it wasn't nothing. Ezra knew better. His works had a habit of unsettling people, though they could rarely articulate why.

It wasn't just their **hyperrealism** or the depth of emotion he infused into them. It was something more—something Ezra himself didn't fully understand.

Until the night he stayed late at the gallery.
The building was silent, the kind of silence that pressed against your ears and made you hyperaware of every creak and rustle. Ezra moved among his paintings, the faint scent of oil and varnish lingering in the air. He paused before the piece Marianne had admired earlier.
"Why do you look so terrified?" he murmured, his eyes tracing the woman's features.
"I'm afraid of what you'll uncover."
The voice was soft, trembling, and unmistakably real. Ezra stumbled back, his breath catching in his throat. His eyes darted around the room, but he was alone.
"Who's there?" he demanded, his voice louder than he intended.
Silence. Then, faintly: "I am here. You brought me to life, after all."
Ezra turned slowly back to the painting. The woman's expression had changed. Her lips were now pressed together, her gaze more piercing, as though she were **scrutinizing** him.
"This isn't possible," he whispered.
"And yet," the painting replied, "here we are."
Ezra's heart hammered in his chest as he stepped closer. "What... what are you?"
"I am what you made me," the woman said. Her voice was steady now, laced with an edge of bitterness. "You painted me, poured your soul into every brushstroke, and in doing so, you gave me... awareness."
He shook his head, disbelief warring with the evidence before him. "This isn't real. Paintings don't speak."
"Perhaps not all paintings," she replied. "But yours do."

Ezra stumbled back into a bench, sitting heavily. His mind raced. Had he gone mad? Was exhaustion playing tricks on him?

"I know your secrets," the woman continued, her voice soft but insistent. "Every thought you had while creating me, every memory you drew upon. It's all here, embedded in the layers of paint."

Ezra stared at her, his throat dry. "What do you want from me?"

"What do you want, Ezra?" she countered. "Why do you paint us with such sorrow, such desperation? What is it you're trying to exorcise?"

He couldn't answer.

The days that followed were a blur of unease. Ezra avoided the gallery, yet the whispers followed him. At home, his older works seemed to watch him from their frames, their painted eyes glinting with something akin to accusation.

Then, one evening, Marianne called.

"Ezra," she said, her voice tight. "You need to come to the gallery. Now."

"What's wrong?" he asked, already pulling on his coat.

"It's… hard to explain. Just come."

When he arrived, the gallery was buzzing. A small crowd had gathered around his painting of the seated woman, their faces pale and drawn.

"What's going on?" Ezra demanded, pushing through.

Marianne grabbed his arm, her nails digging into his sleeve. "It's your painting. It… it spoke."

Ezra froze. "What do you mean?"

"I mean," Marianne said, her voice trembling, "it accused someone. A man. Of… murder."

The words hit him like a blow. He stared at the painting. The woman's expression had changed again; her eyes blazed with intensity, her mouth set in a grim line.

"It was him," she said, her voice clear and cold. "He killed me."

The crowd murmured in shock. A man standing at the back of the room turned and fled, shoving his way through the throng.

Ezra's legs felt like lead as he stepped closer to the painting. "What have you done?" he whispered.

"What you were too afraid to do," the woman replied. "I told the truth."

The incident made headlines. "Painter's Work Solves Cold Case!" the tabloids screamed. Overnight, Ezra's fame skyrocketed, but so did the scrutiny. People flocked to his exhibitions, not for the art but for the secrets they hoped the paintings would reveal.

His studio became a prison. He worked feverishly, his mind consumed by fear and **obsession**. The more he painted, the more his creations spoke, their voices a **cacophony** of truths and confessions.

One evening, as he stared at a half-finished portrait, a thought struck him.

"What about my secrets?" he asked aloud.

The painting before him—a young man with a **wistful** smile—tilted his head. "What about them?"

"Do you know them?" Ezra demanded, his voice rising.

The man in the painting smiled faintly. "Of course. We all do."

Ezra's blood ran cold. "Then why haven't you said anything?"

The painting's smile widened. "Because you haven't painted the one who will."

Ezra's hands trembled as he stepped back. "No," he whispered. "I won't. I'll stop painting."

"Can you?" the painting asked, its voice echoing in the quiet room.

Ezra fled.

For weeks, he avoided his studio, the unfinished works gathering dust. But the urge to paint gnawed at him, relentless and **insidious**. He dreamed of canvases and colors, of faces begging to be brought to life.

One night, unable to resist, he returned to his easel. His hands moved of their own accord, the brush gliding across the canvas

as though guided by an unseen force.
When he finished, he stepped back, his chest tight with dread.

The face on the canvas was his own.
"You knew this was inevitable," the painting said, its voice a mirror of his own. "You've spent your life hiding behind us, using us to speak truths you couldn't face. But now, it's time."
Ezra stared at his painted likeness, the weight of its words pressing down on him. "Time for what?" he whispered.
"To reveal the secrets you've buried," the painting replied. "Starting with the one that haunts you the most."
Ezra sank to his knees, his breath coming in shallow gasps. The truth clawed its way to the surface, dark and unrelenting.
And the painting began to speak.

Comprehension Questions:

1. **How does Ezra's relationship with his paintings change after he discovers they can speak, and how does it affect his perception of his work?**
   Ezra initially sees his paintings as a means of artistic expression, but his perception changes drastically when they begin speaking, revealing secrets and unsettling truths. He becomes increasingly fearful of their power, realizing they reflect his deepest thoughts and emotions. This newfound awareness leads to obsession and paranoia, as he struggles to reconcile his role as their creator with the truths they reveal.

2. **What is the significance of the painting accusing someone of murder, and how does it impact Ezra's life and reputation?**
   The painting's accusation of murder shocks the public and catapults Ezra into fame, as people begin seeing his work as a conduit for hidden truths. However, this event also brings immense scrutiny and pressure, trapping Ezra in a cycle of fear and compulsion to create. It

highlights the duality of his art's power—both as a source of justice and as a personal burden.

Vocabulary List (C2 Level):

1. **Uncanny** - Strange or mysterious in a way that is unsettling or difficult to explain.
   The way Ezra's paintings captured emotion was so uncanny it felt alive.
2. **Scrutinize** - To examine or inspect closely and thoroughly.
   Ezra tilted his head, scrutinizing his latest painting for flaws.
3. **Ethereal** - Extremely delicate or light in a way that seems otherworldly.
   The woman in the painting had an ethereal beauty, as though she weren't real.
4. **Treacherous** - Dangerous or deceptive.
   The calm in Ezra's studio felt treacherous, masking the chaos of his thoughts.
5. **Hyperrealism** - A genre of art characterized by extremely realistic imagery.
   The hyperrealism in Ezra's paintings made them seem like photographs.
6. **Obsession** - A persistent preoccupation or fascination with something.
   Ezra's obsession with his paintings grew as they began revealing secrets.
7. **Cacophony** - A harsh, discordant mixture of sounds.
   The voices of the paintings created a cacophony in Ezra's mind.
8. **Insidious** - Proceeding subtly but with harmful effects.
   The urge to paint crept back into Ezra's life, insidious and relentless.

9. **Accusation** - A claim that someone has done something wrong or illegal.
   The painting's accusation of the man in the crowd sent ripples through the room.
10. **Wistful** - Having a feeling of vague or regretful longing.
    The portrait of the young man bore a wistful smile that seemed full of secrets.

4. THE MEMORY-SWAPPERS

The Memory Exchange Pavilion stood at the center of the city like a **monolithic** temple of progress. Its glass facade reflected a **kaleidoscope** of colors, symbolic of the memories it held within. Everyone in this society had the ability to trade their memories—a privilege, they called it. Others thought it a dangerous liberty, **fraught** with risks no one was prepared to confront.
"I just need a brief distraction," Elena muttered as she adjusted the hem of her coat. The queue outside the pavilion moved briskly, and she tightened her grip on her identification bracelet, the device that would facilitate the exchange. She had been here before, swapping mundane recollections for fleeting moments of thrill or serenity. But this time, her desperation was **palpable**.
"Next!" called an attendant, ushering her forward.
Elena hesitated, her eyes darting to the ceiling where undulating lights mimicked the **neural** waves of active memories.
"You seem nervous," the attendant remarked, scanning her bracelet. "Anything in particular you're looking for today?"
"Something to take my mind off things," she said quickly. "Something... adventurous, perhaps."
The attendant nodded, his expression neutral as he gestured toward the Memory Archive. "We have a selection in the 'Adventurer's Vault.' Take your pick, but remember: exchanges

are **irreversible** for the mandatory 72-hour period. No exceptions."

She nodded absently and entered the chamber, the walls lined with glowing panels. Each panel contained a memory encapsulated in liquid light, waiting for a recipient. Her fingers hovered over a few—a mountaineer's ascent, a deep-sea dive—before she settled on one labeled "The Thrill of the Chase."

"Perfect," she murmured.

The exchange was seamless. She felt the familiar prickle at the base of her neck as her **neural** pathways adjusted to accommodate the new memory. Moments later, she exited the pavilion, her heart racing with the vivid imprint of a memory that wasn't hers.

At first, it was exhilarating. She felt the rush of wind as she darted through darkened streets, the adrenaline coursing through her veins as though she were being pursued. But as the scenes played out in her mind, she noticed something peculiar: a **visceral** dread that didn't align with the adventurous narrative she had expected.

Then came the images—**fragmented**, chaotic. A shadowed figure, a flash of silver, a **muffled** scream. Elena froze mid-step, her breath catching in her throat.

"This isn't right," she whispered, clutching her head as the memories surged forward.

She hurried home, her hands trembling as she locked the door behind her. Sitting at her kitchen table, she replayed the memory, focusing on the details. The chase wasn't a game; it was an escape. The shadowed figure wasn't a competitor but a pursuer. And the **muffled** scream...

Her stomach churned as she realized what she had unwittingly inherited. This was no fabricated thrill. It was the memory of a crime.

Panic set in. The identity of the person who had committed this act was now interwoven with her own recollections. She knew the feel of their footsteps, the sweat on their brow, the surge of satisfaction that followed the act of violence. But the memory was incomplete, **fragmented** by the limits of **neural** compatibility.

Elena paced the room, her thoughts racing. She couldn't keep this memory. But if she reported it, she might be implicated herself. The Memory Exchange Pavilion had strict rules about responsibility: once you acquired a memory, its consequences became yours.

"Think, Elena, think," she muttered, rubbing her temples.

Her thoughts were interrupted by a knock at the door. She froze, her breath hitching. Another knock, this one more insistent.

"Elena Clarke?" a voice called. "This is Detective Morris with the Bureau of Memory Regulation. We need to speak with you."

Her blood ran cold. How did they know? Had the memory been flagged? Slowly, she opened the door, her expression carefully neutral.

"Detective," she said, her voice steadier than she felt. "What's this about?"

Morris, a tall man with sharp eyes, studied her for a moment before stepping inside. His partner, a younger woman with a no-nonsense demeanor, followed.

"We're investigating an **anomaly** in the Memory Exchange system," Morris began. "It appears a classified memory was **inadvertently** released into the general archive."

Elena swallowed hard. "Classified?"

He nodded. "A high-priority case involving a violent crime. The memory was supposed to remain sealed as evidence but somehow ended up accessible to the public. We're tracking down everyone who might have accessed it."

Her mind raced. Did they know she had it? Or was this just a routine inquiry?

"I haven't noticed anything unusual," she lied, keeping her voice even.

The younger detective raised an eyebrow. "You seem nervous,

Ms. Clarke."

"Wouldn't you be?" she countered. "Having two detectives show up unannounced is hardly calming."

Morris gave her a tight smile. "Fair enough. We just need to scan your identification bracelet to confirm your recent exchanges."

Elena's heart pounded as she extended her wrist. The bracelet beeped softly as Morris scanned it. He frowned, glancing at the results.

"'The Thrill of the Chase,'" he read aloud. "Interesting choice."

"I thought it would be exciting," she said, forcing a laugh.

"Exciting," he repeated, his tone measured. "Did you experience anything... unexpected?"

She hesitated, her mind scrambling for an answer. "It felt a bit intense," she admitted. "But isn't that the point?"

Morris exchanged a glance with his partner, who nodded subtly.

"We may need to **confiscate** your bracelet temporarily," he said. "For analysis."

"I'm afraid that's not possible," Elena said, her voice rising. "It contains personal memories—my memories."

"That's precisely why we need it," the younger detective said. "To ensure there's been no **tampering**."

Tampering. The word sent a jolt of fear through her.

"I'll need to consult a lawyer," she said, stepping back.

Comprehension Questions:

1. **What dilemma does Elena face after acquiring the memory labeled "The Thrill of the Chase," and how does it affect her decision-making?**
   Elena discovers that the memory she acquired isn't an adventurous thrill but the fragmented recollection of

a violent crime. This puts her in a moral and legal dilemma: reporting the memory risks implicating her in the crime, while staying silent could endanger others. The weight of the memory and its consequences forces her to confront her role in uncovering the truth.

2. **How do the detectives' investigation and Elena's reaction highlight the risks and ethical complexities of the Memory Exchange system?**

   The detectives' inquiry into a classified memory being released exposes the potential dangers of the Memory Exchange system, where personal and sensitive experiences can be misused. Elena's panic and hesitation underscore the ethical complexities of owning memories that carry serious consequences, raising questions about identity, responsibility, and the impact of shared experiences.

Vocabulary List (C2 Level):

1. **Monolithic** - Large, powerful, and uniform, often immovable or unchanging.
   The Memory Exchange Pavilion stood like a monolithic symbol of progress in the city.
2. **Kaleidoscope** - A constantly changing pattern or sequence of elements.
   The glass facade reflected a kaleidoscope of colors, mesmerizing passersby.
3. **Palpable** - So intense as to seem almost tangible.
   Elena's desperation was palpable as she approached the exchange counter.
4. **Irreversible** - Incapable of being undone or altered.
   The attendant reminded Elena that memory exchanges were irreversible for 72 hours.
5. **Visceral** - Relating to deep, inward feelings rather than intellect.

Elena felt a visceral dread as she relived the memory of the crime.

6. **Fragmented** - Broken into smaller, incomplete parts.
   The memory was fragmented, with chaotic images and disconnected sensations.
7. **Inadvertently** - Without intention; accidentally.
   A classified memory was inadvertently released into the public archive.
8. **Anomaly** - Something that deviates from the norm or expectations.
   The detectives were investigating an anomaly in the Memory Exchange system.
9. **Tampering** - Interfering with something to cause damage or alteration.
   The younger detective suspected tampering with Elena's identification bracelet.
10. **Neural** - Relating to the nerves or nervous system.
    The memory exchange altered Elena's neural pathways to accommodate the new recollection.
11. **Confiscate** - To take something officially, often as a penalty.
    The detective wanted to confiscate Elena's bracelet for further analysis.
12. **Muffled** - Not loud because of being obstructed in some way.
    The voices of the detectives became muffled as the memory overwhelmed her.

5. THE SILENCE OF SOUND

5. The Silence of Sound

The town of Galdora was **unnervingly** quiet. No whispers, no footsteps, no rustling leaves or distant hum of traffic. Sound had been stolen, replaced by an almost **tangible** void. For years, its residents had adapted, learning to rely on gestures, written words, and the nuances of facial expressions. But to most, the loss of sound was an enduring grief.

Except for Anton.

Anton had been deaf since birth, and silence had always been his companion. While others mourned the absence of sound, he remained unburdened. He had spent his life learning to "listen" with his body—the **vibration** of a slammed door, the rhythmic pulse of machinery, the faint tremor of footsteps on wooden floors. To him, sound was never something to be heard; it was something to be felt.

But Galdora's silence wasn't like the quiet Anton had known. It wasn't natural. There was no **vibration**, no **resonance**, no tactile hum of life. It was as though the air itself had been drained of energy, leaving a vacuum. Anton could feel the emptiness pressing against his skin.

One evening, as the sun dipped below the horizon, Anton sat at his weathered piano, his fingers hovering over the keys. The instrument had been a lifelong companion, though he had never heard it. His hands knew the movements, the patterns

that translated into melodies. He pressed a key—a soft C—and waited.
Nothing.
He frowned and struck another, harder this time. Still nothing. Not even the faintest **reverberation** beneath his fingertips.

Frustrated, he slammed both hands down on the keys, his palms smacking the polished wood. And then, something peculiar happened. A faint pulse rippled through his hands, up his arms, and into his chest. It was faint, but it was there. A **vibration**, a whisper of sound felt rather than heard.
Anton froze, his heart quickening. Slowly, deliberately, he pressed a single key again. This time, he focused not on the absence of sound but on the sensation beneath his fingertips. There it was—subtle, almost **perceptible**, but undeniably real.

Excitement coursed through him. Could it be that sound still existed, not as something to be heard but as something to be experienced?
The next day, Anton shared his discovery with Lila, the town's librarian and one of the few people who had always treated him as an equal. She was a petite woman with sharp, observant eyes and a perpetual air of curiosity.
"You felt **vibrations** from the piano?" she signed, her hands moving **fluidly**.
Anton nodded, his own hands animated as he replied. "It's faint, but it's there. I think sound hasn't disappeared—it's just hidden. We've been looking for it with our ears, but maybe that's the wrong approach."
Lila tilted her head, considering his words. "If you're right, this could change everything. But how do we prove it? The town has tried everything to bring sound back—experiments, rituals, even those absurd 'noise machines' from the city."
"None of them focused on **vibration**," Anton signed. "We need to start there."

Over the next few weeks, Anton and Lila worked tirelessly.

They began by experimenting with instruments—pianos, drums, violins—feeling for the faintest quivers of sound. They moved on to other objects: tuning forks, glass bottles, even their own voices.

One evening, as they worked in Lila's study, Anton struck a tuning fork against the edge of a table. He held it up, his fingers grazing its surface.

"Feel this," he signed, handing it to Lila.

Her eyes widened as she touched the vibrating metal. "It's like a heartbeat," she signed back.

Encouraged, they devised a plan to **amplify** the **vibrations**. Using an old phonograph as their base, they crafted a crude device with a large diaphragm and strings stretched taut like a spider's web. When Anton played the piano, the strings trembled in response, their **vibrations** magnified by the diaphragm.

The result was extraordinary. The **vibrations** were strong enough to be felt through the floor, resonating like a silent **symphony**.

The day they unveiled their invention to the townspeople, the square was packed. Anton sat at the piano, his fingers poised over the keys. The crowd watched in anticipation, their faces a mix of **skepticism** and hope.

He struck a chord.

A ripple spread through the ground, subtle at first but growing stronger. The crowd gasped as the **vibrations** coursed through their feet, their bodies. It was as if the town itself had come alive, pulsing with a silent rhythm.

Tears streamed down the faces of many in the crowd. They couldn't hear the music, but they could feel it, and for the first time in years, the void of silence was filled with something **profound**.

As the weeks passed, Anton's discovery transformed Galdora. The town embraced the idea of "felt sound," creating spaces where **vibrations** were **amplified**—concert halls with resonant floors, classrooms where students learned through tactile rhythms, even vibrational alarms for emergencies.

For Anton, the change was **bittersweet**. He had always lived in silence, and now his way of experiencing the world was shared by everyone. But he also knew that sound was more than just a physical phenomenon; it was a bridge, connecting people in ways he had never imagined.

One evening, as he and Lila sat on a bench overlooking the town, she turned to him and signed, "You've given Galdora its soul back."

Anton shook his head, a small smile on his lips. "No," he signed. "The soul was always there. We just needed to learn how to feel it."

And in the silence that wasn't truly silent, the town of Galdora thrummed with life once more.

Comprehension Questions:

1. **How does Anton's unique perspective on sound help him discover the hidden vibrations in Galdora, and how does this discovery transform the town?**
   Anton, being deaf since birth, perceives sound as vibrations rather than something heard. His sensitivity to tactile sensations allows him to realize that sound still exists in the form of vibrations. His discovery leads to the invention of a device that amplifies these vibrations, enabling the townspeople to experience sound through touch. This transformation revitalizes the community, creating new ways of connecting and experiencing the world.

2. **What role does Lila play in supporting Anton's discovery, and how does her collaboration contribute to their success?**
   Lila acts as a confidant and collaborator, validating

Anton's ideas and helping him experiment with instruments and devices. Her intellectual curiosity and belief in his perspective provide the encouragement and resources needed to refine his discovery. Together, their teamwork leads to the creation of a vibrational device that revolutionizes how the town experiences sound.

Vocabulary List (C2 Level):

1. **Unnervingly** - In a way that causes discomfort or unease.
   The town of Galdora was unnervingly quiet, with no sound at all.
2. **Tangible** - Perceptible by touch; clear and definite.
   The void of silence felt almost tangible, pressing against Anton's skin.
3. **Vibration** - A continuous, rapid motion or trembling.
   Anton felt the vibration of the piano keys beneath his fingers.
4. **Perceptible** - Able to be seen, heard, or felt.
   The vibrations from the tuning fork were faint but perceptible.
5. **Resonance** - The quality of a sound being deep, full, and reverberating.
   The town's new concert halls were designed to enhance tactile resonance.
6. **Symphony** - A complex and harmonious arrangement of sounds or elements.
   The vibrations created a silent symphony that everyone could feel.
7. **Amplify** - To increase the strength or effect of something.
   The device amplified the vibrations, allowing the entire crowd to feel them.
8. **Profound** - Deep, meaningful, or intense.

The townspeople felt a profound connection through the vibrations.

9. **Fluidly** - In a smooth and continuous manner.
   Lila signed fluidly, her hands moving gracefully as she communicated with Anton.
10. **Skepticism** - Doubt or disbelief about something.
    The townspeople watched Anton's demonstration with a mix of skepticism and hope.
11. **Reverberation** - The persistence of a sound or effect as it echoes or reflects.
    Anton missed the reverberation he usually felt while playing the piano.
12. **Bittersweet** - Both pleasant and painful or regretful.
    Anton found the transformation of Galdora to be bittersweet, as it changed his unique experience of the world.

6. THE LAST BREATH

The room was dim, the only light a flickering candle by the bedside. Elias stood in the shadows, his gloved hands resting at his sides. He wasn't there to comfort or mourn—his role was far stranger, a gift he never asked for. As the old man in the bed drew his final, **labored** breath, Elias inhaled deeply.

It was like catching smoke in a glass jar—**intangible** yet utterly real. The final breath entered him, a phantom whisper that flooded his senses. Memories, emotions, secrets—all unraveled in a moment. He staggered slightly, steadying himself against the wall as the torrent of the old man's life washed over him.

The man had been a clockmaker, Elias learned, **meticulous** and lonely. He had loved once, fiercely, but his pride had driven her away. Decades later, regret weighed heavier than the hands of his finest clock. Elias exhaled slowly, releasing the breath into nothingness, and with it, the truth of the man's existence.

"That's the last one tonight," murmured Clara, leaning in the doorway. Her sharp green eyes observed him with a mix of curiosity and pity. She was the only one who knew his secret, the only one he trusted to shield him from the questions that inevitably arose when death followed him like a shadow.

"I wish it weren't," Elias muttered, removing his gloves and rubbing his temples. "Sometimes I think this gift is more curse than blessing."

Clara smirked, her tone laced with **sardonic** humor. "Most people would kill for the ability to unearth the truth. You, of course, see it as an eternal burden. Typical Elias."

He shot her a look but said nothing. Clara's **irreverence** was her shield, her way of keeping the world at arm's length. He had learned long ago not to take her jibes too personally.

"What did he leave you with?" she asked, stepping further into the room.

"Regret," Elias said simply. "More than I care to feel."

She sighed. "They always do. Maybe one day you'll catch someone's last breath and find nothing but peace. Wouldn't that be a novelty?"

Elias didn't respond. He wasn't sure peace existed in the way Clara imagined. After years of collecting final breaths, he had seen the deepest corners of human nature—love, hate, joy, despair. Peace was always **transient**, like trying to grasp water in your hand.

The next evening, as the sun dipped below the horizon, Elias found himself called to another deathbed. It was a young woman this time, her face pale and serene against the white sheets. The illness that claimed her had been swift, leaving little time for suffering.

Elias inhaled her final breath, his chest tightening as her life unfurled before him. She had been an artist, her world filled with color and light. Her final days were tinged with sorrow, not for herself but for the unfinished work she left behind.

"She painted sunsets," he told Clara later, as they walked back through the cobblestone streets. "Hundreds of them, each one different. She said the sky never repeated itself."

Clara looked up, her expression uncharacteristically soft. "Sounds like she understood something most people never do."

Elias nodded, lost in thought. The weight of the breaths he had taken was a constant presence, a silent companion he couldn't shake. But tonight, as he thought of the artist's **vivid** sunsets, the burden felt a little lighter.

Weeks turned into months, and Elias continued his strange work. He met people at their most vulnerable, their lives condensed into a single exhalation. Some breaths were heavy with sorrow, others light with gratitude. He saw wars, love affairs, betrayals, and quiet acts of kindness.

But then, one fateful night, everything changed.

He was called to the home of a man who had lived as a **recluse**. No one seemed to know much about him—not even Clara, whose network of informants usually had answers. Elias entered the dimly lit room, the air thick with an **unplaceable** tension.

The man's eyes were closed, his breathing shallow. Elias moved closer, waiting for the inevitable. But when the moment came, when the man's chest rose and fell one final time, Elias inhaled—and felt nothing.

No memories. No emotions. No truth.

He froze, his mind racing. This had never happened before. Every breath he had taken carried the essence of a life, yet this one was void, an empty whisper that left him cold.

"What's wrong?" Clara asked when he returned to their meeting place, his face ashen.

"I don't know," Elias replied, his voice barely audible. "There was… nothing."

"Nothing?" she repeated, frowning. "That doesn't make sense. Everyone has a story."

"Not him," Elias insisted. "It was like he didn't exist."

Clara's skepticism gave way to unease. "Maybe he was just—different. An **anomaly**."

But Elias couldn't shake the feeling that there was more to it. Over the following days, he became consumed by the mystery of the man without a story. He searched for records, spoke to neighbors, even visited the cemetery where the man was buried. But every path led to a dead end.

"Maybe it's a sign," Clara suggested one evening, her tone unusually serious. "Maybe not every life needs to be understood. Maybe some things are meant to remain unknown."

Elias shook his head. "I can't accept that. If his breath held nothing, what does that mean for the rest of us? For me?"
Clara didn't have an answer, and for once, neither did her sharp wit.

Elias began to withdraw, his once unshakable resolve eroded by doubt. The man without a story haunted him, a **phantom** presence that refused to be ignored. He questioned everything—the purpose of his gift, the truth of the breaths he had collected, even the nature of existence itself.

Then, one night, as he sat alone with his thoughts, he had a revelation. Perhaps the absence of a story wasn't an emptiness but a fullness too vast to comprehend. Perhaps the man's life had transcended the limits of memory and emotion, leaving behind something so **profound** that it defied understanding.

The thought both comforted and unsettled him. If it were true, it meant that his gift—his ability to capture the essence of a life—wasn't **infallible**. There were truths beyond even his reach.

Elias returned to his work with a renewed sense of **humility**. He continued to take final breaths, but now he did so with the understanding that not every story could be told, not every life reduced to a single exhalation.

And when his own time came, when he lay on his deathbed and felt the weight of his final breath leave him, he wondered if it, too, would carry a truth beyond comprehension—or if it would simply vanish, like the man who had taught him the value of the unknowable.

Comprehension Questions:

1. **What does Elias's experience with the man who left an empty breath reveal about his understanding of life and his gift?**

Elias's encounter with the man who left an empty breath challenges his belief in the comprehensibility of every life. It leads him to consider that some truths may be too profound to capture, shifting his perspective on the nature of his gift and teaching him to embrace the unknowable aspects of existence.

2. **How does Clara's perspective help Elias navigate the emotional burden of his gift, and what does her role suggest about their relationship?**
Clara's wit and grounded perspective provide Elias with both companionship and a counterbalance to his introspective nature. Her suggestion that not all lives need to be understood helps him accept the limits of his ability, highlighting her role as a supportive yet pragmatic confidant who helps him find clarity in moments of doubt.

Vocabulary List (C2 Level):

1. **Labored** - Requiring great effort or difficulty.
   The old man's labored breathing filled the quiet room.
2. **Meticulous** - Showing great attention to detail; precise.
   The clockmaker was meticulous in his craft, ensuring each gear aligned perfectly.
3. **Sardonic** - Grimly mocking or cynical.
   Clara's sardonic humor often masked her genuine concern for Elias.
4. **Irreverence** - A lack of respect for things generally taken seriously.
   Clara's irreverence toward Elias's gift was her way of keeping things light.
5. **Transient** - Temporary or fleeting.
   Elias realized that peace in life was often transient, never lasting long.

6. **Unplaceable** - Difficult to identify or categorize.
   The tension in the reclusive man's room was thick and unplaceable.
7. **Profound** - Deep, intense, or having great meaning.
   The emptiness of the man's breath left Elias with a profound sense of unease.
8. **Anomaly** - Something that deviates from the norm or expectations.
   The man without a story was an anomaly that Elias couldn't explain.
9. **Recluse** - A person who lives a solitary life and avoids others.
   The man whose breath revealed nothing had been a recluse, known by no one.
10. **Vivid** - Producing strong, clear, and detailed images in the mind.
    The artist's sunsets were described as vivid, each one unique in its beauty.
11. **Phantom** - A ghost or an illusionary presence.
    The man without a story became a phantom in Elias's thoughts.
12. **Humility** - A modest view of one's own importance.
    Elias's experience with the empty breath instilled a newfound humility.
13. **Infallible** - Incapable of making mistakes or being wrong.
    Elias realized that his gift was not infallible, as it couldn't capture every truth.

7. THE COLORLESS WORLD

The day I realized I was different wasn't marked by a dramatic **revelation**. It came slowly, like dawn breaking over the horizon, as I noticed the way people looked at me—or, more accurately, through me.
"Vera, can't you see it?" my sister, Amara, asked one afternoon, pointing toward the young couple arguing in the marketplace. Her voice was tinged with **incredulity**, as though my inability to understand was a deliberate choice. "Their anger—it's all red. Crimson streaks radiating off them like heat."
I squinted, hoping against hope to glimpse the hues she described, but saw only the same muted tones I always did. "I don't see it," I said flatly, averting my gaze. "And you know that."
Amara sighed, her frustration barely masked. "You're so strange. Everyone sees emotions. It's the easiest way to understand people."
Everyone except me, I thought bitterly.

In our world, emotions weren't **abstract** concepts—they were **tangible**, visible as auras of color surrounding people. Happiness shimmered in golden yellows, sorrow draped in deep blues, jealousy crackled in greenish hues. From the moment a child was born, they were taught to read these emotional spectrums. It was as natural as breathing. But for me, the colors were non-existent. I was the only one who had never seen them.

It wasn't just a personal inconvenience; it was a societal **anomaly**. People relied on the visibility of emotions for everything—communication, **empathy**, even trust. Without the ability to interpret the hues around me, I was perpetually at a disadvantage, navigating a world I couldn't fully comprehend.

"Have you tried looking harder?" my mother suggested once, as though I could will the colors into existence through sheer determination.

"I can't see what's not there," I replied, my voice edged with frustration. "Do you think I enjoy being... **defective**?"

She flinched at the word but didn't argue. No one could deny that my condition set me apart, and not in a way that inspired admiration. If anything, it bred **skepticism**. People couldn't fathom how I interpreted their emotions without color. Did I guess? Pretend? Lie? To them, my perception—or lack thereof—made me unreliable, even dangerous.

One day, in the shadow of these doubts, I met Lucien.

It was at the library, my refuge from the constant **scrutiny** of the outside world. The shelves were my sanctuary, filled with words that required no color to understand. He was sitting at a table near the window, flipping through a book with absentminded ease. His dark eyes caught mine as I walked past, and he smiled—a gesture so genuine it startled me.

"You seem... **pensive**," he said, his voice light but inquisitive.

I hesitated. "I didn't realize my thoughts were that transparent."

"They're not. Your face is," he replied, the corners of his mouth **quirking** up. "Most people's emotions announce themselves before they speak, but yours... they're subtle. Intriguing."

I sat down cautiously, unsure whether his words were a compliment or a veiled critique. "You don't find it disconcerting? My lack of color?"

"Disconcerting? No. Refreshing, perhaps," he said, leaning

back in his chair. "It must be exhausting for you, though. Living in a world obsessed with appearances."

"You have no idea," I murmured.

Lucien wasn't like most people. He didn't recoil from my difference or bombard me with questions about how I "managed" without seeing emotions. Instead, he seemed genuinely curious, not about what I lacked, but about how I navigated the world in my own way. For the first time, I felt seen—not as an **anomaly**, but as a person.

Over time, Lucien and I became inseparable. He had a knack for explaining emotions in ways I could understand, not through colors but through words, gestures, and tones. "Happiness feels like sunshine warming your skin," he would say, or "Jealousy is like a vine, creeping and constricting." His metaphors painted pictures in my mind more **vivid** than any color could.

"Why do you bother with me?" I asked him one evening, as we sat on the hill overlooking the village. "You could have anyone—someone normal."

He looked at me with an intensity that made my breath catch. "Normal is overrated. You see the world differently, Vera. That's not a flaw—it's a gift."

I wanted to believe him, but the weight of my difference was a constant reminder of how isolated I truly was. No matter how kind Lucien was, I couldn't escape the feeling that I was an outsider in my own life.

Then, one fateful night, everything changed.

A storm had rolled in, fierce and unrelenting. The wind howled through the village, tearing at rooftops and uprooting trees. Lucien and I were caught in the chaos as we tried to help secure supplies at the town square. Amid the frenzy, a child's cry pierced the air.

"There!" Lucien shouted, pointing to a **precariously** leaning structure. A small boy was trapped beneath the debris, his face pale with terror.

Without thinking, I ran toward him. The ground was slick with rain, and the air was thick with fear—fear I couldn't see, but I could feel it, **palpable** and suffocating. I crouched beside the boy, speaking in soothing tones as I worked to free him.
"It's okay," I murmured. "You're going to be okay."
His eyes locked onto mine, wide and uncertain. "You're not afraid?" he whispered.
"I am," I admitted. "But we'll get through this together."

When we finally pulled him free and returned to the safety of the square, something remarkable happened. The villagers who had always regarded me with **skepticism** looked at me with newfound respect. For the first time, they didn't see what I lacked—they saw what I had done.
"Maybe you don't need to see colors to understand emotions," Lucien said later, as we sat by the fire. "You felt his fear, didn't you? And you calmed him."
I nodded, a realization dawning on me. My inability to see emotions didn't mean I couldn't connect with people. I had always assumed my difference was a barrier, but perhaps it was a bridge—one that required me to listen, to observe, to truly understand.

From that day forward, I stopped trying to chase the colors I couldn't see. Instead, I focused on what I could feel, what I could hear in people's voices and see in their eyes. Lucien was right: my **perspective** wasn't a flaw. It was a gift—a different kind of vision in a world blinded by appearances.
And though the colors never came, I found something far more valuable: the ability to see people for who they truly were, not through the hues they projected, but through the depth of their **humanity**.

Comprehension Questions:

1. **How does Vera's inability to see emotions as colors shape her interactions with others, and how does Lucien help her reinterpret her difference?**
   Vera's inability to see emotions as colors isolates her, making her feel misunderstood and mistrusted in a society that relies on visual emotional cues. Lucien helps her reinterpret her difference by explaining emotions in ways she can understand and showing her that her unique perspective is a strength rather than a flaw.
2. **What changes in the villagers' perception of Vera after the storm, and how does this moment redefine her understanding of herself?**
   After Vera rescues a child during the storm, the villagers view her with newfound respect, recognizing her ability to connect with emotions in ways beyond color. This moment helps Vera realize that her difference isn't a barrier but a bridge, allowing her to connect with others deeply and meaningfully.

Vocabulary List (C2 Level):

1. **Incredulity** - The state of being unwilling or unable to believe something.
   Amara's voice was tinged with incredulity as she asked Vera if she could see the colors.
2. **Abstract** - Existing as an idea but not having a physical form.
   In Vera's world, emotions were not abstract but visible as tangible colors.
3. **Anomaly** - Something that deviates from the norm

or expectations.
Vera's inability to see emotions made her an anomaly in her society.

4. **Scrutiny** - Close and critical observation.
   The villagers' constant scrutiny made Vera feel like an outsider.
5. **Tangible** - Perceptible by touch; clear and definite.
   For most people, emotions were tangible as visible auras of color.
6. **Defective** - Imperfect or faulty.
   Vera resented being considered defective because of her inability to see colors.
7. **Pensive** - Engaged in deep or serious thought.
   Lucien noted that Vera seemed pensive when he first met her in the library.
8. **Quirk** - A peculiar aspect of someone's personality or behavior.
   Lucien's quirk of explaining emotions through metaphors intrigued Vera.
9. **Empathy** - The ability to understand and share the feelings of another.
   Despite her lack of color perception, Vera demonstrated deep empathy for others.
10. **Skepticism** - Doubt or disbelief about something.
    The villagers initially viewed Vera with skepticism because of her difference.
11. **Precarious** - Not securely held or in position; dangerously likely to fall.
    The boy was trapped under a precarious structure during the storm.
12. **Palpable** - So intense as to seem almost tangible.
    The fear in the storm was palpable, even though Vera couldn't see it.
13. **Revelation** - A surprising and previously unknown fact that is made known.
    The storm brought Vera a revelation about her ability to

connect with people.
14. **Perspective** - A particular attitude or way of viewing something.
Lucien helped Vera see her difference as a unique perspective rather than a flaw.
15. **Humanity** - The quality of being compassionate and understanding toward others.
Vera discovered that her inability to see colors helped her connect to the depth of people's humanity.

8. THE ETERNAL ECHO

"You're telling me... my voice echoes into the future?" Desmond asked, his voice tinged with **incredulity** as he leaned forward, gripping the edge of the rickety wooden table. His knuckles whitened with the effort, though his tone carried the quiet desperation of a man clinging to reason in an unreasonable world.

"Yes," the old woman replied, her voice raspy yet steady, like the whisper of sandpaper across wood. "Not just your voice—the sound of you. Every word, every sigh, every breath. It ripples outward, like a stone dropped in a pond, reaching lives you cannot yet see."

Desmond exhaled sharply, the sound punctuating the stillness of the cramped, dimly lit room. "But how? And why me?"

She shrugged with an **infuriating** lack of concern, her ancient hands tracing patterns in the dust that coated the table. "Why you? Why anyone? The universe doesn't concern itself with such trivialities. It just is."

"But I don't hear these so-called echoes," Desmond protested, the words tumbling out in a rush. "How am I supposed to believe any of this? What proof do you have?"

The old woman chuckled, the sound low and dry, like dead leaves rustling underfoot. "You don't hear them because they are not for you. They belong to the future, to the people who will come after you. But they will hear you, Desmond, and they will feel the weight of your words."

He slumped back in his chair, the wood creaking beneath him. His mind churned, trying to process the enormity of what she had said. Every sound he made, every careless utterance, could ripple into the lives of strangers yet unborn. It was absurd—and yet, something in her tone, in the ancient **gravity** of her gaze, made him hesitate.

"What happens if I say the wrong thing?" he asked, his voice barely above a whisper.

The old woman tilted her head, considering him. "You already have. And you will again."

The simplicity of her response hit him like a blow. His mind reeled, conjuring memories of words spoken in anger, in frustration, in jest. How many of them had carried unintended consequences? How many had twisted lives, altered paths, created unforeseen ripples in the fabric of time?

"Can I undo it?" he asked, a note of panic creeping into his voice. "Can I take back what I've said?"

"No," she replied, her tone devoid of sympathy. "But you can choose differently from now on."

The next morning, Desmond awoke with a newfound awareness of the sounds he made. The creak of the floorboards as he rose from bed, the whistle of his breath as he exhaled, the faint hum of his voice as he muttered to himself—all of it felt imbued with a significance he hadn't noticed before.

He stepped outside, the crisp morning air biting at his skin. The village was already stirring, the sounds of daily life rising around him like a **symphony**. Children laughed as they chased each other through the cobblestone streets. Vendors called out, their voices tinged with the sing-song cadence of familiarity. A blacksmith's hammer rang against metal, each strike **resonating** with purpose.

For the first time, Desmond didn't hear these sounds as mere background noise. They were threads in a vast, unseen tapestry, each one contributing to the story of the world.

But his own voice—his own contribution—felt heavier now. He hesitated before speaking, weighing each word as though it were a precious gem. Was it too harsh? Too **frivolous**? Too inconsequential? The pressure of it all threatened to **suffocate** him.

"You're quiet today," remarked Elise, the baker's daughter, as she handed him a loaf of bread. Her auburn hair caught the sunlight, and her blue eyes sparkled with curiosity. "Cat got your tongue?"

"Something like that," Desmond replied, forcing a smile. Even those three words felt like too much. What if his tone was misinterpreted? What if his smile seemed insincere? The possibilities were endless, and they were maddening.

"Are you feeling well?" Elise pressed, her brow furrowing.

"I'm fine," he said quickly, but the lie lodged itself in his throat like a stone. What future had he just altered with that single falsehood? What chain of events had he set in motion?

Desmond couldn't shake the feeling that every word he spoke was a gamble, a dice roll with stakes he couldn't comprehend. He began avoiding people, retreating into the solitude of his small, **modest** home. The silence was a comfort at first—a reprieve from the burden of his voice—but it soon became oppressive.

One night, as Desmond sat by the window, staring out at the moonlit village, he heard a faint knock at the door. His heart leapt, both with anticipation and dread. Who would seek him out at such an hour?

He opened the door to find a young boy standing on the threshold, his face pale and tear-streaked. "Mr. Desmond," the boy stammered, "my mother—she's sick. We don't know what to do."

Desmond's throat tightened. He wanted to help, but the weight of his voice, the fear of saying the wrong thing, **paralyzed** him. What if his words gave false hope? What if they made things worse?

"Please," the boy pleaded, his voice breaking. "You have to come."

Desmond took a deep breath, the sound trembling in the still night air. "I'll do what I can," he said finally, the words heavier than any he had ever spoken.

He followed the boy to a **modest** house at the edge of the village, where the woman lay pale and trembling on her bed. Her **labored** breaths filled the room, each one a reminder of the fragility of life.

Desmond knelt beside her, his mind racing. What could he say? What could he do? He reached for her hand, his touch **tentative**. "You're not alone," he said softly. "We're here with you."

The woman's eyes fluttered open, and for a moment, a faint smile played on her lips. "Thank you," she whispered, her voice barely audible.

Desmond stayed by her side through the night, speaking in low, soothing tones. He told her stories of the village, of the laughter of children and the warmth of the baker's hearth. His words were simple, **unadorned**, but they carried a **sincerity** that transcended time.

When the dawn broke, the woman's breathing had steadied, and the color had returned to her cheeks. The boy looked at Desmond with wide, grateful eyes. "You saved her," he said.

Desmond shook his head. "No. She saved herself. I only reminded her of the strength she already had."

As he walked home, the village waking to the sounds of another day, Desmond felt a strange sense of peace. His voice might echo into the future, shaping lives in ways he could never predict, but that wasn't something to fear. It was a responsibility, yes, but also a gift—a chance to make the world a little brighter, one word at a time.

Comprehension Questions:

1. **How does Desmond's understanding of his voice as an echo into the future change his behavior, and what does he learn from his interaction with the sick woman?**
   Desmond initially becomes paralyzed by the responsibility of his voice, overthinking every word and avoiding people to prevent unintended consequences. However, his interaction with the sick woman teaches him that his voice can bring comfort and hope. He learns that sincerity and intention matter more than perfection, and his words can positively influence others.
2. **What does the old woman's explanation about the ripples of Desmond's words reveal about the interconnectedness of actions and their consequences?**
   The old woman's explanation highlights the idea that every action, no matter how small, creates ripples that affect others in unforeseen ways. This interconnectedness emphasizes the importance of mindfulness and intentionality in how people interact with the world and each other.

Vocabulary List (C2 Level):

1. **Incredulity** - The state of being unable or unwilling to believe something.
   Desmond's voice was tinged with incredulity as he questioned the old woman's claims.
2. **Tangible** - Perceptible by touch; clear and definite.
   The old woman described the ripples of Desmond's words

as though they were tangible forces.

3. **Infuriating** - Causing extreme irritation or frustration.
   Desmond found the old woman's lack of concern infuriating as she explained his gift.
4. **Ripple** - A small wave or series of waves caused by a disturbance.
   The old woman compared Desmond's words to ripples spreading across a pond.
5. **Gravity** - Seriousness or importance.
   The gravity of the old woman's words left Desmond feeling overwhelmed.
6. **Unadorned** - Simple or plain, without embellishment.
   Desmond's stories to the sick woman were unadorned but deeply heartfelt.
7. **Symphony** - A harmonious arrangement of sounds or elements.
   Desmond began to hear the village's daily noises as part of a greater symphony.
8. **Suffocate** - To feel trapped or overwhelmed.
   Desmond felt suffocated by the weight of responsibility his voice carried.
9. **Frivolous** - Lacking seriousness or importance.
   Desmond questioned whether his words were too frivolous to matter.
10. **Modest** - Humble or simple in nature.
    The boy led Desmond to a modest house where his mother lay ill.
11. **Tentative** - Uncertain or hesitant.
    Desmond's touch was tentative as he reached for the woman's hand.
12. **Paralyzed** - Unable to move or act, often due to fear or uncertainty.
    Desmond was paralyzed by the fear of saying the wrong thing to the boy.

13. **Sincerity** - The quality of being genuine or truthful.
    Desmond's sincerity in his words brought comfort to the sick woman.
14. **Resonating** - Producing a lasting, meaningful effect.
    The sound of the blacksmith's hammer resonated with purpose in Desmond's ears.
15. **Unforeseen** - Not anticipated or predicted.
    Desmond feared the unforeseen consequences of his words.

9. THE WHISPERING EARTH

The first time it happened, Mira was alone in the garden, her fingers sunk deep into the cool soil. She loved the way the earth felt against her skin, the grainy texture, the faint, damp scent of life and decay intertwined. Gardening was her **reprieve**, a temporary escape from the noise of the world, and that day had started no differently. She was planting marigolds, humming softly to herself, when she felt it: a strange, rhythmic **tremor** beneath her fingertips.

At first, she dismissed it as her imagination. The earth moved, of course. Tremors, the shifting of tectonic plates, roots growing unseen—it wasn't unheard of. But this was different. It wasn't random or erratic; it had a deliberate **cadence**, a pulse that seemed to echo the steady beat of a heart.

Mira froze, her breath catching in her throat. She pressed her hands deeper into the soil, her ears straining for some sound, though she knew instinctively that this wasn't a thing to be heard. It was to be felt. The vibrations coursed through her, subtle but undeniable, and as she focused, they coalesced into something she couldn't quite believe—words.

"Remember... remember..."

She jerked her hands back, staring at the earth as though it had physically spoken. Her mind reeled, trying to rationalize the experience. Stress, she told herself. A trick of the mind, amplified by her solitude. She shook her head and stood up, brushing the dirt off her palms.

But the next day, it happened again. And the day after that.
The vibrations grew more insistent, the words clearer, though they were **cryptic** and fragmented, like a half-forgotten melody. "The roots... the sky... buried truths." Mira began to feel **unmoored**, her reality splintering under the weight of something incomprehensible. The earth was talking to her, she was certain of it, and the enormity of that realization made her head spin.

She didn't tell anyone at first. Who could she confide in? Her neighbors already thought she was **eccentric**—always out in the garden, muttering to herself as she tended her plants. Her friends, the few she had, would think she'd lost her mind. And yet, the more she listened, the more convinced she became that the earth wasn't merely whispering nonsense. It was trying to tell her something.

One evening, as the sun dipped below the horizon and the world was bathed in hues of gold and crimson, Mira sat cross-legged in her garden, her hands resting lightly on the soil. "What do you want from me?" she asked aloud, her voice trembling. She felt ridiculous, but the question hung in the air, heavy with expectation.

For a moment, there was only silence, the stillness of twilight wrapping around her like a shroud. Then, the vibrations began again, stronger than before. This time, there was no mistaking the message. "Beneath... the roots... lies the truth."

Mira frowned, her brow furrowing as she tried to decipher the **cryptic** phrase. "What truth?" she whispered.
The vibrations shifted, less like words now and more like an urgent rhythm, a summons. It seemed to draw her toward the old oak tree at the edge of her property, its gnarled branches reaching skyward like twisted arms.

Heart pounding, Mira grabbed a spade and began to dig. The soil was dense, **resistant**, as though it didn't want to yield its secrets, but she persisted. Sweat dripped from her brow, and her arms ached, but she didn't stop. Something primal, something beyond logic, drove her forward.

After what felt like hours, her spade struck something hard. She knelt, her fingers trembling as she brushed the dirt away to reveal a small, rusted box. Her breath caught. Carefully, she pried it open, revealing its contents: a bundle of yellowed papers, **brittle** with age, and a strange, metallic disc etched with symbols she didn't recognize.

The papers were covered in dense, spidery handwriting, the ink faded but still legible. As Mira scanned the words, her pulse quickened. The writings spoke of ancient civilizations, of a time when humanity and the earth existed in perfect harmony. They described a **catastrophic** event, a rift that severed the connection, plunging the world into chaos and forgetfulness.

"The earth remembers," the final page read. "It whispers to those who will listen, to those who can mend what was broken."

Mira stared at the page, her mind racing. Was this what the vibrations had been telling her? Was she meant to be some kind of **intermediary**, a bridge between the earth and humanity? The thought was both exhilarating and terrifying.

She turned her attention to the metallic disc. It was cool to the touch, surprisingly heavy for its size. The symbols etched into its surface seemed to shift and shimmer in the fading light, defying her attempts to decipher them. Tentatively, she placed her hand on it, and a shock of energy shot through her, making her gasp. Images flooded her mind: towering forests, crystalline rivers, mountains that seemed to breathe. And then, destruction—flames consuming the land, oceans rising in fury, a **cacophony** of voices crying out in despair.

Mira pulled her hand back, her chest heaving as she tried to process what she'd seen. The earth wasn't just communicating

—it was pleading. It needed her to understand, to act, but how?

Over the following weeks, Mira devoted herself to unraveling the mysteries of the whispers. She pored over the papers, their **archaic** language testing the limits of her comprehension. She studied the symbols on the disc, consulting every book and resource she could find. Gradually, a picture began to emerge, a puzzle coming together piece by painstaking piece.

The earth, she learned, was alive in ways humanity had long forgotten. It was a **sentient** entity, its voice embedded in the vibrations of the soil, the rustle of leaves, the crash of waves. For millennia, it had guided and nurtured life, but humanity's insatiable greed and disregard had driven it into silence. The whispers Mira heard were a desperate attempt to reestablish the connection, to warn of the consequences of continuing down the path of destruction.

One evening, as she sat by the oak tree, the disc in her lap, Mira felt the vibrations intensify. They **resonated** through her entire body, a deep, resonant hum that seemed to align with the very core of her being. She closed her eyes, letting the sound envelop her, and for the first time, she didn't just hear the earth—she understood it.

The earth's message was clear: humanity had a choice. It could continue to exploit and destroy, or it could remember its **symbiotic** relationship with the planet and strive to restore balance. The path forward wouldn't be easy, but the earth believed in the resilience and capacity for change that lay within humanity's heart.

Mira opened her eyes, her **resolve** hardening. She didn't know how she would convince others to listen, but she had to try. The whispers of the earth weren't just a plea; they were a gift—a second chance to set things right. And Mira, the unlikely messenger, would do everything in her power to ensure the whispers were heard.

Comprehension Questions:

1. **What prompts Mira to begin digging beneath the oak tree, and what does she discover that changes her perspective on the earth's whispers?**
   The earth's vibrations intensify and direct Mira to the old oak tree, urging her to uncover the truth beneath its roots. She discovers a rusted box containing ancient writings and a metallic disc. The writings reveal a forgotten harmony between humanity and the earth, while the disc provides visions of both the planet's past beauty and its potential destruction, changing Mira's understanding of her role as a bridge between humanity and the earth.
2. **How does Mira's interpretation of the earth's whispers evolve, and what does she ultimately decide to do with the knowledge she gains?**
   Initially, Mira is confused and skeptical of the cryptic whispers but gradually realizes they are a plea from the earth to restore balance. With the writings and the visions from the metallic disc, she understands the earth's message of warning and hope. She resolves to act as an intermediary, spreading awareness and striving to reconnect humanity with the planet's rhythms and needs.

Vocabulary List (C2 Level):

1. **Reprieve** - A temporary relief or escape from something unpleasant.
   Gardening was Mira's reprieve from the noise of the world.

2. **Tremor** - A slight shaking or vibrating movement.
   Mira first noticed the earth's whispers as a faint tremor beneath her fingers.
3. **Cadence** - A rhythmic flow or sequence of sounds or movements.
   The tremors had a deliberate cadence, like the steady beat of a heart.
4. **Cryptic** - Mysterious or difficult to understand.
   The vibrations formed cryptic messages that Mira struggled to decipher.
5. **Unmoored** - Lacking stability or a sense of direction.
   The whispers left Mira feeling unmoored, her reality splintering under their weight.
6. **Eccentric** - Unconventional or slightly strange.
   Her neighbors thought Mira was eccentric for spending so much time in her garden.
7. **Resistant** - Opposed or difficult to move or change.
   The soil felt resistant as Mira dug toward the secrets beneath the oak tree.
8. **Brittle** - Fragile and easily damaged.
   The yellowed papers inside the rusted box were brittle with age.
9. **Catastrophic** - Involving great damage or suffering.
   The writings described a catastrophic event that severed humanity's connection to the earth.
10. **Intermediary** - A mediator or go-between in communication.
    Mira realized she was meant to be an intermediary between the earth and humanity.
11. **Symbiotic** - Mutually beneficial, often referring to relationships between organisms.
    The ancient writings described humanity's symbiotic relationship with the earth.
12. **Resonant** - Deep, clear, and continuing to sound or affect.
    The vibrations Mira felt were resonant, aligning with the

core of her being.
13. **Archaic** - Very old or outdated, often referring to language or customs.
    The writings were filled with archaic language that tested Mira's comprehension.
14. **Sentient** - Able to perceive or feel things; conscious.
    The earth was revealed to be a sentient entity, alive in ways humanity had forgotten.
15. **Resolve** - Firm determination to achieve something.
    Mira's resolve to act as the earth's messenger grew stronger with each discovery.

10. THE END OF SHADOWS

The city of Umbra was a **paradox** of light and darkness. Its inhabitants lived in perpetual twilight, a world where shadows were not mere extensions of bodies, but the very essence of one's identity. Each shadow was unique, a living manifestation of its owner's emotions, thoughts, and truths. For centuries, the people of Umbra **revered** their shadows, treating them as sacred mirrors of their souls.
But then, the shadows began to vanish.

It started subtly, almost **imperceptibly**. A flicker here, a momentary dimming there. Most dismissed it as an oddity, a trick of the dim light that bathed their world. But when entire shadows began disappearing, leaving people eerily disconnected from themselves, panic set in. Without a shadow, one was an empty vessel, a husk stripped of depth and authenticity. The afflicted became pale, listless, and disturbingly detached, their voices devoid of emotion, their movements mechanical.

This was when the Shadow Hunters were formed—a **clandestine** group tasked with unraveling the mystery of the vanishing shadows. Cassian, the reluctant leader of this motley crew, had never sought such a role. He was a shadow cartographer by trade, a quiet man whose days were spent meticulously mapping the **contours** and shifts of shadows to decipher their meanings. But his expertise in shadow lore made him the obvious choice, and so, reluctantly, he had accepted the mantle.

"Cassian," whispered Leira, his second-in-command, as they crouched behind a crumbling wall in the abandoned district. Her shadow trembled slightly, mirroring her unease. "Do you hear that?"

Cassian tilted his head, straining to catch the faint sound. It was barely audible, a low, mournful hum that seemed to emanate from the air itself. It wasn't the sound that unnerved him, but the absence of shadows in this forsaken place. The buildings loomed like hollow specters, their edges sharp and unnatural without the softening embrace of shadowplay.

"It's here," he murmured, his voice barely above a breath.

The rest of the team tightened their formation, their own shadows flickering with anticipation. Shadows, though alive, could not act independently of their owners. They were bound, **tethered**, but in moments of heightened emotion, they reflected their bearers' states in unsettlingly precise ways. Cassian's own shadow rippled like water, betraying his internal turmoil.

The hum grew louder as they advanced, a dissonant melody that seemed to scrape against their minds. Suddenly, the air grew thick, heavy with an unseen force. And then they saw it—a roiling mass of darkness, shifting and pulsating like a living void. It wasn't a shadow in the traditional sense; it was something else entirely, an entity that devoured light and the very essence of shadows.

"What in Umbra's name is that?" Leira gasped, her voice quivering.

Cassian's jaw tightened. He had read about such phenomena in ancient texts—obscure references to the Abyssal Maw, a force born of imbalance and neglect. It was said to be the **antithesis** of shadows, an entity that fed on their **vitality** and left behind emptiness.

"It's what's been taking them," he said grimly. "The shadows are being consumed."

Before anyone could react, the mass surged toward them, moving with unnatural speed. The team scattered, their movements instinctive, but one member wasn't fast enough. As the darkness enveloped him, his scream pierced the air, chilling Cassian to his core. When the mass receded, the man stood motionless, his shadow gone. His eyes were vacant, his face an expressionless mask.

"Fall back!" Cassian barked, his voice cutting through the rising panic. They retreated, their shadows trailing behind them like desperate animals seeking refuge. When they reached a safe distance, Cassian turned to face his team, his expression grave.

"We can't fight it," Leira said, her voice shaking. "It's... unstoppable."

"No," Cassian said, his tone resolute. "Everything has a weakness. The question is, what does it want?"

"It's feeding," another hunter, Tarek, said. "But why? Shadows aren't tangible. What could it possibly gain?"

Cassian didn't respond immediately. His mind raced, piecing together fragments of knowledge, half-forgotten legends, and his own observations. Shadows were more than mere projections; they were **repositories** of truth, memory, and emotion. If the Abyssal Maw was consuming them, it was likely after those very elements.

"We need to understand its origin," he said finally. "If we can uncover what created it, we might find a way to stop it."

Their search led them deep into the Archives, a labyrinthine repository of Umbra's oldest and most **arcane** knowledge. Cassian spent days poring over crumbling manuscripts and faded tomes, his shadow flickering with intensity as his frustration mounted. It was Leira who eventually stumbled upon the answer.

"Cassian," she called, holding up a fragile scroll. "I think this is it."

The scroll spoke of an ancient pact between the people of Umbra and the shadows. The shadows had willingly bound themselves to humanity, offering guidance and balance, but the pact came with a condition: the people were to honor and nurture their connection to the shadows, to live authentically and truthfully. Over time, as humanity grew **complacent** and self-absorbed, the bond weakened, creating a void—a vacuum that birthed the Abyssal Maw.

"It's our own fault," Leira said, her voice heavy with guilt. "We've neglected our shadows, ignored their warnings, and now we're paying the price."

Cassian nodded, a sense of **foreboding** settling over him. "The only way to stop the Maw is to restore the balance. But how do we **rekindle** a connection that's been severed for so long?"

The answer, they realized, lay in the one thing the Maw could not consume: light. Not physical light, but the metaphorical kind—truth, **authenticity**, and the willingness to confront one's own darkness. If the people of Umbra could be made to see this, to reclaim their bond with their shadows, the Maw would be starved of its sustenance.

It was a daunting task, but the Shadow Hunters were relentless. They spread the word, urging the people of Umbra to listen to their shadows, to embrace their truths rather than hide from them. At first, they were met with skepticism and resistance. But as the Maw's attacks grew more frequent and devastating, desperation forced the people to listen.

Cassian led by example, standing before the city and baring his own vulnerabilities. His shadow responded, growing stronger and more vibrant, a testament to the power of honesty. One by one, others followed, their shadows flickering back to life as they embraced the parts of themselves they had long ignored.

The change was slow, arduous, but undeniable. As the people of Umbra reconnected with their shadows, the Abyssal

Maw began to weaken. Its once-imposing mass shrank, its movements faltering. In a final confrontation, Cassian and his team confronted the entity, their shadows blazing with light. The Maw let out a soundless scream before collapsing into nothingness, leaving behind only silence.

Umbra was forever changed. The people had learned a hard lesson, one they vowed never to forget. Shadows were no longer taken for granted; they were cherished, nurtured, and understood. And though the scars of the Maw's reign remained, the city began to heal, bathed in the gentle interplay of light and shadow that had always defined its soul.

Comprehension Questions:

1. **What role do the shadows play in the lives of the people of Umbra, and how does their neglect lead to the creation of the Abyssal Maw?**
   Shadows in Umbra are sacred manifestations of a person's emotions, thoughts, and truths, serving as a mirror of their soul. Over time, the people neglected their connection to their shadows, ignoring their truths and living inauthentically. This neglect weakened the bond between humanity and the shadows, creating a void that birthed the Abyssal Maw, a destructive force that consumed shadows and left people emotionally hollow.
2. **How do the people of Umbra ultimately overcome the Abyssal Maw and restore balance in their city?**
   The people of Umbra overcome the Abyssal Maw by rekindling their connection to their shadows. They embrace truth, authenticity, and vulnerability, strengthening the bond that had been severed. By confronting their inner darkness and nurturing their shadows, they deprive the Maw of its sustenance. In a

final act of collective honesty and unity, they weaken the Maw until it collapses, restoring balance to their city.

Vocabulary List (C2 Level):

1. **Paradox** - A situation or statement that seems contradictory but may hold truth.
   Umbra was a paradox of light and darkness.
2. **Revere** - To regard with deep respect and awe.
   The people of Umbra revered their shadows as sacred mirrors of their souls.
3. **Imperceptibly** - In a way that is so subtle or gradual as to be almost unnoticeable.
   The shadows began to vanish imperceptibly, starting with faint flickers.
4. **Clandestine** - Done in secrecy, often to conceal an illicit or unauthorized purpose.
   The Shadow Hunters operated as a clandestine group to solve the mystery.
5. **Contours** - The outlines or shapes of something.
   Cassian mapped the contours of shadows to decipher their meanings.
6. **Resonance** - A deep, full, and reverberating sound or emotional impact.
   The hum had a resonance that scraped against their minds.
7. **Antithesis** - The direct opposite of something.
   The Abyssal Maw was the antithesis of shadows, consuming their essence.
8. **Vitality** - The state of being full of life and energy.
   The Abyssal Maw fed on the vitality of shadows, leaving emptiness behind.
9. **Repository** - A place where things are stored or accumulated.
   Shadows served as repositories of truth, memory, and

emotion.

10. **Arcane** - Mysterious, understood by only a few, often referring to old knowledge.
    The Archives contained Umbra's oldest and most arcane texts.
11. **Complacent** - Showing smug or uncritical satisfaction with oneself or one's achievements.
    Humanity grew complacent, neglecting their bond with shadows.
12. **Foreboding** - A feeling that something bad is going to happen.
    Cassian felt a sense of foreboding as they uncovered the truth about the Maw.
13. **Tethered** - Tied or connected to something as if by a rope or chain.
    Shadows were tethered to their owners, unable to act independently.
14. **Authenticity** - The quality of being genuine or real.
    The people of Umbra learned to live with authenticity to restore balance.
15. **Rekindle** - To relight or revive something, often an emotion or relationship.
    The people of Umbra had to rekindle their bond with their shadows.

11. THE BODY CLOCK

From the moment they were born, the clocks were there. **Embedded** within the skin, beneath the surface, visible only to the one whose life they marked. Each individual had a unique timepiece, a countdown, an ever-present reminder of mortality. The clocks didn't tell you the day, the hour, or the minute of your death; they simply counted down in a soft, rhythmic pulse, ticking away silently but steadily until that final moment arrived.

For most, the clock was an invisible companion, a silent whisper of **inevitability**. But for some, it was a source of obsession. People would often find themselves glancing at the back of their hands or the nape of their necks, checking, just to see how much time they had left. It was a reality they couldn't escape, a certainty they couldn't ignore. And yet, most learned to live with it, as they would with any other facet of life.

It was a societal norm, accepted and understood. But then, one day, something inexplicable happened to two strangers.

Leah had always been acutely aware of the constant presence of her clock. It rested just beneath the skin on her left wrist, visible only when she focused on it—subtle, yet persistent. From a young age, she had learned to ignore it. After all, what was the point of worrying about something inevitable? She had grown up with the concept, as had everyone else. It wasn't a curse, or a burden; it was simply part of who she was, part of who they all were. Every morning, her clock ticked on, and every night, she would lay in bed listening to its faint tick-tick-

tick.

But the moment she first saw Jonah, it all changed. It wasn't the way he looked, though he was handsome in a quiet, unassuming way, nor was it the way he smiled at her, as if they shared some invisible connection. No, it was something far stranger. It was the moment their clocks **synchronized**.

It started subtly. They met by chance at a café, where Leah sat in a corner booth, tapping away at her laptop. Jonah had come in to escape the dreariness of his own apartment, his eyes scanning the room for an empty seat. He had noticed Leah, the quiet intensity with which she typed, the way her eyes flicked down to her wrist every so often. Something had drawn him to her, a pull he couldn't explain.

"Mind if I sit here?" he had asked, his voice soft but confident.

Leah had nodded, not thinking much of it, though something had lingered in the air between them. Jonah sat, ordered a coffee, and they exchanged polite words about the weather, the city, anything and nothing. It was when their conversation fell into a lull that it happened.

Leah, half-absentmindedly, glanced down at her wrist. Her clock, which had been ticking steadily for the past few years, suddenly began to pulse more rapidly. She raised an eyebrow, puzzled, and checked it again. The ticking had grown quicker, almost **erratic**. She glanced around, wondering if anyone else had noticed, but the rest of the café was oblivious, lost in their own worlds.

Jonah was looking at her now, his brow furrowed in confusion. "What's wrong?" he asked, a trace of concern in his voice.

Leah didn't answer at first. Her mind was racing. She had learned to ignore her clock, to treat it like the background hum of life. But now, there was something undeniably strange about it. It was as though it was responding to something outside of her, something far beyond her control.

"Nothing," she muttered, more to herself than to him, and tried to focus on their conversation. But she couldn't shake the feeling that something was off. The sound of his voice, the slight increase in his **proximity**—she checked her wrist again, and it was as if the clock was in perfect sync with Jonah's.

"What the hell?" she whispered under her breath, her eyes widening as she looked up at him.

Jonah, too, had checked his wrist. His face was pale, his hands shaking slightly as he stared at the clock **embedded** into his skin. For the first time in his life, he was acutely aware of its presence. It had always been there, ticking quietly in the background, but now it was impossible to ignore. And to his horror, the rhythm of his clock matched Leah's.

The two clocks were in perfect harmony. Both ticking in unison, as though they were bound together in some unseen way.

Leah stood up, her legs shaky, her heart pounding in her chest. "What is this? This isn't possible. This can't be real."

Jonah had followed suit, his face flushed with confusion and fear. "I don't know. This is... this is insane." He grabbed his jacket, pacing nervously. "What's happening?"

Neither of them understood. Neither of them knew what it meant. But they both felt it—the undeniable sense of urgency, the inexplicable pull that they had to figure this out before it was too late.

For days, they tried to go on with their lives as normal. But every time they met, the clocks would **synchronize**, and the realization grew clearer: Their time was somehow connected. They could feel it, in every glance, in every word spoken. It was as if their fates had become **intertwined**, their destinies locked in an **immutable** dance of time.

It was Jonah who first suggested they investigate.

"We need to understand why this is happening," he said one evening, after their clocks had **synchronized** once more. "What does this mean?"

Leah hesitated, unsure. "But how? What could we possibly find out? People have lived with these clocks their whole lives, and they've never reacted like this. It's just… impossible."

But Jonah's **insistence** was undeniable. They sought out the wisest people in their community, the scholars who had dedicated their lives to understanding the nature of the clocks. The answer they found was as **cryptic** as it was **chilling**: When two people's clocks **synchronize**, it signals the crossing of destinies—an event of cosmic **significance**. It is a rare phenomenon, but it is always a **prelude** to a shared fate, a challenge that must be faced together before time runs out.

Leah and Jonah had no idea what this challenge might be. But they both knew one thing: their time was running out. Their clocks were ticking down, faster now, as if racing toward the moment they would find out what it meant.

As the days passed, they became inseparable. They delved deeper into their own lives, their histories, trying to understand what had brought them together. But no answers came, only more questions, and the creeping sensation that they were being drawn toward something neither of them was prepared for.

One evening, as the sun set and the world around them grew darker, Leah glanced at her wrist and felt the final pulse of her clock. The ticking stopped.

Jonah, beside her, looked down at his own wrist. His clock, too, was silent. The silence stretched between them, a **profound** stillness that seemed to stretch on forever.

And then, as if the world had been holding its breath, they both knew. Whatever had brought their clocks together, whatever had tied their fates, was about to be revealed.

In the silence, they held each other, knowing that the end—and the answer—was just beyond the horizon.

Comprehension Questions:

1. **How did Leah and Jonah first discover that their clocks were synchronized, and what was their initial reaction to this phenomenon?**
   Leah and Jonah first noticed their synchronized clocks during a chance meeting at a café. Leah observed her clock ticking more rapidly and erratically when Jonah was nearby, and Jonah experienced the same. Both were shocked and confused, unsure of what was happening but undeniably drawn to investigate the connection.
2. **What did the scholars explain about synchronized clocks, and how did this revelation affect Leah and Jonah's understanding of their shared fate?**
   The scholars revealed that synchronized clocks signal a rare crossing of destinies, marking a cosmic event that requires the individuals to face a shared challenge. This explanation deepened Leah and Jonah's sense of urgency and led them to accept that their fates were intertwined, propelling them to search for the meaning behind their connection.

Vocabulary List (C2 Level):

1. **Inevitability** - The quality of being certain to happen; unavoidable.
   The ticking of the clock was a reminder of the inevitability of time.

2. **Embedded** - Fixed firmly and deeply in a surrounding mass.
   The clock was embedded beneath the skin, visible only to its owner.
3. **Synchronize** - To cause to occur at the same time or rate.
   Leah and Jonah's clocks began to synchronize, ticking in perfect unison.
4. **Erratic** - Unpredictable, inconsistent, or irregular.
   Her clock's ticking became erratic as she sat near Jonah.
5. **Proximity** - Nearness in space, time, or relationship.
   The proximity between them seemed to influence the behavior of their clocks.
6. **Immutable** - Unchanging over time or unable to be changed.
   Their intertwined destinies felt immutable, bound by forces beyond their control.
7. **Cryptic** - Mysterious, obscure, or difficult to understand.
   The scholars offered cryptic explanations about the synchronized clocks.
8. **Chilling** - Causing a sudden and intense sense of fear or unease.
   The revelation about their clocks was as cryptic as it was chilling.
9. **Prelude** - An action or event serving as an introduction to something more important.
   The synchronization of their clocks was a prelude to a shared fate.
10. **Significance** - The quality of being important or meaningful.
    The synchronization of their clocks signified an event of cosmic significance.
11. **Intertwined** - Twisted together or closely connected in a complex way.
    Leah and Jonah realized their lives were intertwined

through the ticking of their clocks.
12. **Insistence** - The act of demanding something forcefully or not accepting refusal.
Jonah's insistence on understanding the clocks drove their investigation.
13. **Profound** - Very great or intense, or having deep meaning.
The silence between them carried a profound weight as their clocks stopped ticking.

12. THE FACTORY OF DREAMS

In the neon-lit city of Sapiros, nestled deep in the heart of a dystopian future, dreams were not the personal sanctuaries they once were. Instead, they were a currency, a **commodity** to be bought and sold, meticulously **harvested** from those who could afford the luxury of sleep. At the heart of this booming industry was the Factory of Dreams, an imposing complex where dreamworkers, highly specialized technicians, extracted, manufactured, and sold dreams to the highest bidder. It was an enterprise that defined the economy, shaped societal hierarchies, and blurred the lines between reality and illusion. For most, dreams were no longer spontaneous or abstract; they were meticulously **curated** experiences designed for consumption.

Alena had been a dreamworker for almost a decade. A member of an elite class of individuals capable of entering the minds of others, she was responsible for weaving dreams into products, mass-produced and marketed like any other luxury item. Her job was precise, calculating, and clinical. Using advanced neural interfaces, she would tap into the minds of sleeping individuals, extracting their subconscious musings, desires, and fantasies. These dreams would then be carefully edited, remixed, and packaged to meet the demands of the rich, the powerful, and the bored.

But Alena's expertise was not confined to simply **harvesting** and editing dreams; she had a rare gift—one she had kept hidden from her supervisors for years. She had discovered, by accident, that she could not only extract dreams but also alter them. She could rewrite them, shaping them into new narratives, bending reality into whatever form she desired. It was a skill that had emerged gradually, unnoticed at first. It began as small shifts, slight changes in the fabric of the dreams she was editing—subtle shifts in perspective, a brief change in the storyline—but over time, it became clear that her influence extended far beyond mere manipulation.

Alena had always been aware of the **ethical** dilemmas that her work posed. The Factory of Dreams was not a place of **liberation**, but of control. It took away a person's most intimate thoughts and memories, **commodifying** what was once sacred. The dreams she crafted were often empty, hollow illusions—products designed to satisfy the needs of people who had long since lost the ability to dream for themselves. Dreams of idyllic vacations, of heroic battles, of romantic conquests—these were the fantasies people desired, and Alena was paid handsomely to provide them. But there was always a nagging feeling in the back of her mind, a growing sense of unease, that what she was doing was not just unethical—it was immoral.

One night, as Alena worked late into the darkened hours of the Factory, her fingers trembling over the glowing interface, she made a mistake. She had been editing a dream for one of the wealthiest clients in Sapiros, a man known for his insatiable hunger for pleasure and control. His request was simple—he wanted a dream of absolute power, a vision where he ruled the world with no opposition, no consequences. But as Alena adjusted the dream's parameters, something unexpected happened. She didn't just alter the dream; she changed it. She rewrote it.

The dream she created was no longer the vision of control the client desired. Instead, it was a dream of **vulnerability**, a nightmare where he was trapped in a world where his power had crumbled, where he was powerless, and where every decision he made led to his downfall. Alena watched, horrified, as the narrative she had woven spiraled out of control. The man's mind, unprepared for such a jarring shift, began to fracture. He screamed, a sound that reverberated through the neural interface, as if the dream had crossed the boundary between consciousness and the waking world. The moment the dream ended, the man awoke in a cold sweat, his mind disoriented and shaken.

Alena's heart raced. She had never seen anything like this before. The dream had not just affected the client's mind; it had altered his perception of reality. The boundaries between dream and waking life had been obliterated, and she feared what this might mean. The ability to manipulate someone's reality so fundamentally was dangerous, **unprecedented**, and yet...it was also **intoxicating**.

For the first time, Alena considered the possibilities her gift presented. She had always adhered to the rules of the Factory, maintaining the delicate balance of editing dreams to fulfill a client's wishes. But now, she realized that she had the power to do more than that. She could change the very fabric of reality for those who experienced the dreams she crafted. She could rewrite their lives. She could influence the decisions they made, the paths they chose, the fates they would encounter.

But as she explored this new frontier, Alena soon realized that there were dangers beyond her understanding. The next time she attempted to rewrite a dream, she found that the changes she made had unintended consequences. People began acting strangely. Some were more withdrawn, others more aggressive. There were reports of people waking up with no memory of their past lives, **disoriented** and confused. It became clear that when Alena rewrote dreams, she wasn't just altering the individuals who experienced them—she was also creating **ripples** in the fabric of reality itself. The more she tampered with the dream world, the more chaotic and unpredictable the real world became.

Despite the growing risks, Alena continued to experiment. She sought out individuals whose lives seemed stagnant or hopeless, people who were stuck in **monotonous** routines or painful existences. She rewrote their dreams, shaping them into stories of triumph, of change, of possibility. She wanted to give them something they could never have—an opportunity to experience a different life, a different reality.

One such person was Miko, a low-ranking clerk who worked in the administrative offices of the Factory. Miko was quiet, reserved, and seemed to have little ambition. Her clock, **embedded** in her skin, ticked relentlessly, marking time in a way that seemed to drain the joy from her life. Alena decided to change that. She entered Miko's mind, rewriting her dreams to reflect the life Miko had always dreamed of—a life where she was powerful, successful, and loved.

When Miko awoke the next morning, she was a different person. She stood taller, her eyes shining with a newfound purpose. The changes were subtle at first, but they grew more pronounced with each passing day. Miko began speaking out, asserting herself in ways she had never done before. She became more confident, more bold, and began making decisions that changed the **trajectory** of her life.

But the effects were not as simple as they appeared. As Miko's life improved, the world around her began to shift. The Factory's operations began to **malfunction**, workers grew agitated, and the once-ordered systems of Sapiros began to break down. Alena realized with a growing sense of dread that her actions, her alterations, were not just creating positive changes—they were **distorting** the delicate balance of society itself.

The Factory of Dreams was never just a factory. It was a reflection of the delicate balance between the mind and the world it inhabited. When that balance was disturbed, when the line between reality and illusion blurred, the world itself became unstable.

Alena had to make a choice: continue rewriting dreams and risk destroying everything, or find a way to restore the original order before it was too late. But as she gazed into the horizon of a city spiraling out of control, she realized that the future of Sapiros—and perhaps the future of dreams themselves—now lay in her hands.

Comprehension Questions:

1. **How did Alena first realize her unique ability to alter dreams, and what consequences did her actions have on her clients and the world around her?**
   Alena discovered her ability to alter dreams gradually, initially through small, unnoticed changes. However, when she rewrote a wealthy client's dream into a nightmare of vulnerability, the boundaries between dream and reality blurred, leaving the client mentally shaken. As she experimented further, her alterations caused unintended consequences, such as erratic behavior in people and disruptions in societal balance.
2. **What ethical dilemmas did Alena face in her work at the Factory of Dreams, and how did they influence her decisions to experiment with rewriting dreams?**
   Alena struggled with the morality of commodifying dreams and the emptiness of the illusions she created for clients. This unease motivated her to experiment with

rewriting dreams to give individuals a sense of purpose or triumph. However, her actions posed ethical dilemmas as they began to destabilize reality, forcing her to confront the unintended harm her interventions caused.

Vocabulary List (C2 Level):

1. **Commodity** - A product or resource that can be bought or sold.
   In Sapiros, dreams were treated as a valuable commodity traded among the wealthy.
2. **Harvested** - Collected or gathered, often with effort or precision.
   Dreamworkers harvested dreams from the minds of sleeping individuals.
3. **Curated** - Carefully selected and organized.
   The dreams sold by the Factory were curated to satisfy specific desires.
4. **Ethical** - Relating to moral principles or the rightness of actions.
   Alena questioned the ethical implications of commodifying people's subconscious.
5. **Meticulously** - Showing great attention to detail; very carefully.
   Dreams were meticulously edited to meet the demands of the clients.
6. **Unprecedented** - Never done or known before.
   The effects of Alena's dream alterations were unprecedented, destabilizing reality.
7. **Commodified** - Turned into a product or object for commercial use.
   Personal dreams were commodified and sold in the dystopian economy.
8. **Intoxicating** - Exciting or exhilarating to the point of being overwhelming.

Alena found the power to rewrite dreams both dangerous and intoxicating.

9. **Trajectory** - The path or progression of an event or development.
   Miko's life took a new trajectory after Alena rewrote her dreams.
10. **Ripple** - A small wave or series of effects spreading outward.
    Alena's dream manipulations created ripples that affected the entire city.
11. **Monotonous** - Dull, repetitive, and lacking in variety.
    Alena sought to rewrite the monotonous lives of those stuck in routine.
12. **Disoriented** - Confused and unable to understand one's surroundings.
    Clients woke up disoriented after experiencing Alena's altered dreams.
13. **Malfunction** - A failure to function properly.
    The Factory began to malfunction as Alena's changes disrupted its systems.
14. **Distorted** - Twisted out of shape; misrepresented.
    The blurred boundaries between dreams and reality distorted people's perceptions.
15. **Liberation** - The act of freeing someone or something from constraints.
    Alena initially hoped her dream manipulations would bring liberation to others.

13. THE GARDEN OF BROKEN THOUGHTS

In the heart of the **tranquil** village of Elmswick, **nestled** between towering oak trees and bordered by fields of wildflowers, lay a garden unlike any other. It was a place few ventured into, and even fewer knew existed. This was the Garden of Broken Thoughts, a magical realm where thoughts, memories, and **fleeting** ideas, discarded or forgotten, grew into plants. The garden was hidden from the world, tucked away in a **secluded** corner of the village, accessible only to those who knew how to find it—or to those who were fated to stumble upon it.

Sylas, a young gardener, had been working in the garden for as long as he could remember. His role was simple yet profound: tend to the thoughts that had been **abandoned**, neglected, or discarded. The thoughts took root in the **fertile** soil, transforming into peculiar plants with strange, delicate flowers. Each thought, once **abandoned**, found a new life in the garden, its essence forever captured in the form of a living plant. Some of the plants grew large and twisting, their petals reaching for the sky, while others were small and modest, hidden beneath layers of moss. It was a place where even the most forgotten ideas, once deemed unworthy, could bloom again.

Sylas loved the garden deeply, although he could never quite shake the feeling that it was more than just a sanctuary for broken thoughts. There was an aura of mystery surrounding it

—an **ethereal** quality that seemed to hint at something greater, something that connected the garden to the very fabric of the universe. The plants, despite their otherworldly appearance, seemed to possess a wisdom of their own, as if they knew the secrets of the world beyond the garden's walls.

One afternoon, while tending to a particularly lush patch of forget-me-nots, Sylas stumbled upon something unusual. It was a small sprout, no larger than his thumb, but it was unlike any other thought he had encountered before. It was not the gentle, faded hue of a forgotten memory, nor the deep purple of a discarded idea. Instead, it shimmered with an **iridescent** glow, casting a faint light in the otherwise shadowy corner of the garden. Sylas knelt down to inspect it more closely. The sprout seemed to hum with an energy all its own, as though it were waiting for something—someone.

Sylas's heart raced. He had spent his entire life tending to the garden, but he had never seen a plant like this. It wasn't broken or discarded—it was whole, **vibrant**, and brimming with potential. Something about it felt important, as though it had a purpose beyond its mere existence in the garden.

Without thinking, Sylas reached out and gently cupped the sprout in his hands, feeling the soft pulse of its energy. As soon as he touched it, a rush of memories flooded his mind. He saw flashes of faces, places, and events—some familiar, some strange, all connected by a single thread. There was a deep longing in those memories, a sense of loss that echoed through him. It was a thought that had been lost long ago, a thought that had once meant something to someone but had been forgotten.

The realization hit Sylas like a bolt of lightning: this thought, this plant, was not just any **abandoned** memory—it was a forgotten thought, lost to its owner. It had been discarded, and now it had found its way into the garden, where it had taken root and begun to grow. But why? What had happened to the thought's original owner, and why had they allowed it to slip away?

Determined to find answers, Sylas decided to embark on a quest to return the forgotten thought to its rightful owner. The idea was both thrilling and terrifying. He had never before ventured beyond the borders of the garden. The world outside was vast and unknown, and the prospect of leaving the safety of the garden filled him with uncertainty. Yet, the thought's pull was irresistible. It called to him, urging him to take action.

Sylas carefully placed the sprout in a small pot, cradling it as though it were the most fragile thing in the world. He set out from the garden, walking through the village with a sense of purpose he had never felt before. He asked the villagers if they recognized the plant, if they could recall any memories of a lost thought. But no one could offer any answers. The villagers knew little of the garden's magic, and even less of the forgotten thoughts it housed.

Days turned into weeks as Sylas traveled from town to town, seeking any clue, any sign that might lead him to the owner of the thought. Along the way, he encountered people who had lost things—memories, loves, moments—but none of them seemed to recognize the sprout or the feelings it evoked. It was as though the thought had disappeared from the world entirely, leaving no trace behind. The more Sylas searched, the more he began to feel the weight of the thought's absence. It was as if the world itself had forgotten it, and with it, the person who had once owned it.

Exhausted and disheartened, Sylas sat on a hill one evening, the pot with the sprout cradled in his arms. The sun was setting, casting long shadows across the landscape. He looked down at the sprout, now beginning to blossom into a delicate flower, its petals glowing faintly in the twilight. He wondered if he had been wrong to seek out the owner of the thought. Perhaps it was better that some things remained forgotten, lost to time. But as he stared at the flower, something within him stirred. The thought, despite its lost origins, had a beauty all its own. It had flourished despite being forgotten. It had found its way into the world, its existence in the garden a testament to the **resilient** nature of thoughts, even those discarded and left behind.

Suddenly, a voice broke through the silence, a voice that seemed to come from nowhere yet echoed in Sylas's mind. "You've been searching for me," the voice said softly. "But I've been waiting for you."

Sylas's heart skipped a beat. He looked around, but there was no one in sight. The voice seemed to come from the very air around him, as though the wind itself had spoken. "Who are you?" Sylas whispered, his voice trembling.

"I am the thought you have been seeking," the voice replied. "I was lost, but not forgotten. And now, you have found me."

With those words, the flower in Sylas's hands began to glow brighter, its petals opening wider. The sprout had **transformed** into a fully bloomed flower, and as it did, Sylas felt a deep sense of peace wash over him. The quest had not been about returning the thought to its original owner. It had been about understanding the thought's journey—its transformation from something broken and forgotten into something beautiful and alive.

As the last rays of sunlight disappeared behind the horizon, Sylas realized that he had not only restored the thought but had also discovered something much deeper. The Garden of Broken Thoughts was not just a place of forgotten memories—it was a **sanctuary** for rebirth, a place where even the most discarded parts of the human experience could find new meaning. Sylas's journey had been one of self-discovery as much as it had been about returning something lost. And in that quiet, magical moment, as the flower glowed softly in his hands, he understood that the garden was not just a place of broken thoughts—it was a place of healing, where even the most **fractured** parts of the soul could be made whole again.

Comprehension Questions:

1. **What was Sylas's role in the Garden of Broken Thoughts, and how did his discovery of the iridescent sprout change his perspective on the garden's purpose?**
   Sylas tended to the garden, nurturing plants that grew from discarded and forgotten thoughts. The discovery of the iridescent sprout, unlike any he had seen before, led him to realize that the garden wasn't just a sanctuary for broken thoughts but a place where they could transform and find new meaning.
2. **What was Sylas's quest with the forgotten thought, and what did he ultimately learn about its significance?**
   Sylas set out to return the forgotten thought to its original owner, seeking answers about its origins. Through his journey, he realized that the thought's value wasn't tied to its owner but to its ability to flourish and transform, symbolizing resilience and the beauty of renewal.

Vocabulary List (C2 Level):

1. **Tranquil** - Peaceful, calm, and undisturbed.
   The tranquil village of Elmswick was surrounded by towering oak trees and fields of wildflowers.
2. **Nestled** - Positioned comfortably or cozily in a sheltered spot.

The garden was nestled between the trees, hidden from the rest of the village.
3. **Ethereal** - Extremely delicate and light in a way that seems too perfect for this world.
The garden had an ethereal quality, hinting at its connection to the universe's mysteries.
4. **Iridescent** - Displaying luminous colors that seem to change when viewed from different angles.
The sprout shimmered with an iridescent glow, casting light in the shadowy garden.
5. **Abandoned** - Left behind or given up on.
The plants in the garden grew from abandoned thoughts and forgotten memories.
6. **Secluded** - Quiet and private, away from other people or activity.
The garden was in a secluded corner of the village, known to very few.
7. **Fertile** - Capable of producing abundant growth.
The fertile soil of the garden allowed even forgotten thoughts to take root and grow.
8. **Transform** - To change completely in form or appearance.
The thought transformed into a glowing flower, symbolizing its journey of renewal.
9. **Vibrant** - Full of energy, life, or color.
Unlike the other plants, the sprout was vibrant and brimming with potential.
10. **Fleeting** - Lasting for a very short time.
The garden held fleeting memories that had been discarded by their owners.
11. **Resilient** - Able to recover quickly from difficulty or adversity.
The thought's transformation into a flower demonstrated its resilient nature.
12. **Sanctuary** - A place of refuge or safety.
The garden served as a sanctuary for discarded thoughts,

allowing them to find new meaning.
13. **Fractured** - Broken into pieces.
    The garden symbolized a place where fractured parts of the soul could be made whole again.

14. THE SOUNDLESS WORLD

In a world **devoid** of sound, silence reigned supreme. People moved about, their lips parting only to form silent words, their footsteps muffled against the soft, smooth ground. There were no echoes of laughter, no hum of conversation, no rush of wind or sound of nature. The world was in a state of **profound** quiet, a quiet that had existed for as long as anyone could remember. It wasn't the absence of noise—it was the absence of sound itself. People had learned to live with it, communicating with gestures, expressions, and the unspoken language of the eyes. The concept of sound was as foreign to them as the notion of color might be to someone born blind.

From the moment she was born, Lira knew only silence. Her parents, like everyone else in the world, had accepted this reality. They whispered softly to her, their voices lost in the still air. They taught her to read and write, to communicate through hand gestures and the language of the mind. But there was one thing they did not know—that Lira had begun to hear.

It started faintly, like a whisper at the edge of her **consciousness**. At first, it seemed like nothing—just a **fleeting** sense of movement in the air, a sensation that couldn't quite be explained. But then, as she grew older, the sounds became clearer, sharper. It wasn't like the soft murmur of thoughts or the sounds that might be imagined in dreams. No, this was music—real, **tangible**, beautiful music. She would hear it when she was alone, when she closed her eyes, when the world around her seemed to fade away. The music would rise and fall in waves, sometimes slow and gentle, sometimes fast and intense. She could hear melodies she could not describe, **harmonies** she could not name. The sound of violins, the beat of drums, the soft whispers of a flute. It filled her with a joy she could not explain.

At first, Lira thought it was something everyone experienced. She didn't question it—how could she? Her parents could not hear it, of course, but neither could anyone else in the village. She assumed that everyone had their own internal music, a personal symphony that played just for them. It was only when she began to play in the fields, spinning in circles with the music in her ears, that she noticed something strange. When she looked around, no one else seemed to hear the music. They would watch her, their faces filled with confusion as she danced and laughed, moving to the invisible rhythm that seemed so real to her.

Lira tried to explain it to them, but her words fell flat. She used her hands to describe the beats, miming the rise and fall of the music she could hear, but they only smiled kindly and patted her on the head, as if humoring a child who had an overactive imagination. Her parents were the same. They saw her joy, her excitement, but they couldn't hear what she heard. They told her that she must be mistaken, that the silence of the world was all there was.

But Lira knew. She had come to understand that the music she heard wasn't just a figment of her imagination—it was something more. She could feel the rhythm deep within her chest, a pulse that seemed to sync with the beat of her heart. It was as if the music was part of her, an extension of herself. She could hear it even in her dreams, and when she woke, it was still there, lingering in the back of her mind.

One day, when she was older, Lira decided to explore the source of the music. She wandered deep into the forest beyond the village, where no one ever went. The trees here were ancient, their trunks twisted and **gnarled**, their branches weaving together like the fingers of an old, wise being. It was here, in this forgotten corner of the world, that Lira hoped to find answers.

As she walked, the music grew louder, more **insistent**. It seemed to **emanate** through the trees, swirling around her like a whirlwind. Her heart raced with excitement, and she hurried to follow the sound, her feet light on the soft earth. She pushed through the dense undergrowth until she came to a clearing, a place where the air was thick with the hum of the music. It was overwhelming now—so beautiful, so full, that it seemed to surround her on all sides.

And then, in the center of the clearing, she saw it: a stone, ancient and worn, its surface covered in strange symbols. The music seemed to **emanate** from it, vibrating through the air, pulsing like the rhythm of life itself. Lira stepped closer, her breath shallow, her hands trembling. She reached out to touch the stone, and the moment her fingers brushed against its surface, everything went silent. The music stopped.

Confused, Lira pulled her hand back, but the silence didn't fade. It was as if the stone had absorbed the sound, as if it had absorbed her very **consciousness**. Her mind felt heavy, weighed down by a sudden sense of emptiness. She closed her eyes, trying to process what had happened. And then, in that silence, something strange occurred.

The stone seemed to **shimmer** with a faint light, and in that light, Lira saw something she had never seen before—a vision of herself, standing at the edge of the clearing, her hands outstretched, her eyes wide in awe. But this version of her was different. It wasn't the Lira she knew, but a reflection, a deeper version of herself that had never existed before. In that moment, Lira understood the truth: the music she had been hearing all her life wasn't external—it was a **manifestation** of her own **consciousness**, a creation of her mind.

The realization hit her like a wave, sweeping over her with a force she hadn't expected. The music, the rhythm, the melodies—all of it had been generated within her. It wasn't something that existed in the world; it was something she had been creating all along. The music was her own mind, her own thoughts, her own **perception** of the world, translated into sound. She had thought it was something external, something magical, but in truth, it was a **manifestation** of her own **consciousness**.

Lira sat down on the stone, her mind racing with the implications of this discovery. She had spent her entire life believing in the existence of something outside of herself, something that had brought her joy and wonder. But now she understood that it was all a part of her, a reflection of her inner world. The music was no different from her thoughts, her emotions, her desires. It was a part of her, as much as anything else.

As the sun began to set, casting long shadows over the clearing, Lira stood up and turned to leave. She knew now that she could never look at the world in the same way again. The silence around her would always remain, but now, she understood its depth. The music, once so real and **vibrant**, was nothing more than the echo of her own soul.

And as she walked back toward the village, the music softly resumed in her mind, not because the world had changed, but because she had.

Comprehension Questions:

1. **How did Lira first discover the music, and how did it differ from the world around her?**

Lira began hearing faint music as a child, which gradually became clearer and more beautiful over time. Unlike the silent world she grew up in, this music was vibrant and filled her with joy. However, no one else could hear it, leading her to realize it was unique to her.

2. **What did Lira discover about the source of the music, and how did it change her understanding of herself and her world?**
    Lira found that the music she heard came from within her own consciousness, not from the external world. This revelation helped her understand that the music was a manifestation of her inner self, showing her the depth and richness of her own mind despite the silent world she lived in.

Vocabulary List (C2 Level):

1. **Devoid** - Completely lacking or free from something.
    The world was devoid of sound, existing in profound silence.
2. **Profound** - Deep, intense, and meaningful.
    The silence was profound, shaping the very fabric of their existence.
3. **Tangible** - Perceptible by touch; real and concrete.
    The music Lira heard felt tangible, as though it existed outside of her mind.
4. **Harmony** - A pleasing combination or arrangement of different elements.
    The music was filled with harmonies she couldn't name but found mesmerizing.
5. **Unassuming** - Modest, not seeking attention.
    The forest beyond the village appeared unassuming but held ancient secrets.
6. **Insistent** - Demanding attention or action; persistent.

The music grew louder and more insistent as Lira approached the clearing.

7. **Gnarl** - To twist or knot, often describing old, weathered objects.
   The trees in the forest were ancient and gnarled, their branches like twisted fingers.
8. **Manifestation** - An event, action, or object that embodies something, especially an abstract concept.
   The music was a manifestation of Lira's inner world, created by her consciousness.
9. **Perception** - The ability to see, hear, or become aware of something through the senses.
   Lira's perception of the music revealed it to be a reflection of her own mind.
10. **Emanate** - To flow out or spread from a source.
    The music seemed to emanate from the ancient stone in the clearing.
11. **Shimmer** - To shine with a soft, flickering light.
    The ancient stone shimmered with a faint light, revealing its mysterious power.
12. **Consciousness** - The state of being aware of one's thoughts, surroundings, and existence.
    Lira's journey revealed that the music was a creation of her own consciousness.

15. THE CLOCKWORK SUN

In a world where the sun was not a **celestial** body but a carefully engineered mechanism, the people lived beneath the surface, beneath a great expanse of metal gears, turbines, and levers. The sky, as they understood it, was not a natural phenomenon, but a carefully crafted illusion, its light generated by the movement of massive gears deep beneath the earth's crust. This great clockwork, an **intricate** system of **precision** and power, was the lifeblood of their civilization, controlling not only the day and night cycles but also the very seasons themselves. Without it, there would be nothing but endless darkness, and the cold of eternal night would descend upon them all.

The gears had been forged centuries ago, their origins lost to time. No one remembered who had built them, nor did anyone understand the full extent of the technology that powered the sun. It was simply the way things were. People were born to live their lives in the constant glow of this mechanical sun, never questioning its source, its workings, or its future. Until Elara came along.

Elara was a young engineer, a prodigy who had been fascinated by the great clockwork system since childhood. She had studied the blueprints, learned the ancient designs, and spent years in the great workshop, tinkering with small machines and gears, always trying to understand how it all fit together. Her fascination with the sun was more than mere curiosity—

it was an **obsession**. She had often wondered why the light of the sun, despite being artificial, seemed to have a power over people's lives. It affected their moods, their health, and even their dreams. It was as if it wasn't just a machine but a living thing, a force that controlled everything.

One day, while deep within the belly of the machine, she discovered something that no one else had noticed: the gears were rusting. They were **corroded**, the once-smooth surfaces now jagged and worn, as if time itself was **eroding** the very foundation of their world. The turbines, which once hummed with a steady, rhythmic energy, now sputtered and groaned, struggling to keep up with the demands placed on them. The sun, once bright and steady, had started to dim, its light weakening with each passing day. It was subtle at first—an imperceptible shift in the warmth of the light, the length of the shadows—but Elara knew what it meant. The sun was dying.

In a panic, she rushed to the archives, searching for any reference to a failure of the great machine. But the records were sparse, and what she did find only deepened her fear. The sun had never failed before. There had been no plans for its repair, no mention of any **contingency** for its eventual demise. The engineers who had come before her had built the system to last forever, or so it seemed. But now, it was becoming clear that the clockwork sun was not eternal. It had a **finite** lifespan, and that lifespan was running out.

Elara knew she had to act quickly. The rusting gears needed to be replaced, the turbines repaired, and the great machine restored to its former glory. But as she ventured deeper into the system, she encountered more problems than she had anticipated. The rust wasn't just on the surface—it was everywhere. The gears were beyond simple repair; they needed to be completely **dismantled**. The turbines, too, were failing at an alarming rate. She couldn't do it alone.

She sought help from the council of engineers, the wise and seasoned elders who had overseen the machine for generations. But when she brought her concerns to them, they dismissed her. "The sun has never failed," they told her, "and it won't fail now. The gears are fine. You're just overreacting."

But Elara couldn't ignore the truth. She had seen it with her own eyes. The machine was breaking down, and if it wasn't fixed soon, the consequences would be **catastrophic**. Without the sun, the entire world would fall into chaos. People would starve, the crops would wither, and the darkness would engulf them all. The end of time itself was on the horizon, and no one seemed to care.

In desperation, Elara turned to the underground tunnels, where the oldest and most forgotten parts of the machine were hidden. It was there, deep beneath the earth's surface, that she uncovered something that no one had dared to speak of— a **blueprint** for a new system, one that could replace the old clockwork sun and ensure that the world would continue to thrive. It was a **radical** design, one that defied the traditional understanding of how the sun worked. Instead of relying on gears and turbines, it proposed a system based on a renewable, natural source of energy. It was a gamble, a leap of faith, but it was their only chance.

With no time to waste, Elara rallied a group of young engineers who shared her vision. Together, they set to work, **dismantling** the old machine and building the new system. It was dangerous work, and there were many moments when it seemed like they wouldn't succeed. The rusted gears resisted their every effort to remove them, and the old turbines seemed determined to fail at the most critical moments. But Elara was **relentless**, pushing through the exhaustion, the fear, and the uncertainty. She knew that the future of their world depended on their success.

As the days passed, the work became more and more intense. Elara hardly slept, barely ate, consumed by the task at hand. The sun grew dimmer by the day, and with each passing hour, the pressure mounted. But she couldn't stop. There was no room for failure. She had to finish the new system before it was too late.

And then, one fateful night, as the last gear was removed from the crumbling machine, Elara and her team activated the new system. The moment the switch was flipped, the world held its breath. For a brief moment, there was silence, and then, the sun flickered. It pulsed once, twice, and then it blazed to life, brighter and stronger than it had been in years. The gears, no longer rusted and weak, hummed with a renewed energy, spinning effortlessly. The turbines roared to life, sending a surge of power through the system. The sun, no longer a dying relic, was reborn.

The people emerged from their homes, blinking in the intense light, amazed at the brilliance of the sun. It was as if the world had been given a second chance. Elara stood at the heart of the machine, her hands trembling with exhaustion, but her heart soaring with triumph. She had done it. She had saved them all.

But as she looked up at the bright, shining sun, she couldn't help but wonder: how long would it last? Would they be able to keep it alive? Or would they eventually find themselves facing the same fate once again? The clockwork sun was no longer dying, but time, as it always had, was ticking away.

Comprehension Questions:

1. **What discovery did Elara make about the clockwork sun, and how did she respond to the crisis?**
   Elara discovered that the gears and turbines of the

clockwork sun were rusting and failing, threatening the entire system. She sought help from the council of engineers, who dismissed her concerns, so she took it upon herself to find a solution, ultimately designing and building a new renewable energy system with a team of young engineers.

2. **What challenges did Elara and her team face in replacing the old clockwork sun, and how did they overcome them?**

   Elara and her team encountered extensive rust, resistant gears, and failing turbines, making their work dangerous and grueling. Through relentless effort, innovation, and determination, they managed to dismantle the old system and successfully implement the new design, saving their world.

Vocabulary List (C2 Level):

1. **Celestial** - Relating to the sky or heavens.
   The sun in their world was not a celestial body but a mechanical construct.
2. **Intricate** - Very complicated or detailed.
   The clockwork system was an intricate network of gears and turbines.
3. **Corrode** - To gradually wear away or destroy by chemical action.
   The gears of the sun were beginning to corrode, threatening the system's integrity.
4. **Contingency** - A plan or measure prepared for a possible future event or circumstance.
   There was no contingency plan for the failure of the clockwork sun.
5. **Relentless** - Oppressively constant; unyielding.
   Elara worked relentlessly to repair the failing system and save their world.

6. **Obsession** - A persistent preoccupation or intense focus on something.
   Elara's obsession with understanding the sun drove her to uncover its flaws.
7. **Dismantle** - To take apart a machine or structure for repair or disposal.
   Elara and her team dismantled the old gears to make way for the new system.
8. **Blueprint** - A detailed plan or design.
   Elara discovered a blueprint for a revolutionary system to replace the sun.
9. **Precision** - The quality of being exact and accurate.
   The clockwork system required precision in its construction and maintenance.
10. **Radical** - Relating to or affecting the fundamental nature of something; revolutionary.
    The new system Elara designed was a radical departure from traditional methods.
11. **Finite** - Having limits or bounds.
    Elara realized that the clockwork sun had a finite lifespan, contrary to belief.
12. **Erode** - To gradually wear away, often by time or natural forces.
    Time had eroded the gears of the clockwork sun, leaving them jagged and weak.
13. **Catastrophic** - Involving sudden and widespread disaster.
    If the sun failed, the consequences would be catastrophic for their civilization.

16. THE PAPER GOD

In the dimly lit studio of a **reclusive** artist, the world was silent except for the soft scratch of pencil on paper, the occasional rustle of ink as it flowed onto delicate sheets, and the occasional flick of a paintbrush. This was the domain of Enzo, a paper artist whose skill and passion for his craft were unmatched in the world. His work was revered for its breathtaking **intricacy**; the lifelike sculptures he created from paper were not only beautiful but seemed to carry a certain presence—an **aura** of life within their folds.

Enzo's **obsession** with paper had begun when he was a child. The texture, the way it could be manipulated, folded, and torn, fascinated him. His room was a testament to his craft—shelves upon shelves of paper sculptures, delicate creations that seemed to defy the **fragility** of their medium. Animals, people, trees, and even abstract forms—everything he made from paper seemed to pulse with a quiet energy, as if it were not just an object of art, but something more, something alive.

But there was one sculpture Enzo had never quite finished. It was an unfinished figure—a humanoid figure with arms outstretched as if embracing something, as if **yearning**. The sculpture was meant to be his masterpiece, the culmination of years of work, but something had always felt missing. It was as if the paper didn't quite capture the soul he intended to **imbue** it with. There was no emotion, no depth. And so, he'd left it untouched, hidden away in the farthest corner of his studio.

One evening, as the sky darkened and the wind picked up

outside, Enzo sat before the unfinished figure. He stared at it intently, studying the delicate folds, the crisp edges of the paper. Something inside him stirred—a sudden, inexplicable urge to complete it. Perhaps it was the storm, the energy in the air, or perhaps it was the culmination of years of craftsmanship. But Enzo knew, deep down, that this figure had to come to life. It wasn't just an artistic creation; it was something greater, something more **profound**.

With careful hands, Enzo began to work, folding, creasing, and shaping the paper. He wove **intricate** patterns into the figure's clothes, each fold designed to create the illusion of movement. He added layers upon layers of delicate paper, each one more detailed than the last. He sculpted the face, giving it a depth and expression he had never attempted before. The eyes were slightly closed, as if the figure were waiting for something—a promise, a revelation. Enzo worked long into the night, until the last shred of paper had been molded into place. When he finished, the figure was beautiful—almost too beautiful. The paper gleamed in the low light, catching the glow of the lamps as if it were somehow alive, waiting.

For the first time, Enzo stepped back, admiring his work. He marveled at the lifelike quality the figure now possessed. It was as though the figure could breathe. He could almost feel the warmth of its skin, the pulse of its veins beneath the surface. It stood there before him, the embodiment of his **obsession**, his creation, and his dream. Yet, there was something more—something unspoken between them. For the first time in his life, Enzo felt as if the paper had become more than just an object. It was his creation, yes, but it was also something beyond him, beyond the boundaries of art. It was real.

He whispered into the quiet of the studio, almost as if he were speaking to the figure itself, "What are you?"

To his surprise, the figure's eyes opened, the slightest flicker of motion, as though it were waking from a long, deep slumber. The figure turned its head toward him slowly, its gaze locking with Enzo's. For a long moment, neither of them moved. There was a stillness in the room that made the air thick, heavy with something undefinable. The figure blinked, its eyes gleaming with an almost knowing expression.

Then, without warning, the figure spoke, its voice a soft rustling sound, like paper caught in the wind. "I am... bound."

Enzo's heart skipped a beat. Bound? What did it mean? The figure, seemingly aware of his confusion, continued.

"I can only exist until the first drop of rain falls," it said. "Then, I will return to paper. To dust."

Enzo's mind raced. The rain? The storm outside? His creation—his masterpiece—was alive, yes, but it was **ephemeral**, bound to the very element that had given it life. The rain, the one thing that could undo everything. It was as if fate itself had intervened to create a ticking clock for his creation's existence.

"I don't understand," Enzo said, his voice shaking with disbelief. "Why? How do I keep you alive? What do I have to do?"

The figure stepped forward, its movements slow and deliberate. "You must find the mystery before the storm comes," it said. "The answer lies in your own heart. Only then can I survive. Only then can I be free."

Enzo's mind was a whirl of confusion and fear. What mystery? What did it mean? The storm was nearing. The wind howled outside, and in the distance, the sound of thunder rumbled, signaling the storm's approach. He had no time to waste. He had to figure out the mystery, or his creation—his only chance at understanding what he had achieved—would be lost forever.

With a sense of urgency, Enzo grabbed a piece of paper,

scribbling furiously, his thoughts spiraling. As the rain began to patter softly against the windows, he realized something **profound**. The figure was not just a reflection of his artistic abilities; it was a **manifestation** of his own desires, his own **yearnings**. He had created it to be something perfect, something that could exist beyond the realm of paper. And yet, it was still bound by the very limitations he had set for it. The mystery was not in the figure—it was in himself. His fear, his doubts, his desire for control. The figure was a mirror of his own need to create, to dominate, to preserve something that was fleeting.

With trembling hands, Enzo reached out to the figure, his voice barely a whisper. "I understand. You're not just a creation. You're a part of me. You always were."

The figure nodded slowly, its form flickering slightly, like paper in the wind. "And you are a part of me," it said softly. "Now, let me be free."

As the first drop of rain fell from the sky, a strange warmth filled the room, and the figure, with its delicate paper form, began to dissolve into the air, fading into the ether, leaving behind only the faintest trace of its existence.

Enzo stood alone in the studio, his hands trembling, not from fear but from the realization that his creation had **transcended** the limitations he had set for it. The mystery had been solved—it was not about saving the figure from the storm; it was about letting it go, letting go of the need for permanence, for control. The storm had come, and with it, the realization that some things, no matter how beautifully crafted, were meant to fade away.

And in the silence that followed, Enzo understood the true nature of his art—everything, even the most fragile creation, had its moment in time.

Comprehension Questions:

1. **What was special about Enzo's paper sculpture, and why did he feel compelled to finish it during the storm?**
   Enzo's sculpture was his unfinished masterpiece, a humanoid figure meant to embody emotion and depth. During the storm, he felt an overwhelming urge to complete it, believing it held a greater significance beyond mere art.
2. **What realization did Enzo come to about his creation, and how did it influence the sculpture's fate?**
   Enzo realized that the sculpture was a reflection of his own desires and limitations, representing his struggle with control and impermanence. This understanding allowed him to accept the sculpture's ephemeral nature and let it dissolve with the rain, embracing the transient beauty of creation.

Vocabulary List (C2 Level):

1. **Reclusive** - Avoiding the company of others; solitary.
   Enzo lived a reclusive life, devoting himself entirely to his art.
2. **Intricacy** - The quality of being complex or detailed.
   The intricacy of his paper sculptures left viewers in awe of his skill.
3. **Fragility** - The quality of being delicate or easily broken.
   The fragility of the paper made each sculpture seem more precious.

4. **Obsession** - A persistent preoccupation with something.
   Enzo's obsession with paper art consumed every waking moment.
5. **Profound** - Very deep or intense, especially in a meaningful way.
   The creation of the sculpture was a profound experience for Enzo.
6. **Aura** - A distinctive atmosphere or quality surrounding something.
   The sculpture emanated an aura of life, as if it were more than just paper.
7. **Ephemeral** - Lasting for a very short time.
   The ephemeral nature of the sculpture mirrored the fleeting beauty of life.
8. **Resonate** - To evoke or suggest emotions or memories.
   The figure's eyes resonated with a deep, unspoken emotion.
9. **Imbue** - To fill or inspire with a feeling or quality.
   Enzo worked to imbue the sculpture with a sense of life and purpose.
10. **Transcend** - To go beyond the limits of something.
    The sculpture seemed to transcend its paper origins, becoming something more.
11. **Manifestation** - The expression or display of an idea or quality.
    The sculpture was a physical manifestation of Enzo's deepest aspirations.
12. **Yearning** - A deep longing or desire.
    The unfinished figure seemed to convey a yearning for something unattainable.

17. THE DREAM CATCHER'S CURSE

The dreamcatcher had always been a **relic**, a curiosity from another era, one that had been passed down through the generations in the Morrow family. As a child, Daniel had been fascinated by the **intricate** patterns woven into the web of its delicate frame, the small feathers that fluttered ever so slightly, and the shimmering beads that adorned its length. He had always believed it to be just a trinket, a mere symbol of his heritage. But now, standing in the dim light of his grandmother's attic, it seemed far more **ominous** than the charming keepsake he had once imagined.

His grandmother, Eleanor, had often spoken of it in passing, her voice heavy with unspoken history, but she had never explained why the dreamcatcher was so important. It wasn't until her death that Daniel inherited the object, wrapped in the faded cloth of a **bygone** era, tied with a **fraying** string. At first, he had dismissed it as just another old family **relic**, something to gather dust in the corner of his room. Yet, there was something unsettling about it that gnawed at the edges of his mind, a feeling that seemed to persist no matter how often he tried to ignore it.

The first night he hung the dreamcatcher above his bed, the air seemed unnaturally still. The soft moonlight filtering through the window cast eerie shadows across the room, and for the first time in years, he felt a strange unease creeping along his spine. He tried to shake it off, but sleep, when it came, was restless. His dreams were jumbled, **disjointed**—a maze of images that made no sense, but left him with an overwhelming sense of dread upon waking.

But it was the following night that things began to change.

As Daniel drifted off into a fitful sleep, he found himself trapped in a nightmare. It was a strange, hollow world, one that felt like a **fractured** memory, where the sky was an unnatural shade of red, and the ground beneath him was cracked and barren. Figures, grotesque and shadowed, moved in the distance, their whispers growing louder with each passing second. Daniel tried to scream, but his voice was **muffled**, swallowed by the **oppressive** silence of the dreamscape. He ran, but there was no escape—no matter which direction he took, the nightmare persisted, closing in on him, suffocating him.

Then, just as he thought he could endure no more, a shadowed figure emerged before him. It was cloaked in darkness, its face obscured by a veil of mist, but its eyes glowed with an unnatural light. It spoke in a voice that **resonated** deep within his soul, chilling him to the core.

"You have disturbed the balance," it whispered, its voice soft but laden with **menace**. "You dared to inherit the Dream Catcher's Curse."

Daniel awoke with a start, his heart pounding, sweat soaking his clothes. The room was still, but the **oppressive** feeling lingered, heavy in the air. He glanced up at the dreamcatcher, which now seemed less like a **relic** and more like a **harbinger** of something **sinister**.

The next morning, the nightmare continued to haunt him, even as he tried to convince himself it was just a bad dream. But as the day wore on, things began to take a turn for the worse. His thoughts were clouded by a pervasive sense of dread, and even the simplest tasks seemed insurmountable. He couldn't shake the feeling that something was watching him, waiting for him to make a mistake.

Then, that evening, as he sat at his kitchen table, something strange happened. The air around him grew colder, a sudden chill that crept up his spine and made his skin prickle with fear. The lights flickered, and for a brief moment, the dreamcatcher—hanging in the far corner of the room—began to sway. At first, Daniel dismissed it as a trick of the light or a draft, but then he heard it—a faint whisper, like the sound of rustling feathers.

His heart stopped. He could feel the hairs on the back of his neck stand up, his instincts screaming at him to run, to flee. But before he could react, the door to his bedroom creaked open, and from the shadows of the hallway, a figure emerged. It was cloaked in darkness, a silhouette with indistinct features, its eyes glowing faintly in the dim light. Daniel's pulse raced as the figure moved closer, and with each step it took, the temperature in the room seemed to drop further, until he could see his own breath in the air.

The figure spoke, its voice a rasping whisper that sent shivers down his spine. "You have been chosen, Daniel Morrow. The curse cannot be undone."

The figure's presence was overwhelming, its energy suffocating, and Daniel could do nothing but watch in terror as it advanced toward him. He stumbled backward, but the figure's gaze held him captive, paralyzed in place. The dreamcatcher above him swayed once more, and for the first time, he understood the truth.

The nightmare he had encountered was no mere figment of his imagination—it had been real. The dreamcatcher didn't simply collect dreams. It harvested nightmares, trapping them in its web, and now those nightmares had begun to bleed into the waking world. The curse his grandmother had spoken of was not just a legend—it was a terrible truth.

Panic surged within him, but the figure merely raised a hand, its long fingers reaching toward him with a slow, deliberate motion. "You are bound to this fate. Your nightmares will become reality, one by one, until you confront them. Until you destroy the dreamcatcher itself."

Daniel's mind raced. He had to act. He had to find a way to stop this, to sever the connection between the nightmares and the waking world. He didn't know how, but the answer seemed to lie within the very object that had brought him this curse. With trembling hands, he reached for the dreamcatcher, its feathers now rustling like dry leaves, its beads gleaming with an unsettling light.

The figure laughed—a cruel, mocking sound—as Daniel grasped the dreamcatcher and attempted to remove it from the wall. The moment his fingers touched the web, a shock of energy coursed through him, as though the very fabric of the universe had jolted in response to his actions. His vision blurred, and for an instant, he found himself back in the nightmare—trapped in the red-tinged world of shadows and whispers.

But he refused to succumb. With every ounce of willpower, Daniel willed himself to fight back, to confront the nightmare head-on. "I won't let you control me!" he shouted, his voice shaking but determined.

And in that moment, something shifted. The figure faltered, its presence weakening, and the dreamcatcher—now pulsing with a dark energy—began to **unravel**. With a final, desperate scream, Daniel hurled the cursed object across the room. It shattered upon impact, its web **unraveling**, its dark power dissipating into the air like smoke.

For a moment, everything was still. Then, as if a weight had been lifted from his chest, Daniel felt the darkness recede.

The figure vanished, and the chill in the air evaporated. The room was silent, save for the soft sound of his breathing. The nightmares, for now, were gone.

But Daniel knew that the curse was not truly broken. The dreamcatcher had been destroyed, but its power lingered in the air, a reminder that some forces were not easily **vanquished**. And though the nightmares were quiet for now, Daniel would never forget the terrifying truth: that the line between dreams and reality was far thinner than he had ever imagined. And the nightmare... could return.

Comprehension Questions:

1. **What did Daniel discover about the dreamcatcher's true nature, and how did it begin to affect his life?**
   Daniel discovered that the dreamcatcher was cursed, harvesting nightmares and allowing them to bleed into the waking world. This began to manifest as terrifying nightmares, a pervasive sense of dread, and encounters with shadowy figures that brought his fears to life.
2. **How did Daniel confront the curse, and what happened when he destroyed the dreamcatcher?**
   Daniel confronted the curse by attempting to destroy the dreamcatcher, despite the overwhelming presence of the shadowy figure and the fear it induced. When he shattered the dreamcatcher, its dark energy dissipated, and the nightmares receded. However, the lingering presence of its power hinted that the curse might not be fully broken.

Vocabulary List (C2 Level):

1. **Relic** - An object from the past that holds historical or

sentimental value.
The dreamcatcher was an old relic passed down in the Morrow family.
2. **Ominous** - Suggesting that something bad is going to happen.
The dreamcatcher cast an ominous shadow in the dimly lit attic.
3. **Bygone** - Belonging to an earlier time; past.
The faded cloth wrapped around the dreamcatcher was from a bygone era.
4. **Fractured** - Broken or damaged, often figuratively describing something fragmented.
The nightmare felt like a fractured memory, disjointed and surreal.
5. **Harbinger** - A person or thing that signals the approach of something.
The dreamcatcher seemed to be a harbinger of nightmares.
6. **Oppressive** - Weighing heavily on the mind or spirits; causing discomfort.
The silence in the nightmare was oppressive, suffocating Daniel's thoughts.
7. **Menace** - A threatening or dangerous quality.
The shadowy figure's voice was laden with menace, chilling Daniel to the core.
8. **Sinister** - Giving the impression that something harmful or evil is happening or will happen.
The dreamcatcher exuded a sinister energy that unnerved Daniel.
9. **Fraying** - Unraveling or becoming worn at the edges.
The string tied around the dreamcatcher was old and fraying.
10. **Disjointed** - Lacking a coherent sequence or connection.
His dreams were disjointed, filled with jumbled images that made no sense.

11. **Resonating** - Evoking a feeling of connection or significance.
    The figure's whispered words resonated deeply with Daniel's fears.
12. **Muffled** - Muted or softened in sound.
    Daniel's scream in the nightmare was muffled, as though swallowed by the dreamscape.
13. **Vanquished** - Defeated or overcome.
    Though the shadowy figure was vanquished, Daniel knew the curse might still linger.
14. **Unraveling** - Coming apart or breaking down, figuratively or literally.
    As the dreamcatcher shattered, its web began unraveling into nothingness.

18. THE BREATH OF TIME

In the land of Zaria, time was not measured by clocks or calendars. It was counted by breaths, each one marking the passage of life. From the moment a person took their first breath, a small, invisible counter began ticking. Every inhale and exhale, every heartbeat, was tallied and stored in the air around them, invisible to the human eye but perceptible in the most fundamental of ways. For each individual, their life was governed by the number of breaths they were allotted, and once their final breath was taken, they ceased to exist entirely.

People in Zaria lived their lives knowing that every moment was precious, for their breaths were **finite**, and once the last one was drawn, they vanished, never to be remembered. Their bodies **dissolved** into the air, their memories fading like mist. It was a world governed by the certainty of the countdown, and every day was a reminder that the end was **inevitable**. Some embraced it, savoring every breath as a gift. Others lived in denial, desperately clinging to the hope that they could somehow stretch out their time, extend their breaths beyond their natural limit.

For most, there was no escape. But for Soren, there was only one thought that consumed him: What if time could be bent, even broken?

Soren had always been different. While the others around him accepted the limitations of their breath-counting existence, he couldn't help but question the very nature of their reality. He had seen people live their lives in dread of the end, constantly aware of the ticking clock that would eventually take them. But Soren wasn't content with simply waiting for the **inevitable**. He knew there had to be more to life than this linear march toward expiration.

He had spent years researching ancient texts, forgotten philosophies, and **obscure** theories. And then, one night, in the dusty corner of a hidden library, he had discovered it: The Breath of Time, a legend passed down through whispered stories of those who had dared to defy the very nature of existence. According to the legend, there was a way to escape the countdown, a secret buried deep in the **fabric** of time itself. But the knowledge was **cryptic**, and the cost of uncovering it was said to be beyond comprehension.

Still, Soren was determined. He had no family to lose, no connections that bound him to this world. His mind, however, was sharp, and he was willing to sacrifice anything to uncover the truth.

For days, he worked tirelessly, experimenting with the boundaries of his own breaths. He had long since learned to control his body's rhythms, slowing his heartbeat, regulating his respiration, even suspending the act of breathing for moments at a time. But it was never enough. His breaths were still counted, still ticking away in the quiet of his mind, reminding him that time was running out.

And then, one fateful evening, as the setting sun cast a crimson glow over the land, he felt it—a shift, a subtle **tremor** in the air around him. For a moment, his breaths faltered, and then, like a distant whisper, the world seemed to exhale in unison with him. The very **fabric** of time itself seemed to loosen, as if the invisible thread that held it all together had momentarily frayed.

In that instant, Soren understood: the key to escaping the countdown was not in defying time itself, but in learning to harmonize with it. Time, it seemed, was not an enemy to be defeated but a rhythm to be embraced. The challenge was not to outlast time, but to become one with it, to move in sync with the very **pulse** of the universe.

The following weeks were a blur of experimentation and discovery. Soren pushed his mind and body to the limits, mastering the art of breath control until his every inhale and exhale was as **deliberate** as a dancer's movements. He learned to stretch his breaths, to synchronize them with the heartbeat of the world around him, until he no longer felt like a prisoner to the countdown but a part of something greater.

And then, on the night of the full moon, when the stars aligned and the air shimmered with an almost palpable energy, Soren took his final step. He stood in the heart of the ancient forest, where the trees whispered secrets older than time itself. His breaths were steady, deep, and unhurried. As he inhaled, he felt the energy of the universe surge through him, aligning his own rhythm with the **pulse** of the world. With each exhale, the boundaries of his existence seemed to fade, his body becoming lighter, his **essence** expanding beyond the confines of his physical form.

For the first time in his life, he felt free—not from time, but from the fear of it. He no longer cared about the countdown, for he had discovered a truth far more **profound**. Time was not something to be feared or resisted. It was not something that could be conquered or escaped. It was a force that connected all things, a universal rhythm that flowed through everything and everyone.

As he stood there, bathed in moonlight, Soren realized that the secret to escaping the countdown was not to halt it, but to **transcend** it. By becoming **attuned** to the rhythm of the universe, he had unlocked a state of being that allowed him to exist beyond time itself. His breaths no longer counted toward an end. They became part of an **eternal** cycle, a continuous flow that could never be measured or numbered.

And so, Soren disappeared from the world, not in the way people had always feared—not in the finality of death, but in a quiet, unseen transformation. His body, his mind, his very **essence** became one with the breath of the universe, existing beyond the limitations of the countdown. He was neither bound by time nor free from it. He simply was.

The people of Zaria never saw Soren again. They continued to live their lives, counting their breaths, aware of the **inevitable** end that awaited them all. But sometimes, when the wind whispered through the trees or the stars shone just a little brighter, they felt a strange, comforting presence—an inexplicable sense of peace, as if time itself had momentarily paused, just long enough for them to breathe. And in those moments, they would remember Soren and wonder if perhaps, in the end, the countdown was never meant to be an end at all, but a beginning.

As for Soren, he existed now in the breath of time itself—an **eternal** rhythm that **transcended** all boundaries. He had not escaped time, but had learned to move with it, to dance with it, until he became one with the **pulse** of the universe. Time was no longer his master. It was his companion, his guide, and in the silence between breaths, he found the peace that he had long sought.

Comprehension Questions:

1. **What realization did Soren come to about time, and how did it change his approach to escaping the**

countdown?

Soren realized that time was not an enemy to be conquered but a rhythm to harmonize with. Instead of resisting the countdown, he embraced the flow of time and synchronized his breaths with the pulse of the universe, transcending the limitations of mortality.

2. **How did Soren's final transformation reflect his understanding of time?**

Soren's transformation into the breath of time itself showed that he had moved beyond the constraints of individual existence. By becoming one with the rhythm of the universe, he transcended the countdown, existing in a state that was neither bound by time nor free from it.

Vocabulary List (C2 Level):

1. **Finite** - Having limits or an end.
   In Zaria, people knew their breaths were finite, marking the limits of their existence.
2. **Inevitable** - Certain to happen; unavoidable.
   The countdown of breaths in Zaria was an inevitable aspect of life.
3. **Obscure** - Not well known or difficult to understand.
   Soren studied obscure texts to uncover the secrets of time.
4. **Profound** - Very great or intense; having deep meaning.
   Soren experienced a profound realization about the nature of time.
5. **Cryptic** - Mysterious or difficult to interpret.
   The legend of The Breath of Time was cryptic, offering more questions than answers.
6. **Tremor** - A slight shaking movement or vibration.
   Soren felt a tremor in the air, signaling a shift in the

fabric of time.

7. **Harmony** - A pleasing or consistent arrangement of parts.
   Soren learned to exist in harmony with the rhythm of the universe.
8. **Fabric** - The basic structure or framework of something.
   Soren believed the secret to transcending time was hidden in the fabric of the universe.
9. **Deliberate** - Done consciously and intentionally.
   Every breath Soren took became deliberate, part of his synchronization with time.
10. **Transcend** - To go beyond the limits of something.
    Soren transcended the countdown by attuning himself to the pulse of the universe.
11. **Attuned** - Brought into harmony with.
    Soren became attuned to the rhythm of the universe, allowing him to escape the countdown.
12. **Essence** - The intrinsic nature or indispensable quality of something.
    Soren discovered the essence of time within the flow of his own breaths.
13. **Pulse** - A regular beat or rhythm, often used metaphorically.
    Soren synchronized his breathing with the pulse of the world around him.
14. **Dissolve** - To disappear or fade away.
    In Zaria, people dissolved into the air when their final breath was taken.
15. **Eternal** - Lasting forever; infinite.
    By transcending the countdown, Soren became part of an eternal rhythm beyond time.

19. THE UNSEEN PATH

The morning mist hung low in the dense forest as I **trudged** along the winding path, my boots sinking softly into the damp earth. I had been walking for hours, the silence only broken by the occasional rustle of leaves and the distant call of birds. The forest was thick, **unnervingly** still, as though the trees themselves were holding their breath. My map was useless here—no marked trails, no signs, no indication of what lay ahead. The wild expanse was meant to be a test, a rite of passage, for anyone who dared navigate through the deep woods of Caelum Forest. It was a place I had heard of only in hushed, fearful whispers—few ever ventured in, and fewer still came out the same.

I paused to check my compass, the needle spinning wildly, refusing to settle on a direction. My instinct told me I was not lost, but something—some unseen pull—beckoned me deeper into the woods, toward a path that seemed both present and absent at the same time. The feeling was **imperceptible**, like the very forest was aware of me, watching, waiting. And then, as I took another step forward, it appeared—an invisible trail, no more than a faint disturbance in the air that I could not explain. It wasn't visible in the traditional sense—no marked dirt or worn grass. It was as if the very air around me shifted, forming a subtle, almost **imperceptible** line cutting through the trees.

At first, I thought it might be a trick of the light, or perhaps the fatigue from hours of travel was beginning to take its toll on my mind. But as I took a tentative step forward, the sensation of walking upon solid ground was unmistakable. I could feel the earth beneath my feet, and with each step, the sensation grew stronger. Something about it felt deliberate, like I was being guided down a path that had always been there, hidden from others.

I tried to shake off the sense of unease that crept up my spine. After all, it was just a trail. But the deeper I ventured, the stranger the forest became. The trees, once towering and unyielding, now seemed to **warp** in size, some stretching upwards to impossible heights, while others bent toward the ground, their branches twisting unnaturally. The air around me **shimmered** faintly, as though reality itself was bending under some unseen force. I continued to walk, feeling an odd weightlessness in my chest, as though the path was leading me not through the forest, but through something much deeper, something beyond ordinary perception.

As I advanced, the normal sounds of the forest—birds chirping, the rustling of leaves—ceased. A **profound** silence enveloped me, thick and impenetrable. It wasn't the kind of silence that was peaceful; it was unsettling, as though even the very essence of sound had been swallowed up by the invisible trail. I glanced around, only to see that the world seemed to **blur** at the edges, as if my perception was being distorted. The air felt cooler here, and yet there was a strange warmth in the way the path seemed to glow faintly, leading me forward with an almost **magnetic** pull.

Suddenly, a faint glow appeared at the edge of my vision. I stopped, my heart thudding louder in my chest. It was a light, soft and diffused, not coming from any obvious source but radiating outward, like the light of a distant star peering through a fog. The further I walked, the stronger the glow became, illuminating a space just ahead of me—an empty clearing, but not like any clearing I had seen before.

The trees in the clearing were twisted, their trunks curled in unnatural angles, their leaves **shimmering** in hues that I had never seen before—deep purples, bright blues, and vivid oranges, all gleaming with an **ethereal** glow. The ground was soft and spongy beneath my feet, like walking on an endless bed of moss. The air itself seemed to hum with energy, charged with a strange and ancient force.

I stepped into the clearing, drawn by an inexplicable curiosity, my mind racing with questions. What was this place? Where was I? The path I had followed had disappeared behind me, and I could no longer trace the invisible line that had led me here. I was completely alone in this strange, surreal world—surrounded by towering trees with bark that glittered as though dusted with stardust. And yet, it felt as though I had always been here, as though this moment had been **predestined**.

I knelt to touch the ground, the soft moss yielding beneath my fingers. As I did, the world around me shifted, and for a fleeting moment, I saw something—or someone—out of the corner of my eye. A figure stood in the shadows of the trees, draped in flowing robes that shimmered with the same **ethereal** glow as the landscape itself. I blinked, and the figure was gone, as though it had never existed.

A surge of energy coursed through me, and I staggered back to my feet, my mind reeling. My breath quickened, the air around me thickening. I had entered a realm that was not just disconnected from reality, but distorted by it. Time here seemed to bend and stretch, the edges of the world **blurring** with every passing second. How long had I been walking? Minutes? Hours? Or perhaps... it had been no time at all.

My thoughts were interrupted by a soft voice—calm, clear, and distant, as if carried on the wind.

"The path you walk is not for the faint of heart," it said, its tone both comforting and **foreboding**. "You have crossed into a world where time and space hold no **dominion**. Here, the line between reality and illusion **blurs**. You must choose carefully, for your journey is one of **discovery** and consequence."

I froze, looking around for the source of the voice, but saw nothing. The air hummed, the ground beneath my feet pulsing with a strange rhythm. I had been guided here, but to what end? What was the purpose of this unseen trail, and where would it lead?

As if in answer, the light in the clearing grew brighter, and the trees began to sway in a wind that I could neither see nor feel. The path I had walked—an invisible trail that no one else could see—seemed to beckon me once more, urging me onward.

I stood at the crossroads of my decision. Should I turn back, returning to the known world, or should I continue forward, deeper into this distorted realm? The forest around me seemed to **pulse** with life, as if it were alive with waiting, as if it knew that the choices I made here would ripple through not just time, but the very **fabric** of existence.

I **hesitated**, my mind racing. And then, with a deep breath, I stepped forward again, knowing that this path, though unseen, was the only one that would lead me to the answers I sought.

Comprehension Questions:

1. **What unusual phenomena did the narrator experience as they followed the invisible trail through the forest?**
   The narrator encountered a spinning compass, distorted trees, shimmering air, and profound silence, all of

which created a surreal, unsettling atmosphere. The trail seemed both present and absent, leading them to a glowing clearing unlike anything they had seen before.
2. **What choice does the narrator face at the end of the story, and what implications does it have for their journey?**
   The narrator must decide whether to turn back to the familiar world or continue deeper into the distorted realm. This choice symbolizes a leap of faith and the potential for significant discovery or consequence.

Vocabulary List (C2 Level):

1. **Trudge** - To walk slowly and with heavy steps, often due to exhaustion.
   I trudged along the winding path, my boots sinking into the damp earth.
2. **Unnerving** - Causing anxiety or discomfort; unsettling.
   The unnervingly still forest seemed to hold its breath.
3. **Imperceptible** - So slight, gradual, or subtle as to not be noticed.
   The trail was marked by an imperceptible disturbance in the air.
4. **Warp** - To distort or twist out of shape.
   The trees seemed to warp in size, bending into impossible shapes.
5. **Profound** - Very great or intense; having deep meaning.
   A profound silence enveloped the narrator, amplifying the surreal atmosphere.
6. **Foreboding** - A feeling that something bad will happen; ominous.
   The voice carried a tone both comforting and foreboding.
7. **Ethereal** - Extremely delicate and light, seemingly

not of this world.
The clearing glowed with an ethereal light, like stardust in the air.

8. **Magnetic** - Having an attractive or compelling quality.
The path had a magnetic pull, urging me deeper into the forest.

9. **Shimmer** - To shine with a flickering or wavering light.
The air around me shimmered faintly, distorting reality itself.

10. **Predestined** - Determined in advance; inevitable.
It felt as though this moment had been predestined.

11. **Hesitate** - To pause before doing something, often out of uncertainty.
I hesitated, unsure whether to step forward or turn back.

12. **Blur** - To make or become unclear or less distinct.
The edges of the forest blurred, bending my perception of time.

13. **Dominion** - Sovereignty or control over a domain.
In this place, time and space held no dominion.

14. **Pulse** - A rhythmic vibration or beat.
The ground beneath my feet pulsed with a strange rhythm.

15. **Discovery** - The act of finding or learning something for the first time.
This journey was one of discovery and consequence.

20. THE GRAVITY OF MEMORY

Dr. Evelyn Harris stared intently at the console in front of her, her hands trembling slightly as she adjusted the settings on the advanced memory transfer machine. For years, she had been obsessed with a theory, one that many of her colleagues scoffed at and dismissed as fantastical. What if memories, those **intangible** fragments of our past, were more than mere fleeting images and feelings? What if they were real, physical entities—things that carried weight, energy, even mass? Her early experiments had hinted at the possibility, and now she was on the verge of proving it.

The concept itself was dizzying: memories as mass, capable of being transferred, manipulated, and even transported. It wasn't just a theoretical construct—it was a breakthrough, one that could potentially **revolutionize** neuroscience, quantum physics, and even our understanding of consciousness itself. The implications were staggering, and yet, no one seemed to care. To her peers, it was just another eccentric idea from a scientist more interested in fantastical possibilities than the rigid confines of traditional research.

Her lab was a **sterile**, almost cold place, bathed in the harsh light of fluorescents. The equipment buzzed and hummed around her, the walls lined with papers and equations, some of them half-finished, others full of speculative hypotheses. Despite the dismal surroundings, Evelyn thrived here, in this space where curiosity and ambition collided. Today, she was poised to take a step that could either launch her career into the stratosphere or destroy everything she had worked for.

"Memory transfer test—final attempt," she murmured to herself, reading the words printed on the screen in front of her. The subject for this trial was no ordinary volunteer. It was her own mother, who had suffered from Alzheimer's for the past several years. Her mother's memories were slowly fading, like water slipping through the cracks of a sieve. Evelyn could never bear to watch her mother lose herself, piece by piece, until she was nothing more than a shell of the vibrant, intelligent woman she had once been.

"Okay," Evelyn whispered, as she carefully set the machine into motion. The complex neural network in her lab was designed to tap into the brain's electrical signals and translate those signals into data that could be transferred to a digital storage medium. Her plan was to capture one of her mother's most **cherished** memories: a moment from her childhood when she and her mother had shared a quiet afternoon in the garden, planting roses together. It was a memory Evelyn held onto tightly, even as her mother forgot it.

The machine hummed with life, its complex algorithms and sensors working in tandem to extract the memory. Evelyn had spent weeks perfecting this process. There were risks, of course—she was venturing into unknown territory, and the human brain was an intricately delicate system. But this was her mother's only chance, and Evelyn was determined to save what little of her past remained.

As the memory began to transfer, Evelyn watched in awe as the data flowed seamlessly from the machine into the storage system. The memory was **pristine**, vivid—like watching a scene unfold before her eyes. She could almost feel the warm sunlight on her skin, the scent of roses in the air, and hear the soft laughter of a younger version of herself. Her mother had been right there beside her, their hands covered in soil, their hearts full of joy.

But then something strange happened.

The machine **sputtered**, its lights flickering erratically. The hum of the equipment grew louder, more insistent, as if it were struggling to contain something that had been unleashed. Evelyn's heart raced. She leaned forward, her fingers flying over the keyboard as she tried to stabilize the system, but it was too late.

The memory, once so beautiful and clear, began to **ripple** like a stone thrown into a pond. But this was not a gentle ripple. It was a wave, a force that pushed outward with such intensity that the entire room seemed to tremble. The data flowed faster now, faster than it should have, as if it were being pulled by an invisible gravitational force. And then, without warning, a sharp, high-pitched sound filled the room, followed by a sudden silence.

The memory, the very essence of it, seemed to have vanished. And in its place, there was something else.

Evelyn's breath caught in her throat as she looked at the monitor. Instead of a preserved memory, what appeared on the screen was a dark, swirling mass—an event horizon, like a black hole. The data was pulling in on itself, an **unyielding** vortex that seemed to devour everything it came into contact with. At first, Evelyn thought it was just a glitch, some kind of system error. But then she realized the truth: the machine had created something far more dangerous than she could have ever imagined. It had created a black hole—one made entirely of human memories.

Her heart pounded as she tried to **comprehend** what was happening. Memories, once thought to be fleeting and **intangible**, had weight. And now, they were gathering in a **singularity**, a gravitational force that was capable of sucking in not just data, but everything around it. The room around her seemed to distort, the edges of her vision darkening as if the black hole were pulling her in, too. The data was not just extracting the memory; it was expanding, replicating, feeding off of other memories, both stored and uncontained.

"Evelyn," a voice broke through the tension, startling her. It was a recorded message from her colleague, Dr. Marcus Aldridge, who had warned her about the potential dangers of her experiments. "I warned you about the **instability** of memory transference. You must stop. Do not attempt to manipulate the **gravitational** force of the memories. It will—"

The message cut off abruptly as the machine powered down, leaving only the ominous hum of the black hole, now much larger, much closer. Evelyn's mind raced. She understood now—the mass of human recollections had a pull, a **gravitational** force that could **unravel** the very **fabric** of time and space.

Panic gripped her. She reached for the emergency shutdown button, but it was too late. The black hole of memory had grown too powerful, too consuming. It began to pull everything into it: the data, the walls of the lab, her very thoughts. She tried to hold onto something, anything, but the **gravitational** force of the memories was too much.

And then, as if a great weight had been lifted, the room fell silent.

There was no machine. No console. No lab. Just darkness.

And within that darkness, Evelyn found herself **adrift**—caught in the endless pull of forgotten memories.

Comprehension Questions:

1. **What was Dr. Evelyn Harris's groundbreaking theory about memories, and how did her**

experiment with her mother's memory confirm or challenge it?

Dr. Evelyn Harris theorized that memories were not intangible but physical entities with weight and energy. Her experiment with transferring her mother's cherished memory initially confirmed this idea, but it spiraled out of control, creating a memory-based black hole that challenged her understanding of memory's nature.

2. **How did the experiment lead to the creation of a black hole, and what were the consequences for Evelyn and her surroundings?**

   The experiment's instability caused the extracted memory data to collapse into a singularity, forming a black hole that began to consume the lab and potentially reality itself. The gravitational pull of this memory black hole overwhelmed Evelyn and erased her surroundings, leaving her adrift in darkness.

Vocabulary List (C2 Level):

1. **Intangible** - Unable to be touched or grasped; not having a physical presence.
   Memories, once thought intangible, were revealed to have weight and energy.
2. **Revolutionize** - To change something radically or fundamentally.
   Her discovery could revolutionize the understanding of consciousness.
3. **Sterile** - Free from bacteria or devoid of creativity and warmth.
   The lab was a sterile place, bathed in the harsh light of fluorescents.
4. **Cherished** - To hold something dear or value deeply.
   Evelyn sought to preserve her mother's cherished memory of the garden.

5. **Pristine** - In perfect condition; unspoiled.
   The memory transferred into the machine was vivid and pristine.
6. **Sputter** - To make irregular, explosive sounds; to falter or fail.
   The machine sputtered, its lights flickering erratically.
7. **Ripple** - To form or cause small waves.
   The memory began to ripple, distorting like a stone thrown into water.
8. **Singularity** - A point where conventional understanding breaks down, often associated with black holes.
   The swirling mass resembled a singularity, devouring everything around it.
9. **Unyielding** - Inflexible; unable to be stopped or resisted.
   The vortex created by the memory was an unyielding force.
10. **Comprehend** - To understand or grasp fully.
    Evelyn struggled to comprehend the catastrophic consequences of her experiment.
11. **Instability** - Lack of stability or predictability; prone to change or failure.
    Her colleague had warned about the instability of memory transference.
12. **Gravitational** - Relating to the force that attracts objects toward one another.
    The memory black hole exerted a powerful gravitational force.
13. **Unravel** - To undo or resolve something complex or mysterious.
    Evelyn feared that her discovery might unravel the fabric of reality.
14. **Catastrophic** - Involving or causing great damage or disaster.
    The creation of the memory black hole had catastrophic

consequences.

15. **Adrift** - Without direction or anchor; floating aimlessly.
Evelyn found herself adrift in the endless pull of forgotten memories.

21. THE PAPER THIN SOUL

In a city built on the delicate balance of trade and commerce, there was a **commodity** that held far more power than gold, silver, or land. Souls. They were considered the ultimate possession, the very essence of existence. People didn't just sell their labor or ideas; they sold pieces of themselves, and in return, they received wealth, status, or a certain level of power. But there was one thing that set the soul apart from the rest: it could never truly be bought or sold, at least not without dire consequences.

Or so it was believed.

Lena had lived a humble life. She was a mid-level clerk in the bustling district of Narida, where everything was governed by the unwritten law of transactions. Every item, every action, had a price attached to it. From the smallest favor to the most complex creation, you paid with something of equal value. It was a city where human ambition thrived and every person was a merchant in their own right, whether they knew it or not.

Lena had never considered the idea of parting with her soul. After all, how could she? It was the most intimate, irreplaceable part of her. She had heard the rumors of those who had traded parts of their essence in exchange for power—greedy moguls, influential politicians, and even artists who sold a fragment of themselves to create masterpieces. But Lena was content with the life she had, one that didn't require the glitzy rewards of an overindulgent society.

That is, until one morning, when she woke to find an unsettling **absence**. It wasn't physical—it was something deeper, something invisible but profoundly real. Her soul, once anchored firmly within her, felt... hollow, absent. It was as if someone had quietly plucked it from her being without her knowledge, leaving behind only an echo of its former self.

She searched frantically for an explanation, going from street to street, knocking on doors, asking everyone she knew. Yet, no one seemed to have an answer. It was impossible to track her soul; no one had ever heard of it being taken without consent. Souls, after all, were supposed to be **inviolable**.

"Are you sure you're not just overreacting, Lena?" her colleague Gregor asked, trying to sound reassuring. He was a tall man with sharp features and an **uncanny** ability to manipulate the conversation in his favor. "Maybe you're just stressed. You've been working non-stop for weeks now. Perhaps it's fatigue playing tricks on you."

But Lena could feel the gnawing emptiness. She had always been a practical person, grounded in reason. This, however, was beyond the realm of reason. Her very essence was missing.

That's when she heard about the black market for souls.

There was a whispered rumor that, deep beneath the city, in the forgotten alleys and crumbling underbelly of Narida, souls could be exchanged in the most **insidious** ways. No contracts, no safeguards—just cold, hard transactions for those who had something to sell or something to buy. Those who had lost their souls were left wandering, unaware of what had happened to them, while others used dark arts to pull souls out of their owners without their consent. Lena knew that this underground network, this hidden trade, was where her soul had gone.

Determined to find it, Lena embarked on a journey into the depths of Narida. It was a **perilous** trek, one fraught with danger and deception. The city was a labyrinth of **opulent** mansions on the surface, hiding a darker, more sinister world below. The deeper she ventured, the more she encountered people whose eyes were **vacant**, whose presence felt... **mechanical**. They were soulless, and Lena couldn't help but wonder if they had, too, been victims of this **insidious** exchange.

Finally, after days of searching, she came upon a **dilapidated** building, hidden between two towering skyscrapers that seemed to eclipse the very sky itself. The door creaked open with an unsettling groan as she stepped inside, her heart pounding with both fear and hope.

Inside was a large room filled with strange, glowing objects—vials of light, floating orbs, and shimmering liquid suspended in mid-air. It was like a twisted version of a laboratory, a place where human lives were reduced to commodities. At the far end of the room sat a man with pale, almost **translucent** skin, his eyes gleaming with a **calculating** coldness.

"You must be Lena," the man said, his voice smooth, as though he had been expecting her all along. "I've heard about you. You're looking for something that no one can return."

Lena's voice shook with urgency. "My soul. I need it back. It was taken from me."

The man smiled, a cruel twist of lips. "Taken? No, no. It was sold. And I'm afraid, once a soul is sold in Narida, there is no turning back."

"I never sold it!" Lena protested, her voice rising. "I didn't give permission. I don't even know how it happened!"

The man leaned forward, his hands resting on the table before him. "You misunderstand. Souls don't require permission. Not in this city. The moment your soul became of value, it was ripe for exchange. You see, Lena, souls are like any other form of currency here. The moment they are separated from their owner, they belong to whoever claims them first."

"But I don't understand. Who took it? Who would do this to me?"

The man's smile faded as he narrowed his eyes. "It doesn't matter who. The real question is, what will you do to get it back? Your soul is now a possession. A prized asset. There are those who will pay handsomely for it."

Lena's blood ran cold. "I won't let that happen. I'll fight. I'll fight until I **reclaim** it."

"You can't fight what you don't even know how to retrieve," the man said, shaking his head. "Your soul is **fragmented**. It has been dispersed and absorbed into the trade networks. You'll have to outbid others for it. The question is, do you have what it takes to win it back?"

Lena felt a surge of anger mixed with **resolve**. "I'll do whatever it takes."

The man chuckled softly, then gestured to a stack of papers on his desk. "Then sign. Sign, and enter the game. If you think you can outsmart Narida's elite and reclaim what is yours, I welcome the challenge."

She stared at the papers, her hands trembling. She knew the risks, knew that this was a dangerous gamble. But she also knew that without her soul, she was nothing—just a shell wandering through a city that could never truly be home.

With a sharp breath, Lena picked up the pen. She was ready to fight, to claw her way back from the abyss, and **reclaim** her humanity, no matter the cost. The game had begun.

Comprehension Questions:

1. **What event sets Lena on her journey into the underbelly of Narida, and how does she discover the black market for souls?**
   Lena wakes up feeling an unsettling emptiness, realizing her soul is missing. After hearing rumors about a black market for souls operating in the hidden depths of Narida, she embarks on a perilous journey to retrieve her stolen essence.
2. **What does the man in the black market reveal about how souls are traded in Narida, and how does this challenge Lena's understanding of ownership and value?**
   The man reveals that in Narida, souls are treated as commodities that can be taken and traded without the owner's consent. He explains that Lena's soul was sold because it became valuable, challenging her belief in the inviolability of her own essence.

Vocabulary List (C2 Level):

1. **Commodity** - A valuable item or resource that can be bought and sold.
   In Narida, souls were treated as the ultimate commodity.
2. **Inviolable** - Sacred and unable to be violated or broken.
   Lena believed her soul to be inviolable, yet it was stolen without her consent.
3. **Opulent** - Lavishly rich and luxurious.
   The surface of Narida was adorned with opulent mansions, masking its darker underbelly.

4. **Dilapidated** - Falling apart or in a state of disrepair.
   The black market was hidden inside a dilapidated building, shrouded in secrecy.
5. **Calculating** - Coldly and strategically manipulative.
   The man in the black market had a calculating gleam in his eye as he explained the rules of the trade.
6. **Fragmented** - Broken into pieces or incomplete.
   Lena's soul had been fragmented and dispersed into the trade networks.
7. **Ethereal** - Delicate and otherworldly, often with a spiritual quality.
   The room glowed with ethereal lights from floating orbs and shimmering liquids.
8. **Mechanical** - Emotionless or automatic, lacking vitality.
   The soulless people Lena encountered moved with mechanical precision, their presence hollow.
9. **Perilous** - Full of danger or risk.
   Lena's journey into the depths of Narida was perilous, fraught with deception and threats.
10. **Absence** - The state of being missing or lacking.
    Lena awoke to an absence deep within her, realizing her soul had been taken.
11. **Insidious** - Subtly harmful or deceitful.
    The black market operated through insidious means, exploiting the value of stolen souls.
12. **Resolve** - Determination to accomplish a goal.
    With resolve, Lena decided to sign the papers and fight to reclaim her soul.
13. **Vacant** - Empty or devoid of expression or presence.
    The eyes of the soulless people were vacant, reflecting the loss of their humanity.
14. **Translucent** - Allowing light to pass through, yet not completely clear.
    The man's pale, translucent skin gave him an eerie appearance.

15. **Reclaim** - To retrieve or regain possession of something.
Lena was determined to reclaim her soul, no matter the cost.

22. THE EYES OF SILENCE

In a distant future, where the rapid march of technology had altered the very fabric of society, communication had taken on a form that was foreign to the world once known. The hum of machines, the pulse of digital streams, and the endless barrage of artificial voices had reduced speech to an obsolete art. Words, once the cornerstone of human interaction, had become an **endangered** species, overtaken by whispers and gestures, gestures that no longer carried meaning. The people had grown silent. It was not a choice, but an inevitable consequence of their reliance on machines that thought for them, spoke for them, and whispered into their ears the truths they were no longer willing to hear.

In this society, truth was a rare commodity, something hidden beneath layers of **obfuscation** and misdirection. Information was controlled, tailored, and filtered through digital filters that shaped reality itself. The louder the silence became, the more **distorted** the truth became. Yet, amidst this cacophony of quiet, there existed one person—an **anomaly**—who could see beyond the quiet void and unravel the mysteries that lay buried within.

His name was Elias, and he was a prophet, though not in the traditional sense. Elias was blind, his eyes nothing more than two empty sockets, devoid of light. Yet, his blindness was not a curse, but a gift. For Elias had learned to see the world not through sight, but through the lens of silence. His mind was attuned to the subtle **vibrations** of the world around him, and it was in these **vibrations** that the truths of the world could be heard. To others, it appeared that he wandered aimlessly, a man in darkness, but to him, the world was alive with hidden messages.

He had spent his entire life in this quiet world, living on the **periphery**, observing the silent motions of society. People came to him not for guidance through words, but for guidance through presence. They sought his wisdom, for Elias had the ability to see what others could not—he could hear the whispers of the world. And these whispers told him things that no one else could comprehend.

One day, a delegation came to him. They were from the Council of Silence, a governing body that had maintained the law of **quietude** for generations. Their robes were woven from the finest silks, their faces expressionless, their eyes empty of emotion. They were leaders in a world where words had become a rarity, and every gesture had meaning, every glance laden with expectation. They had come to Elias not for a prediction, but for something far more significant: a guide.

"Elias," the chief councilor spoke, his voice muffled by the silence that enveloped him. "We are at a crossroads. The silence, while bringing peace, has also caused division. The truth has become **fragmented**, concealed beneath layers of misunderstanding. The people no longer know what to believe. The whispers have grown erratic, and the balance of society is threatened."

Elias could hear the tension in the chief councilor's voice, a faint **vibration** that suggested a hidden fear, something far beyond the surface of his words. The silence surrounding him was thick, like a fog, suffocating the very air. Yet, Elias was undeterred. He had lived his entire life in this quiet world, listening to the undercurrents of truth that others ignored. He was the only one who could hear the true pulse of society, the only one who could see the world through the lens of silence.

"What is it that you seek from me?" Elias asked, his voice calm and steady.

"We need you to guide us," the chief councilor replied. "You can hear what we cannot. You see what we cannot. The truth is hidden from us, veiled in whispers and half-truths. We need you to help us restore balance, to **unravel** the knots that bind us and reveal the truths that have been silenced."

Elias nodded, his mind already racing with the weight of their request. The silence was not just a lack of sound—it was a force, a barrier that had been constructed over generations to shield the people from the noise of the outside world. But in this silence, truths had been buried, **manipulated**, and **distorted** beyond recognition. And it was Elias who could unearth them.

"I will help you," Elias said finally, his voice **unwavering**. "But understand this: the truth is not always what you want to hear. The truth is often inconvenient, uncomfortable, and disturbing. It will not be delivered in the way you expect, and it will not be easy to accept."

The councilors exchanged uncertain glances, but they knew that Elias was their only hope. The silence that had once brought peace was now a prison, and they needed the truth to break free.

For the next several days, Elias spent time with the council, listening to the whispers that filled the air. He would sit in the council chambers, his mind attuned to the subtle **vibrations** of the space, and he would listen. The whispers were faint at first, mere echoes of thoughts and emotions that lingered in the background. But as he focused, the whispers grew louder, clearer, until they became voices—voices of truth that had been silenced for far too long.

Elias began to **unravel** the fabric of society's illusion. The whispers told of corruption, **deceit**, and **manipulation** at the highest levels. The Council of Silence, in their desire to maintain control, had **suppressed** the truth for years, using silence as a tool to control the masses. They had **manipulated** the very essence of communication, **distorting** the whispers to suit their own agenda. And now, the people were waking up to the lies, to the truth that had been hidden beneath the surface for so long.

One evening, as Elias sat alone in his chamber, he heard a whisper that made his blood run cold. It was a voice he had never heard before, a voice filled with sorrow and **regret**. It spoke of betrayal, of a deep wound that had been inflicted upon the people, a wound that could never be healed as long as the truth remained hidden. It was then that Elias understood—the silence had not brought peace; it had merely silenced the cries of the oppressed.

The next day, Elias convened with the council. He did not need to speak to them in words. His presence alone was enough. The whispers had already spoken to him, and now it was time for the council to face the truth.

"The truth is simple," Elias said, his voice soft but firm. "The silence you have imposed upon your people has been used as a weapon. You have buried the truth beneath layers of silence, and in doing so, you have created a society built on lies. The truth cannot remain hidden any longer."

The councilors were stunned into silence, their faces a mixture of fear and disbelief. They had known, on some level, that the truth was **elusive**, but they had never imagined that it would be so devastating.

Elias turned to the chief councilor. "You have the power to change this, but it will not be easy. You must restore the voice to the people, allow them to speak, to share their truths, no matter how uncomfortable or inconvenient they may be. Only then will you begin to heal the wounds that have festered in the silence."

The chief councilor nodded, his eyes now filled with a sense of realization. The silence had been a **crutch**, a way to avoid facing difficult truths, but it was no longer sustainable. The people needed to speak, and they needed to listen.

And so, the council began the difficult task of **unraveling** the silence, of allowing the voices of the people to be heard once more. It was not an easy journey, for the truth was often painful, and the whispers were hard to decipher. But with Elias as their guide, they began to rebuild a society where speech was not a tool of control, but a means of **connection**.

In the end, Elias remained as he always had—silent, but no longer blind. For in the silence, he had seen the truth of the world, and in seeing it, he had given others the power to speak it.

Comprehension Questions:

1. **What role does Elias play in the society governed by the Council of Silence, and why do they seek his guidance?**
   Elias, though blind, possesses the ability to hear the subtle vibrations of the world, allowing him to perceive hidden truths. The Council of Silence seeks his guidance to unravel the growing division and fragmentation of truth caused by their imposed silence.
2. **How does Elias reveal the consequences of the Council's imposition of silence, and what solution does he propose?**
   Elias discovers that the silence imposed by the Council

has been used as a tool to suppress truths and control society. He proposes restoring the people's ability to speak freely, encouraging open communication as the path to healing and connection.

Vocabulary List (C2 Level):

1. **Obfuscation** - The act of making something unclear or difficult to understand.
   The Council's policies relied on the obfuscation of truth, burying facts beneath layers of silence.
2. **Endangered** - At risk of being lost or disappearing entirely.
   In the society Elias lived in, spoken words had become an endangered form of communication.
3. **Anomaly** - Something that deviates from what is normal or expected.
   Elias was an anomaly in his silent society, able to perceive truths others could not.
4. **Vibration** - A subtle oscillation or movement felt through a medium.
   Elias detected the vibrations of hidden truths in the quiet air around him.
5. **Quietude** - A state of calm and quiet.
   The Council of Silence enforced quietude across society, silencing voices in the name of peace.
6. **Periphery** - The outer edges or boundaries of an area or subject.
   Elias lived on the periphery of society, observing its flaws without participating directly.
7. **Unwavering** - Steadfast and resolute, not faltering.
   Elias's voice was unwavering as he revealed the Council's misuse of silence.
8. **Elusive** - Difficult to find, catch, or achieve.
   The truth in Elias's world was elusive, hidden beneath

layers of manipulated silence.

9. **Manipulate** - To control or influence something or someone cleverly or unscrupulously.
   The Council had manipulated the silence to conceal their misdeeds.
10. **Suppress** - To forcibly put an end to something or prevent it from being expressed.
    The Council suppressed speech to maintain their control over society.
11. **Resonance** - A deep, full sound that reverberates or an idea that evokes a strong emotional response.
    Elias felt the resonance of unspoken truths within the silence.
12. **Deceit** - The act of concealing or misrepresenting the truth.
    The whispers revealed the Council's deceit, hidden beneath their strict rules of silence.
13. **Fragmented** - Broken into smaller parts that are disconnected or incomplete.
    Elias observed that society's understanding of truth had become fragmented over generations.
14. **Dominion** - Control or sovereignty over something.
    The silence had held dominion over society, dictating every interaction.
15. **Unravel** - To solve or clarify something complex or mysterious.
    Elias's role was to unravel the hidden truths that had been buried by the silence.
16. **Distorted** - Twisted or altered out of its true, natural, or original state.
    The Council's manipulation of silence had distorted the people's perception of reality.
17. **Revelation** - A surprising or previously unknown fact that is revealed.
    Elias's revelation about the Council's misuse of silence shocked the members into reflection.

18. **Regret** - A feeling of sadness or disappointment about something that has happened.
    The whispers carried a deep sense of regret for the harm caused by prolonged silence.
19. **Crutch** - Something used for support, often relied on excessively.
    The Council used silence as a crutch to avoid confronting difficult truths.
20. **Connection** - A relationship in which people or things are linked.
    Elias believed restoring communication would rebuild the lost connection among the people.

23. THE WANDERER WHO FORGOT

There was once a wanderer, a traveler of realms, who journeyed across worlds that were beyond **comprehension**. The traveler, whose name had long since slipped from memory, roamed from one reality to the next with a sense of awe and wonder. Each world offered new sights, new experiences, new possibilities. The wanderer had no destination in mind, only the relentless desire to explore what lay beyond. But with each new world, something changed. The landscapes, the people, and the very **fabric** of existence shifted, as if the traveler was perpetually chasing an **elusive** dream.

The wanderer wandered without purpose, for purpose had become an **abstract** concept. In each reality, the traveler found themselves assuming a new identity, taking on the **guise** of someone else, someone shaped by the unique laws of that world. In one world, the traveler was a philosopher, contemplating the nature of existence. In another, a soldier, wielding a sword in battles that seemed endless and futile. In yet another, the traveler was an artist, painting visions of landscapes that were **indescribable**, captured on canvases that warped and bent like time itself.

But with every passing world, the traveler began to feel something slipping away. It wasn't the identities they assumed that they began to lose; it was themselves. At first, it was a vague sensation, like a distant echo, barely noticeable in the bustle of their adventures. The traveler would forget the name of a person they had met just hours ago, or lose track of where they had been the day before. At times, they would wake up in a new world, unsure of how they had arrived there or what they were meant to do. The continuity of their being started to **fray** at the edges.

One day, in a world that was a mixture of ancient ruins and futuristic cities, the traveler stood in front of a monument —a statue of a figure whose features seemed eerily familiar, yet completely foreign. It was an image of someone who had once been, someone who had traversed this path before. The traveler stared at the statue for what seemed like hours, the feeling of **recognition** growing stronger. But as the **recognition** deepened, so did the confusion. Who was this figure? Why did it seem as if they had known them, as if they had once been them?

The traveler shook their head, trying to dispel the intrusive thoughts, but the weight of the question lingered. As they wandered deeper into the world, trying to push the statue and its meaning out of their mind, they encountered a woman sitting on the edge of a crumbling stone wall. Her clothes were worn, her hair unkempt, but there was a knowing look in her eyes, as if she had seen through the very **fabric** of the universe.

"You seem lost," she said without preamble, her voice soft but carrying a weight that seemed to **resonate** with the very air.

The traveler paused, taken aback. "Lost? I don't think so. I am a wanderer, a traveler of worlds."

"Yes," the woman replied, her gaze never leaving the traveler's face. "But even wanderers can lose themselves, can they not? How many worlds have you seen? How many lives have you lived in all these realities?"

The traveler thought for a moment. "I've seen countless worlds. I've been many things: a philosopher, a warrior, a healer. I have lived many lives."

"And yet, you do not know who you are," the woman said, her voice now tinged with a sadness that seemed to bleed into the air around them.

The traveler felt a shiver run through them. "What do you mean? I know who I am. I am... I am—"

But the words caught in the traveler's throat. They couldn't finish the sentence. A deep, unsettling realization began to creep over them, the truth beginning to take shape. They didn't know who they were anymore. The wanderer, the traveler, the many personas—they were all just **fragmented**, pieces of a puzzle that no longer fit together.

"I have forgotten," the traveler whispered, their voice barely audible.

The woman nodded, her expression one of quiet **sympathy**. "Yes. Each world you visit, each life you live, erases another part of you. It is the price of wandering through the many realms. You have lost your **connection** to the original universe, to the person you once were."

The traveler closed their eyes, overwhelmed by the weight of this truth. The woman's words echoed in their mind, each syllable a hammer striking against the walls of their consciousness. They had been to so many worlds, assumed so many lives, that they had forgotten who they truly were. And yet, despite the loss, there was still something deep within them—a spark of **recognition**, a **faint** memory of a time when they had known their purpose.

"I don't remember," the traveler said softly, a hint of **despair** in their voice. "I don't remember who I was before all this."

"You were someone," the woman said, standing up and walking toward the traveler. "But now, you are many things, and yet, nothing at all. You are a wanderer, **adrift** in a sea of worlds. But remember this—every world you visit, every identity you take on, leaves a mark. Even if you forget, those marks remain. And one day, perhaps, you will remember enough to return to the place where you began."

The traveler looked at the woman, a strange sense of peace settling over them. "How can I return if I don't even remember where I came from?"

The woman smiled faintly, her eyes sparkling with an ancient **wisdom**. "You may not remember now, but the path will find you. The journey, though long and filled with forgotten selves, will always lead you back to where you belong."

With those final words, the woman turned and faded into the **ether**, leaving the traveler standing alone. The winds of the world howled around them, carrying with it the sounds of forgotten voices, the echoes of lives once lived.

And in that moment, the traveler understood. They might have forgotten who they were, but the essence of their being, the core of who they truly were, could never be erased. The journey was not just about finding new worlds, new identities —it was about **rediscovering** themselves amidst the **infinite** expanse of existence.

The traveler closed their eyes and took a deep breath. The road ahead was uncertain, but perhaps, just perhaps, they would find their way back home.

Comprehension Questions:

1. **How does the wanderer's journey across countless worlds impact their sense of identity?**
   The wanderer's journey erases parts of their original self with each new world they visit and identity they assume. Over time, they lose their connection to who they once were, becoming a fragmented collection of personas

without a true sense of self.

2. **What wisdom does the mysterious woman impart to the wanderer about their journey and eventual return?**
   The woman explains that although the wanderer has forgotten their original self, the marks left by each world and identity remain. She assures them that the journey, despite its uncertainties and losses, will eventually guide them back to where they belong.

Vocabulary List (C2 Level):

1. **Comprehension** - The ability to understand something.
   The wanderer struggled with the comprehension of their fragmented identity.
2. **Abstract** - Existing in thought or as an idea, but not having a physical or concrete existence.
   Purpose had become an abstract concept to the wanderer.
3. **Fabric** - The underlying structure or framework of something.
   The very fabric of existence seemed to shift with each world the wanderer visited.
4. **Guise** - An external appearance or assumed identity.
   The wanderer took on the guise of a philosopher in one world.
5. **Indescribable** - Too unusual or extreme to be adequately described.
   The artist painted visions of landscapes that were utterly indescribable.
6. **Fray** - To unravel or become worn at the edges.
   The continuity of the wanderer's being began to fray with each new reality.
7. **Recognition** - The ability to identify something as

familiar.
The traveler experienced a moment of recognition upon seeing the statue.

8. **Periphery** - The outer limits or edge of an area.
The wanderer lived on the periphery of their own memories, unable to connect fully.
9. **Resonate** - To evoke a strong emotional or meaningful response.
The woman's words resonated deeply with the wanderer.
10. **Unwavering** - Steadfast and resolute; not shaken.
Despite their despair, the wanderer maintained an unwavering curiosity about their journey.
11. **Sympathy** - Feelings of pity and compassion for someone else's distress.
The woman's expression held quiet sympathy for the wanderer's loss of identity.
12. **Despair** - The complete loss or absence of hope.
The wanderer felt a hint of despair as they realized they could not recall their original self.
13. **Faint** - Slight or barely perceptible.
A faint memory of their purpose lingered in the wanderer's mind.
14. **Adrift** - Without direction or purpose, like a boat floating without control.
The wanderer was adrift in a sea of worlds, disconnected from their origins.
15. **Ether** - The clear sky or the heavens; also, a sense of an intangible realm.
The woman faded into the ether, leaving the traveler alone.
16. **Fragmented** - Broken into pieces; incomplete.
The wanderer's sense of self had become fragmented over countless lives.
17. **Elusive** - Difficult to find, catch, or achieve.
The wanderer pursued an elusive sense of purpose across worlds.

18. **Wisdom** - The quality of having experience, knowledge, and good judgment.
    The woman shared her wisdom about the wanderer's journey and its ultimate destination.
19. **Infinite** - Limitless or endless in extent.
    The wanderer's journey spanned the infinite expanse of existence.
20. **Rediscover** - To find again something that was forgotten or lost.
    The wanderer sought to rediscover their original self amidst the many lives they had lived.

24. THE BREATHE OF THE FOREST

There was something inherently unsettling about the forest that surrounded Elyse's small cottage, though she had lived near it for years. At first, it was the dense **canopy** of trees that seemed to close in on her, their **gnarled** branches reaching out like the fingers of unseen hands. But over time, she had grown accustomed to the forest's vastness and shadowed depths. Still, a whispering **unease** lingered, a sensation that she couldn't quite place—like a **faint murmur** at the edges of her consciousness.

Elyse had always loved the solitude the forest provided. The rhythmic sound of the wind through the leaves, the occasional call of a distant bird, and the rustling of small creatures moving through the underbrush were the music of her life. But recently, things had changed. The air felt thicker, the wind felt heavier, and the trees, once silent, seemed to be speaking to her in ways she couldn't understand.

One evening, as **twilight** descended and the sun cast long shadows over the forest floor, Elyse ventured deeper into the woods than usual. The forest was alive with the **faint murmur** of leaves, a low **murmur** in the distance that she couldn't identify. She had grown used to the quiet, the **serenity** of this wild world, but tonight, it felt different. The wind had picked up, carrying an almost **imperceptible** hum, as if the forest itself was exhaling.

Elyse paused and closed her eyes, letting the breeze sweep across her skin. There it was again—an odd sensation, like a **pulse** in the air. She took a step forward, drawn by an instinct she couldn't explain. The path narrowed, the trees thickening around her, until the woods felt suffocating. She could hear the wind swirling through the branches, but this time, it wasn't just the wind—it was the voices of something **ancient**, something far older than she could comprehend.

The trees, tall and towering, seemed to **sway** in a way that was too **deliberate**, too coordinated. She had always known the forest was old—older than any records could describe, older than even the oldest map of the land. But it had never felt like this before. The air was thick with an energy she had never sensed in all her years of living beside it. The **ancient** oak in front of her creaked as if it were **groaning** in its sleep. The wind shifted, carrying a low **murmur**, a voice too deep and too far away to decipher, but it made her heart race nonetheless.

Curiosity tugged at her, and despite the growing sense of **unease**, she pressed on. She had walked these woods countless times before, but now it felt as though the trees were watching her. She could almost hear the **faintest sigh**, a gust of air that seemed too **deliberate** to be natural. It was as though the forest was **inhaling** and **exhaling**, the rhythm of its breath filling the air around her.

As she ventured further, Elyse's senses heightened. The ground beneath her feet was damp, the rich scent of earth thick in the air. The leaves above her whispered and rustled with the sound of a distant conversation, though the language was alien to her ears. The trees bent in the breeze, creaking as if stretching their limbs after a long, peaceful slumber.

And then, in the silence between the gusts of wind, she heard it —a voice, **faint** but clear. It was soft, almost like a **whisper**, but it seemed to come from all around her.

"Elyse…" the voice murmured, like a distant memory stirring from the depths of time.

She froze, her breath catching in her throat. The voice was **ancient**, filled with the weight of millennia. She had heard nothing like it before, not in all her years of walking the woods. It wasn't human. It wasn't animal. It was the voice of the forest itself, deep and **resonant**, as old as the earth.

"Elyse…" The voice again, this time louder, more urgent, as though calling her from the depths of the trees.

Her heart began to race, the hairs on the back of her neck standing on end. Slowly, she turned around, but there was no one there. No figure, no shadow—only the towering trees, their branches twisting like **gnarled** hands reaching toward the sky. But as she turned back toward the path, she realized that something had changed. The wind had shifted, no longer the soft breeze it had been. Now, it carried with it a sense of purpose, a **pulse** that seemed to emanate from the heart of the forest.

The trees were alive in a way she had never understood before. They were not just silent witnesses to the passage of time; they were **sentient**, breathing entities that had witnessed centuries unfold. She could feel the life of the forest all around her—the slow, **deliberate** movement of the trees, the deep sighs as they **exhaled** through the wind. The **ancient** oak before her, its massive trunk twisted with age, seemed to lean toward her, its bark **groaning** as if it recognized her presence.

"Why do you come?" the voice spoke again, clearer now, the words **resonating** in the air.

Elyse's knees trembled, but she stood her ground. "Who are you?" she whispered, her voice trembling in the weight of the moment. "What are you?"

"I am the breath of the forest," the voice replied, the sound of it vibrating through the ground beneath her feet. "I am the wind that carries the voices of those who came before. I am the **ancient** spirits of the trees, the **pulse** of life that has endured since the beginning of time."

Elyse's mind raced. She had always known the forest was old, but she had never imagined that it could be alive in such a way—that it could speak, feel, and remember. The trees, the leaves, the earth beneath her feet—everything had a voice, a story, a memory. And now, they had chosen to share it with her.

"I did not mean to intrude," Elyse said, her voice barely above a **whisper**. "I didn't know."

The voice softened, and the wind, which had been howling moments before, calmed. "You are not intruding," it said. "You are a part of us, just as we are a part of you. The breath of the forest flows through your veins as it does through ours."

As the words hung in the air, Elyse felt something **profound** stir within her. The **connection** between herself and the forest, once distant and **abstract**, was now clear. She was not merely a visitor in this place. She was connected to it, woven into its very **fabric**, as much a part of it as the roots that reached deep into the earth.

For a long time, she stood there, feeling the **pulse** of the forest—the slow, steady beat that had carried the trees through millennia. And in that moment, she understood. The forest was alive, and it was breathing, living through time, through the ages, and through every person who had walked its paths. It had always watched, always listened, and now, it had chosen to speak.

And Elyse, for the first time, truly listened.

Comprehension Questions:

1. **What changes did Elyse notice in the forest, and how did they lead her to realize its sentient nature?**
   Elyse noticed the air felt heavier, the wind carried an almost deliberate hum, and the trees seemed to sway in a coordinated manner. These changes, along with hearing an ancient voice, revealed the forest's sentient nature and its deep connection to life and time.
2. **How does the voice of the forest describe itself, and what does Elyse learn about her connection to it?**
   The voice describes itself as the breath of the forest, the wind carrying voices of those who came before, and the pulse of life enduring through time. Elyse learns that she is connected to the forest, as its life force flows through her, making her an integral part of its existence.

Vocabulary List (C2 Level):

1. **Canopy** - A covering, typically formed by the tops of trees.
   The dense canopy of the forest blocked out most of the sunlight.
2. **Gnarled** - Twisted and rough, often from age or weathering.
   The gnarled branches of the oak tree reached out like ancient hands.
3. **Murmur** - A soft, indistinct sound made by a person or thing.
   The murmur of the wind through the leaves was both calming and eerie.
4. **Imperceptible** - Impossible or difficult to perceive by the senses.
   An imperceptible hum filled the air, making Elyse pause in her tracks.
5. **Sway** - To move slowly back and forth or side to side.
   The trees seemed to sway in a deliberate rhythm, almost

as if they were alive.

6. **Resonant** - Deep, clear, and continuing to sound or reverberate.
   The resonant voice of the forest vibrated through the ground beneath her feet.
7. **Sentient** - Capable of feeling, perceiving, or experiencing subjectively.
   Elyse realized that the forest was sentient, breathing and observing her presence.
8. **Deliberate** - Done consciously and intentionally.
   The wind carried a deliberate rhythm, as if the forest were trying to communicate.
9. **Ancient** - Belonging to the very distant past.
   The ancient oak groaned under the weight of centuries.
10. **Ethereal** - Extremely delicate and light in a way that seems not of this world.
    The ethereal whisper of the forest filled Elyse with both awe and fear.
11. **Profound** - Very great or intense; having deep meaning.
    Elyse felt a profound connection to the forest as she listened to its voice.
12. **Inhale** - To breathe in.
    It felt as though the forest itself was inhaling deeply around her.
13. **Whisper** - To speak very softly.
    The leaves whispered secrets that Elyse could almost understand.
14. **Fabric** - The essential structure or framework of something.
    She realized she was woven into the very fabric of the forest's existence.
15. **Groan** - A low, mournful sound, often expressing pain or strain.
    The ancient tree groaned as it leaned toward her, creaking under its own weight.

16. **Unease** - A feeling of worry or discomfort.
    An unease settled over Elyse as she ventured deeper into the woods.
17. **Exhale** - To breathe out.
    The forest seemed to exhale, its breath rustling through the leaves.
18. **Twilight** - The soft glowing light from the sky when the sun is below the horizon.
    The forest grew more mysterious as twilight descended.
19. **Serenity** - The state of being calm and peaceful.
    The usual serenity of the forest had been replaced by an unsettling tension.
20. **Pulse** - A rhythmic beat or flow.
    Elyse could feel the pulse of the forest, a steady rhythm that connected everything.

25. THE LAST DREAMER'S GHOST

Vera had always known that her dreams were unlike those of ordinary people. While others wandered through the hazy landscapes of their unconscious minds, she had the **uncanny** ability to control them. She could navigate through her dreams with ease, shaping the scenery, **manipulating** time, and even conversing with people who seemed so real that they might as well have been pulled from the waking world. Her dreams, to her, were a second life, a sanctuary where she could escape, create, and experience the impossible. But recently, something had started to change, and she could feel it like a chill in the air, a **disturbance** in the otherwise **tranquil** world she had cultivated for years.

It began with small things—**flickers** of shadow at the corner of her vision, whispers that echoed just beyond the edge of hearing, and the subtle shifting of objects when she wasn't paying attention. At first, Vera thought it was just a result of spending too much time in the dream world. But over time, these strange occurrences grew more frequent, and one night, as she drifted off into sleep, she found herself in a dream that felt... wrong.

She had just entered the familiar landscape of a sunlit meadow, the kind of place where she often went to think and clear her mind. The grass was a soft green, and the wind carried the sweet scent of wildflowers. It was a place she had visited countless times, a perfect image of **serenity**. But tonight, something was different. The sky above, usually an **ethereal** blue, was now tinged with an unnatural hue, a murky, swirling gray that seemed to **pulse** like a heartbeat. The air felt thick, almost suffocating, and the once soft grass beneath her feet now appeared brittle and sharp.

Vera looked around, confusion settling in. "This isn't right," she whispered to herself. "This is not my dream."

As she turned to leave, a figure emerged from the fog, walking toward her with slow, **deliberate** steps. Vera's breath caught in her throat as she recognized the face. It was her own. The woman who approached her had the same eyes, the same hair, but her expression was one of **unrelenting** sorrow, as if she had been lost for far too long.

"You shouldn't be here," the dream-Vera said, her voice hollow, tinged with an unsettling **desperation**. "You're not supposed to see this."

Vera took a step back, her heart racing. "Who are you?" she demanded, though deep down, she already knew the answer.

"I am you," the figure replied, "or rather, I was. I was a dream. And now, I want to wake up."

The words sent a shiver down Vera's spine. She understood instantly—this wasn't a normal dream. This was a nightmare taking form, a shadow of something that had slipped through the cracks of her carefully controlled dreamscape. She had never felt the weight of fear in her dreams before. But now, she could feel it pressing in from all sides, an **oppressive** force that was threatening to consume her.

"You can't leave," Vera said, her voice trembling despite herself. "You're a part of me. You're just a dream."

The figure smiled, a cruel and twisted smile that didn't belong on her own face. "No," it said, "I'm not just a dream. I am the part of you that you've been hiding, the part you refuse to acknowledge. And now, I'm breaking free."

Before Vera could respond, the landscape around them began to **distort**. The grass twisted into jagged, black tendrils, and the once calm sky above them crackled with lightning. The air grew cold, and the sound of distant, mournful wailing filled her ears. Her surroundings were no longer a peaceful meadow; they had become a place of horror, a reflection of her deepest fears.

In a panic, Vera turned to flee, but the ground beneath her feet began to shift, swallowing her with every step. The nightmare that had once been confined to the edges of her consciousness was now **unraveling** her reality. The boundary between her dreams and the waking world was crumbling, and the horrors that had once only existed in her mind were bleeding into her life.

When Vera awoke, she was not in her bed, but standing at the edge of a cliff overlooking a vast, dark ocean. Her heart pounded in her chest as she struggled to comprehend what had just happened. Was it still a dream? Or had she crossed over into something more dangerous, something that could no longer be controlled?

She looked around in **disbelief**, trying to steady herself. This place… it felt too real, too solid. The wind, the scent of salt in the air, the crashing waves below—it was all too **tangible**. This wasn't supposed to happen. Vera had spent years **cultivating** her ability to control her dreams, but now, it seemed that something had slipped through the cracks, something that had learned how to break the rules.

For days after, Vera could not escape the feeling that the boundaries between her dreams and her waking life were beginning to **fray**. Every time she closed her eyes, she saw glimpses of the nightmare world—shadows lurking in the corner of her vision, muffled voices calling her name, the sound of something breathing just behind her. It was as if the dream was following her, watching her every move, waiting for her to slip again.

And then, one evening, as she sat at her desk, writing in her journal, she heard it—the unmistakable **whisper** of a voice, soft and insistent.

"Vera…"

She froze, her pen hovering above the page. The voice was coming from inside her head, but it was not her own. It was the nightmare that had been chasing her, trying to make its way into the waking world. And it was getting stronger.

"Vera…" The voice repeated, this time louder, more demanding. "You can't hide from me forever."

Suddenly, the room around her began to darken, the walls closing in, the air growing thick with tension. Vera knew she couldn't run any longer. The line between the dream world and reality had been irrevocably shattered. The nightmare she had created in her own mind was now a **manifestation**, and it was determined to claim her.

With trembling hands, she stood up, her heart pounding in her chest. "I won't let you take over," she whispered, but even as the words left her lips, she knew it might be too late. The nightmare had already begun to bleed into her reality, and there was no escaping the **consequences** of having unleashed it.

As she stepped toward the door, the shadows seemed to stretch and writhe, and the haunting voice grew louder, closer, until it was right behind her, whispering in her ear.

"Wake up, Vera," the voice breathed. "Wake up, or we'll both be lost."

Comprehension Questions:

1. **How does Vera's ability to control her dreams begin to change, and what new challenges does she face because of it?**
   Vera notices unsettling changes in her dream world, such as shadows, whispers, and distorted landscapes. These changes culminate in an encounter with a nightmare version of herself that claims it is breaking free, causing the boundary between her dreams and reality to fray.
2. **What is the significance of the nightmare telling Vera to "wake up," and how does it reflect her internal struggle?**
   The nightmare's command to "wake up" signifies Vera's need to confront her fears and the parts of herself she has repressed. It highlights her internal struggle to maintain control over her dreams and reality as the nightmare begins to influence her waking life.

Vocabulary List (C2 Level):

1. **Uncanny** - Strange or mysterious in an unsettling way.
   Vera found the uncanny shadows in her dream unsettling, as if they were alive.
2. **Manipulate** - To skillfully control or influence something.
   Vera could manipulate the landscapes of her dreams with ease.
3. **Tranquil** - Calm, peaceful, and free from disturbance.
   Her dreams were usually tranquil, a sanctuary from the chaos of life.

4. **Disturbance** - A disruption of peace or normalcy.
   The disturbance in Vera's dream world began with subtle whispers and shadows.
5. **Flicker** - A brief or irregular appearance of light or movement.
   Shadows would flicker at the edge of her vision, making her uneasy.
6. **Deliberate** - Done consciously and intentionally.
   The nightmare-Vera's steps toward her were slow and deliberate.
7. **Desperation** - A state of despair, typically resulting in rash behavior.
   The desperation in the nightmare-Vera's voice sent chills down her spine.
8. **Oppressive** - Overwhelming and suffocating, often referring to atmosphere or tension.
   The air in the dream felt oppressive, as if it was pressing down on Vera.
9. **Tangible** - Perceptible by touch; real and concrete.
   The wind and salt in the air felt too tangible to be part of a dream.
10. **Fray** - To unravel or come apart at the edges.
    The boundary between her dreams and reality began to fray.
11. **Inevitable** - Certain to happen; unavoidable.
    Vera felt the nightmare's intrusion into her waking life was inevitable.
12. **Reverberate** - To echo repeatedly.
    The nightmare's voice seemed to reverberate in her mind long after waking.
13. **Unrelenting** - Not yielding in strength, severity, or determination.
    The nightmare's pursuit was unrelenting, following Vera even when she was awake.
14. **Distort** - To twist or change something so it no longer appears normal.

The peaceful meadow began to distort, turning into a jagged, nightmarish landscape.
15. **Manifestation** - An outward or visible expression of something, especially an abstract idea.
The nightmare-Vera was a manifestation of her hidden fears and repressed emotions.
16. **Cultivate** - To develop or improve through careful effort.
Vera had cultivated her dreamscape over the years, but it was now crumbling.
17. **Periphery** - The outer edges or margins of something.
The strange occurrences started at the periphery of her dreams before overtaking them.
18. **Bleed (into)** - To spread or flow into something else.
Her nightmare began to bleed into her waking reality, blurring the lines between the two.
19. **Disbelief** - Inability or refusal to accept something as true.
Vera stared in disbelief at the changes in her dream world.
20. **Consequences** - Results or effects, often of a negative kind.
Vera knew she had to face the consequences of unleashing the nightmare.

26. THE SKY ABOVE THE STARS

In the vast **expanse** of the cosmos, where the ordinary laws of space and time seemed to **wane**, Captain Elara Voss piloted the starship Aurora. Her mission was routine—charting new regions of the universe, mapping stars, and cataloging celestial phenomena. Yet, on this particular voyage, she would encounter something that defied both her understanding and the universe's known paradigms.

As the Aurora glided silently through the star-speckled void, Elara found herself captivated by the **kaleidoscope** of **luminescent** bodies stretching infinitely beyond her view. The stars, those ancient sentinels of light, seemed to whisper secrets of the cosmos, secrets that eluded human comprehension. The vast emptiness, paradoxically teeming with possibilities, was a canvas of **ineffable** beauty.

Suddenly, the onboard navigation system detected an **anomaly**. A region of space, previously uncharted and marked by an inexplicably high concentration of energy, lay ahead. Intrigued and driven by a curiosity that had often been her guiding compass, Elara decided to investigate. As she adjusted the ship's trajectory, the phenomenon revealed itself—a radiant sphere, pulsating with an **ethereal** glow, suspended in the abyss. It was as if the sky above the stars had opened a portal to some **primordial** chapter of the universe.

As the Aurora approached, the ship's sensors went haywire, overwhelmed by the cacophony of data emanating from the **anomaly**. Elara's hands danced over the controls, her mind a tempest of calculations and hypotheses. The sphere seemed to draw the ship closer, its gravitational pull an enigmatic force that defied conventional astrophysics.

The ship's communication system crackled to life, a voice resonating through the cabin, ancient and profound. "Welcome, seeker of truth," it intoned with a **gravitas** that sent shivers down Elara's spine. "You stand on the **precipice** of creation, where the sky above the stars unfolds its mysteries."

Elara, though seasoned in the art of interstellar exploration, found herself speechless. Her voice, when it emerged, was a mere whisper against the grandeur of the moment. "Who, or what, are you?" she inquired, her tone a blend of awe and trepidation.

The voice replied, its resonance a **symphony** of

knowledge and timelessness. "I am the Echo, a remnant of the cosmos's infancy. Within this sphere lies the **tapestry** of existence, woven with threads of time and space, reality and illusion."

As the sphere's **luminescence** enveloped the ship, Elara's consciousness expanded, transcending the **corporeal** confines of her form. She beheld the universe's genesis—a cataclysmic burst of energy birthing galaxies, stars, and worlds. Time unraveled before her, a **continuum** of events cascading like a river of stardust. She perceived the intricate dance of celestial bodies, their gravitational waltz a testament to the universe's **harmonious** chaos.

Yet, amidst this cosmic revelation, another truth emerged—one that challenged the very essence of her understanding. Reality, the Echo revealed, was but a **facet** of a larger, unfathomable existence. The universe was a multiverse, each dimension a reflection of infinite possibilities, each reality a mere shadow of its greater self.

"The sky above the stars," the Echo continued, "is a mirror, reflecting the myriad **facets** of existence. It holds the secrets of creation, the essence of life, and the **boundless** potential of the cosmos. Those who dare to peer beyond its veil glimpse the truth of their own being."

Elara, her mind now interwoven with the **tapestry** of the

cosmos, grappled with the enormity of this revelation. The knowledge was intoxicating, a **symphony** of enlightenment and **enigma**. She pondered her place within this cosmic mosaic, a single thread in a **tapestry** of universes.

"What does this mean for us?" she queried, her voice a fragile bridge between the known and the unknown.

"The journey of understanding," the Echo replied, "is both a gift and a burden. To know the universe is to embrace its infinities, its complexities, and its simplicities. It is to recognize that you are both a creator and a creation, an observer and a participant in the dance of existence."

The sphere's light began to fade, its **luminescence** retreating into the vastness from whence it came. The Echo's voice, now a gentle whisper, imparted a final message. "Carry this knowledge with humility and **reverence**. For in the end, the sky above the stars is not just a phenomenon to be understood, but a reminder of the infinite potential within you."

As the Aurora resumed its journey, the cosmos once again a sea of stars and silence, Elara was left with a profound sense of purpose. The universe, with its myriad mysteries, beckoned her with promises of discovery and understanding. In the solitude of space, she felt an unyielding connection to the cosmos, a kinship with the stars that **transcended** the boundaries of time and space.

With a heart brimming with newfound wisdom and wonder, Elara charted a course for the unknown, ready to embrace the myriad possibilities that awaited beyond the veil of stars. The sky above the stars had revealed its secrets, and she, a humble traveler of the cosmos, was forever transformed by its enigmatic grace.

Comprehension Questions:

1. **What does Captain Elara Voss discover about the nature of the universe after encountering the radiant sphere?**
   Elara learns that the universe is part of a larger multiverse, where each dimension reflects infinite possibilities. The sphere, described as the "sky above the stars," reveals that reality is a facet of a much larger and unfathomable existence.
2. **How does the Echo describe humanity's relationship with the cosmos, and what does it suggest about the journey of understanding?**
   The Echo explains that humanity is both a creator and a creation, an observer and a participant in the universe's dance. The journey of understanding is portrayed as a gift and a burden, requiring humility and reverence for the infinite complexities of existence.

Vocabulary List (C2 Level):

1. **Expanse** - A vast, open area or stretch.
   The ship glided through the endless expanse of the

cosmos.

2. **Wane** - To decrease in strength, intensity, or power.
In this region of space, the ordinary laws of time seemed to wane.
3. **Kaleidoscope** - A constantly changing pattern or scene.
The stars formed a kaleidoscope of colors in the vast void of space.
4. **Luminescent** - Emitting light without heat.
The sphere radiated a luminescent glow, captivating Elara.
5. **Anomaly** - Something that deviates from the norm or expectations.
The region of space ahead was marked by an unexplainable anomaly.
6. **Primordial** - Existing from the beginning of time; ancient.
The radiant sphere seemed to hold a primordial energy.
7. **Ineffable** - Too great or extreme to be expressed in words.
Elara was struck by the ineffable beauty of the cosmos.
8. **Ethereal** - Extremely delicate and light, almost otherworldly.
The sky above the stars glowed with an ethereal light.
9. **Gravitas** - A sense of seriousness or importance.
The voice of the Echo carried an unyielding gravitas.
10. **Precipice** - A point where danger or difficulty begins; a steep cliff.
The Echo described the anomaly as a precipice of creation.
11. **Symphony** - A harmonious arrangement of elements.
The Echo's voice was a symphony of knowledge and timelessness.
12. **Tapestry** - A rich and complex combination of elements or ideas.
The Echo revealed the universe as a tapestry woven with

time and space.

13. **Corporeal** - Relating to the physical, tangible body.
    As her consciousness expanded, Elara felt herself transcend the corporeal world.
14. **Continuum** - A continuous sequence where no distinct divisions exist.
    Time unfolded before Elara as a continuum of stardust and creation.
15. **Harmonious** - Forming a pleasing or consistent whole.
    The celestial bodies moved in a harmonious waltz of gravitational forces.
16. **Facet** - One side of something many-sided, particularly a concept or object.
    The Echo described reality as a single facet of a greater existence.
17. **Boundless** - Unlimited or immense.
    The sphere held the boundless potential of the cosmos.
18. **Enigma** - A person or thing that is mysterious or difficult to understand.
    The sphere remained an enigma, even as it revealed profound truths.
19. **Transcend** - To go beyond the limits of something.
    Elara's mind transcended her physical form, connecting to the universe.
20. **Reverence** - Deep respect for something.
    The Echo advised Elara to carry her newfound knowledge with reverence.

27. THE GRIEF COLLECTOR

In the bustling **metropolis** of New Haven, where the **clamor** of everyday life veiled an undercurrent of unspoken sorrow, the unique profession of a grief collector thrived. This was a world unlike any other, where emotions could be extracted, distilled, and confined into tangible objects, each one a repository of human despair. The city was a **labyrinth** of intricate feelings, with its inhabitants perpetually balancing their lives on the **precipice** of emotional **tumult**.

Eliot Marlowe, a seasoned grief collector, was a man of few words and profound **introspection**. He had spent years mastering the delicate art of grief extraction, a skill that required not only a deft touch but an empathetic heart. His studio, an unassuming space nestled between a quaint bookshop and a café that perpetually smelled of freshly baked bread, served as both a sanctuary and a workshop. Within its walls, shelves groaned under the weight of glass vials and porcelain urns, each containing a fragment of human sorrow awaiting transformation.

Eliot's reputation as the finest grief collector in New Haven was unrivaled. His clients ranged from the inconsolable widow yearning to relinquish the ache of loss to the melancholy poet seeking to liberate his creativity from the shackles of despair. Yet, despite his successes, Eliot harbored a secret—a grief of his own, long buried and untouched. He had never dared to confront it, for fear that acknowledging its existence might unravel the delicate **equilibrium** he had meticulously maintained.

On a blustery autumn morning, as leaves pirouetted through the streets like dancers in a forgotten ballet, Eliot received an unusual request. A letter, delivered in a vellum envelope sealed with crimson wax, bore the insignia of the enigmatic Lumina Institute—a prestigious organization known for its **esoteric** explorations into the human psyche. The missive, penned in elegant script, extended an invitation to retrieve a grief that had eluded capture for decades.

Intrigued yet **apprehensive**, Eliot accepted the task, his curiosity piqued by the challenge. The Lumina Institute, with its austere façade and **labyrinthine** corridors, exuded an air of solemnity befitting its purpose. As Eliot traversed the marble halls, he was acutely aware of the weight of history that permeated the air—a storied past of emotional alchemy and scholarly pursuit.

He was greeted by Dr. Livia Fontaine, a woman whose presence commanded both respect and **reverence**. Her eyes, a shade of azure that mirrored the depths of the sea, regarded Eliot with a mixture of admiration and scrutiny.

"Mr. Marlowe," she began, her voice a melodious cadence that resonated through the room, "our archives indicate that you are uniquely qualified for this endeavor. The grief we seek to reclaim is one of unprecedented magnitude, encapsulated within an **heirloom** of considerable antiquity."

Eliot nodded, his curiosity intensifying. "What form does this grief take?"

Dr. Fontaine gestured towards a mahogany table, upon which rested a delicate music box, its surface embellished with mother-of-pearl inlays that shimmered in the dim light. "This music box belonged to Lady Arabella Everleigh, a luminary of the Victorian era. It is said that her sorrow, born of unrequited love and societal ostracism, is ensconced within."

Eliot approached the music box with **reverence**, his fingers tracing the intricate patterns that adorned its surface. As he lifted the lid, a **haunting** melody unfurled, each note imbued with a palpable sense of longing and despair. The music resonated deep within him, awakening echoes of his own dormant grief—a **haunting** specter that had remained hidden for far too long.

The process of grief extraction was a delicate one, requiring Eliot to navigate the **labyrinth** of emotions with precision and care. As he embarked on this journey, he found himself inexorably drawn into Lady Arabella's world—a **tapestry** of **opulent** ballrooms and clandestine rendezvous, where love and anguish intertwined in a tragic dance.

With each note, Eliot's understanding of Lady Arabella's plight deepened, and he began to unravel the layers of her sorrow. Her unrequited love for a man bound by the shackles of convention and duty had left an indelible mark upon her soul, a wound that festered beneath the veneer of societal **decorum**.

As Eliot delved deeper into her grief, he confronted the shadows of his own past—a **kaleidoscope** of memories tinged with bittersweet nostalgia. He recalled the love he had once known, a love that had been extinguished by the caprices of fate. The loss had left a void within him, a chasm he had sought to fill through the sorrows of others.

It was within this crucible of emotion that Eliot found the strength to confront his own buried sorrow. As he extracted the essence of Lady Arabella's grief, he recognized the **universality** of human suffering—the shared experiences that transcended time and place, binding individuals in a silent, unspoken **kinship**.

In the quiet aftermath of the extraction, Eliot held the vial containing Lady Arabella's grief, its contents a swirling **miasma** of emotion rendered tangible. As he gazed upon it, he felt a profound sense of **catharsis**, a release from the chains that had bound him for so long.

Dr. Fontaine, observing the transformation in Eliot, offered a gentle smile. "You have not only reclaimed a lost grief, Mr. Marlowe, but you have also **liberated** yourself."

Eliot nodded, understanding that his journey as a grief collector was far from over. Yet, he now carried with him a newfound sense of purpose—a recognition of the power inherent in the acknowledgment and release of sorrow. In a world where grief could be collected and stored, Eliot had discovered the most profound truth of all: that healing began with the courage to confront one's own shadows.

As he left the Lumina Institute, the music box safely ensconced within its velvet-lined case, Eliot felt a lightness in his step and a warmth in his heart. The city, with its **clamor** of life and emotion, beckoned him forward, and he embraced it with open arms—a grief collector reborn, ready to face the world anew.

Comprehension Questions:

1. **What unique ability does Eliot Marlowe possess, and how does he use it in his profession?**
   Eliot Marlowe is a grief collector, skilled in extracting and distilling human sorrow into tangible forms like vials and urns. He uses his empathetic heart and delicate expertise to help clients release their pain, from widows mourning loss to poets seeking creative liberation.
2. **How does Eliot's encounter with Lady Arabella's music box affect his personal journey?**
   The process of extracting grief from Lady Arabella's music box forces Eliot to confront his own buried sorrow, stemming from a past love. Through this, he realizes the universality of suffering and experiences a cathartic release, discovering the courage to face his own grief and find purpose in healing.

Vocabulary List (C2 Level):

1. **Metropolis** - A large, densely populated urban area.
   The bustling metropolis of New Haven was alive with activity.
2. **Clamor** - A loud and confused noise, often from a crowd.
   The clamor of the city masked the quiet sorrows of its inhabitants.
3. **Labyrinth** - A complex network of paths or passages; a maze.
   The city was a labyrinth of emotions and hidden stories.
4. **Precipice** - A very steep rock face or metaphorically, a dangerous situation.
   The inhabitants balanced their lives on the precipice of emotional tumult.
5. **Introspection** - The examination of one's own thoughts and feelings.

Eliot was a man of profound introspection, often lost in his thoughts.

6. **Apprehensive** - Anxious or fearful that something bad may happen.
Eliot was apprehensive about accepting the Lumina Institute's request.

7. **Esoteric** - Intended for or likely to be understood by a small, specialized audience.
The Lumina Institute was renowned for its esoteric studies into the human psyche.

8. **Heirloom** - A valuable object passed down through generations.
Lady Arabella's music box was an heirloom steeped in sorrow and history.

9. **Haunting** - Poignant and evocative, often in a way that lingers in the memory.
The melody of the music box was haunting, filled with unspoken anguish.

10. **Reverence** - Deep respect or admiration for something.
Eliot approached the music box with reverence, sensing its emotional weight.

11. **Tapestry** - A rich and intricate combination of events or elements.
Lady Arabella's story was a tapestry of love, anguish, and societal constraints.

12. **Opulent** - Ostentatiously rich and luxurious.
Lady Arabella's world was one of opulent ballrooms and hidden heartache.

13. **Decorum** - Behavior in keeping with good taste and propriety.
Lady Arabella's grief was hidden beneath a façade of societal decorum.

14. **Miasma** - A heavy atmosphere or cloud of something unpleasant.
The vial of grief swirled with a miasma of emotions.

15. **Catharsis** - The process of releasing strong emotions, leading to relief.
    Eliot experienced catharsis as he extracted the grief from the music box.
16. **Universality** - The quality of being shared by all people.
    Eliot recognized the universality of human suffering during the extraction.
17. **Kinship** - A sense of connection or shared experience.
    Eliot felt a silent kinship with Lady Arabella's sorrow.
18. **Liberate** - To set free from confinement or oppression.
    Dr. Fontaine noted that Eliot had liberated himself from his own grief.
19. **Equilibrium** - A state of balance or stability.
    Eliot had carefully maintained his emotional equilibrium for years.
20. **Tumult** - A state of great noise, confusion, or disturbance.
    The city's emotional tumult provided a unique backdrop for Eliot's work.

28. THE INK THAT MOVES

The ink pot was an **unassuming** vessel, elegant in its simplicity, and nestled inconspicuously upon an antique mahogany writing desk. For years, the writer had sought inspiration, searching ceaselessly for the elusive spark that would ignite the dormant pages of his unwritten masterpiece. Each day, he would sit by the window, quill poised, awaiting the muse that evaded him with such maddening persistence.

It was on a dreary afternoon, the sky a drab **tapestry** of grey, that the ink began its subtle **metamorphosis**. With an air of spontaneity that belied its former inertia, the ink swirled with a newfound **vivacity**, as though infused with a life force of its own. The writer, oblivious to the **arcane** phenomena unfolding before him, dipped his quill into the inkpot, unaware of the **portentous** shift that had begun to unfurl.

As the tip of his quill met the parchment, the ink flowed with an ease that was almost **preternatural**. Words, once obstinate in their refusal to be summoned, cascaded forth with a lyrical grace. The writer, entranced, watched as his hand moved of its own accord, guided by an unseen hand that orchestrated the **choreography** of letters. Each stroke of the quill was a note, each word a melody, and together they composed the opus of his soul.

Yet, as the sentences unfurled, he became aware of an **uncanny** peculiarity. The ink, with a wilful autonomy, began to rearrange his prose, altering the very fabric of his narrative. A sentence intended to describe the gentle whisper of the wind through the trees was transformed into an ominous foreboding of an impending storm. Characters, once mere figments of his imagination, took on a sentience that defied the constraints of fiction.

Unable to comprehend the phenomena, the writer paused, his mind a **maelstrom** of befuddlement. It was then that he noticed the ink—moving with deliberate **choreography**—manifesting an intricate script upon the parchment. The words seemed to pulse with an energy that transcended the physical realm, imbued with a **prescient** wisdom that spoke directly to the writer's soul.

"Embrace thy destiny," the ink inscribed, each letter a beacon of enigmatic clarity. The writer, his heart a tumult of **trepidation** and intrigue, pondered the implications of the ink's **exhortation**. What destiny awaited him, hidden within the **labyrinth** of these cryptic symbols?

Determined to unravel the riddle, he resumed his writing, allowing the ink to guide his hand. Each sentence penned was a revelation, a glimpse into a future that was simultaneously exhilarating and terrifying. Reality, once a steadfast anchor, became fluid, malleable to the whims of the ink's inscrutable design.

Days blurred into nights as the writer, enraptured, chronicled the evolution of his reality. Friends and acquaintances began to notice the shift in his demeanor, the gleam of newfound purpose that lit his eyes. They inquired about the source of his inspiration, but he, bound by the sanctity of his communion with the ink, offered only a cryptic smile.

As the narrative unfolded, the writer found himself ensnared in a paradox. The ink, in its **capricious** benevolence, bestowed upon him a destiny replete with triumphs and tribulations. The accolades of literary success were tempered by the poignant solitude of his singular journey. With each stroke, the ink delineated a path that diverged from the mundane, leading him towards an existence both extraordinary and isolating.

In the quiet solitude of his study, the ink revealed the culmination of his odyssey. The final page lay before him, resplendent in its completion. The ink, now **quiescent**, awaited his final **benediction**. As he penned the concluding sentence, a profound serenity enveloped him, the ink's essence interwoven with the **tapestry** of his soul.

The writer, his heart awash with gratitude, pondered the journey that had brought him to this moment. The ink, enigmatic in its origins, had bestowed upon him the greatest gift—a destiny of his own making. And as the final words dried upon the parchment, he understood the true nature of the ink's intention. It was not merely a catalyst for his creativity, but a mirror reflecting the innermost desires of his heart.

With a gentle sigh, he placed the quill beside the inkpot, its purpose fulfilled. The manuscript, a testament to the **symbiosis** between man and ink, lay before him—a masterpiece born of their collaboration. The writer, now a vessel of wisdom and **introspection**, gazed out the window, his spirit buoyed by the limitless horizons of possibility.

The ink, though silent, had spoken volumes. It had rewritten the writer's reality, not as a **capricious** fate, but as a destiny forged through the **alchemy** of word and will. And in its quiet repose, the inkpot awaited the next seeker of dreams, ready to guide another soul toward the realization of their own extraordinary narrative.

Comprehension Questions:

1. **How does the ink transform the writer's creative process, and what impact does it have on his life?**
   The ink transforms the writer's creative process by guiding his hand and reshaping his narrative with a sentient, autonomous force. It allows him to create a masterpiece, but also alters his reality, leading him on a journey of profound self-discovery and isolation, culminating in a deeper understanding of his destiny.
2. **What is the ultimate revelation the writer gains from his experience with the ink?**
   The writer realizes that the ink was not merely a tool for creativity but a mirror reflecting his deepest desires and potential. It helped him forge a destiny through the fusion of his will and imagination, showing him the power of introspection and self-determination.

Vocabulary List (C2 Level):

1. **Unassuming** - Modest and not drawing attention.
   The inkpot was an unassuming vessel, nestled quietly on the desk.
2. **Metamorphosis** - A complete change in form or nature.
   The ink began its subtle metamorphosis, swirling with new energy.
3. **Vivacity** - Liveliness or energy.
   The ink swirled with a newfound vivacity, as if infused with life.
4. **Preternatural** - Beyond what is normal or natural.
   The ink flowed with a preternatural ease, as though guided by unseen hands.
5. **Arcane** - Mysterious or understood by few.
   The writer was oblivious to the arcane phenomena

unfolding before him.

6. **Portentous** - Ominously significant or indicative of future events.
The shift in the ink's behavior was portentous, hinting at a greater destiny.

7. **Maelstrom** - A powerful whirlpool or a situation of turmoil.
The writer's mind became a maelstrom of confusion and wonder.

8. **Choreography** - The art of designing sequences of movements.
The ink moved with deliberate choreography, forming intricate symbols.

9. **Exhortation** - An urgent or emphatic recommendation or advice.
The ink's exhortation, "Embrace thy destiny," resonated with the writer.

10. **Prescient** - Having foresight or knowledge of events before they happen.
The ink seemed imbued with a prescient wisdom that guided the writer.

11. **Capricious** - Given to sudden and unaccountable changes.
The ink's capricious nature bestowed both triumphs and tribulations.

12. **Benediction** - A blessing or act of approval.
The writer offered his final benediction as he completed the manuscript.

13. **Symbiosis** - A mutually beneficial relationship between two entities.
The manuscript was a testament to the symbiosis between man and ink.

14. **Introspection** - The examination of one's own thoughts and feelings.
The ink's guidance led the writer to profound introspection.

15. **Quiescent** - In a state of inactivity or dormancy.
The ink, now quiescent, awaited its next seeker.
16. **Trepidation** - A feeling of fear or agitation about something that may happen.
The writer's heart was a tumult of trepidation and curiosity.
17. **Luminescent** - Emitting light, especially not caused by heat.
The ink's luminescent glow hinted at its mysterious power.
18. **Ineffable** - Too great or extreme to be expressed in words.
The ink revealed truths that were ineffable, beyond human comprehension.
19. **Manifest** - To display or show clearly.
The ink began to manifest a message, its movements deliberate.
20. **Alchemy** - A process of transformation, creation, or combination.
The ink became an alchemy of word and will, forging a new reality.

29. THE CELL OF TIME

The dimly lit cell was a **paradox** of time and space, a cruel experiment in existential dread. As consciousness returned, the individual—an enigma without a name—found themselves **ensconced** in this peculiar chamber, its walls pulsating with an eerie **luminescence**. The air was thick with an indefinable tension, a **palpable** reminder that this was a place where the ordinary rules of the universe had been rendered obsolete.

At first, the cell seemed innocuous, its dimensions modest, its furnishings sparse but functional. Yet, the subtle, disconcerting sensation of time's **aberrant** flow soon became evident. The initial revelation came as a whisper, an instinctual awareness that the passage of time within these walls was not as it was in the world beyond. The realization crystallized with an unsettling urgency: every minute spent here equated to a year outside.

Panic ensued, a **visceral** reaction to the unfathomable implications of this temporal distortion. Each heartbeat echoed the **inexorable** march toward an untimely demise, propelling the individual into a frenetic quest for liberation. The walls, a **melange** of muted colors, seemed to mock their predicament, indifferent to the desperation that permeated the air.

Conversations, or rather, the echoes of conversations, reverberated through the chamber. These were not the product of another's presence but rather the remnants of dialogues once held in the corridors of memory. Each word seemed imbued with a poignant significance, as if the very act of communication could somehow unravel the enigma of this temporal prison.

"How did I arrive here?" the individual mused aloud, their voice a fragile thread in the vast **tapestry** of silence. There was no immediate answer, only the persistent hum of the cell's mysterious mechanisms. The absence of a clear recollection was disconcerting, a void where certainty should reside. Yet, despite the amnesia, there was an unshakable conviction that escape was imperative.

The cell, though **austere**, was not devoid of clues. On its walls were inscriptions, cryptic messages etched into the very fabric of the space. Each inscription was a puzzle, a fragment of a larger narrative that hinted at the origins of this place and the means of **egress**. The language was archaic, a **melange** of symbols and words that defied easy interpretation. Yet, there was a familiarity to it, a resonance that suggested the answers lay within, if only they could be deciphered.

Time, the ever-present adversary, pressed on with relentless resolve. The individual, acutely aware of the sands slipping through the hourglass, set about the task of unraveling the inscriptions. Each symbol was scrutinized, each phrase dissected for meaning. It was a laborious process, one that demanded both intellectual acumen and a profound patience, for the language was a labyrinth of nuance and ambiguity.

"To escape the cell of time," one inscription declared, "you must first understand its essence." This cryptic **admonition** became the cornerstone of their efforts, a guiding principle that illuminated the path forward. The essence of the cell was elusive, a riddle encapsulated in paradoxes. It was a place where time was both a prison and a key, where the boundaries between past, present, and future were blurred and indistinct.

As days turned into minutes, a pattern began to emerge from the chaos. The inscriptions, once a jumble of obscure references, **coalesced** into a coherent narrative. They spoke of an ancient civilization, one that had harnessed the power of time itself. The cell was a relic of their **hubris**, a testament to their attempts to transcend the limitations of mortality. It was a cautionary tale, a reminder of the perils inherent in the manipulation of natural laws.

With this newfound understanding, the individual

turned their attention to the mechanics of escape. The inscriptions hinted at a mechanism, a subtle alteration in the cell's **configuration** that could reverse the temporal flow. It was an intricate process, one that required precision and an unerring comprehension of the cell's underlying principles.

In the end, it was a single word, buried deep within the inscriptions, that provided the key to their salvation. The word was "Aeternitas," an **invocation** of eternity that resonated with profound clarity. It was a command, a supplication to the forces that governed the cell, a plea for liberation from the confines of time.

With trembling hands and a heart fraught with anticipation, the individual uttered the word aloud. The response was immediate and overwhelming. The cell shuddered, its walls **undulating** with a renewed vigor. The **luminescence** intensified, enveloping the space in a radiant glow that seemed to pierce the very fabric of reality.

For a moment, there was nothing but light, a **transcendent** brilliance that consumed all thought and sensation. Then, as abruptly as it began, it was over. The cell, once a bastion of temporal distortion, was now a mere memory, a shadow of its former self.

The individual found themselves standing on the **precipice** of a new beginning, the weight of time's passage lifted from their shoulders. The world outside awaited, a **tapestry** of endless possibilities unfurling before them. Yet, as they stepped into the light of a new dawn, there was an awareness that the experience in the cell had irrevocably altered them.

The lessons learned within those confines were **indelible**, a testament to the resilience of the human spirit in the face of insurmountable odds. In the end, the cell of time was not merely a prison, but a **crucible** of transformation, a place where the boundaries of possibility were expanded, and the essence of existence redefined.

Comprehension Questions:

1. **What challenges did the individual face in the cell of time, and how did they overcome them?**
   The individual faced the challenge of a distorted temporal reality, where every minute in the cell equated to a year outside. They overcame this by deciphering cryptic inscriptions on the walls, which revealed the cell's origins and the key to escaping its confines through the invocation of the word "Aeternitas."
2. **How did the experience in the cell of time transform the individual?**
   The experience in the cell taught the individual resilience, patience, and an understanding of time's essence. It transformed them by redefining their perception of existence and revealing the indelible

strength of the human spirit.

Vocabulary List (C2 Level):

1. **Paradox** - A situation, person, or thing that combines contradictory features or qualities.
   The cell was a paradox of time and space, defying all logical understanding.
2. **Ensconced** - Settled comfortably or securely.
   The individual found themselves ensconced in the peculiar chamber.
3. **Palpable** - Able to be felt or touched; so intense as to be almost tangible.
   The air was thick with a palpable tension.
4. **Aberrant** - Deviating from the normal or expected.
   The aberrant flow of time became evident to the individual.
5. **Visceral** - Relating to deep inward feelings rather than intellect.
   Panic ensued, a visceral reaction to the realization of temporal distortion.
6. **Inexorable** - Impossible to stop or prevent.
   Each heartbeat echoed the inexorable march of time.
7. **Melange** - A mixture or medley of different things.
   The language was a melange of symbols and archaic words.
8. **Austere** - Severe or strict in manner, attitude, or appearance.
   The cell, though austere, was not devoid of clues.
9. **Admonition** - A firm warning or reprimand.
   The inscription carried a cryptic admonition to understand the cell's essence.
10. **Coalesced** - Came together to form one whole.
    The inscriptions coalesced into a coherent narrative.
11. **Hubris** - Excessive pride or self-confidence, often

leading to downfall.
The cell was a relic of an ancient civilization's hubris.
12. **Egress** - The act of going out or leaving a place.
The inscriptions hinted at the means of egress from the cell.
13. **Configuration** - An arrangement of parts or elements.
The escape required an alteration in the cell's configuration.
14. **Invocation** - The act of calling on something for assistance or authority.
The word "Aeternitas" was an invocation of eternity.
15. **Undulating** - Moving with a smooth, wave-like motion.
The cell's walls undulated as the invocation took effect.
16. **Luminescence** - Light emitted by a substance not caused by heat.
The luminescence of the walls grew more intense as the cell responded.
17. **Transcendent** - Beyond the ordinary or physical human experience.
The light was a transcendent brilliance that consumed all thought.
18. **Indelible** - Unable to be forgotten or removed.
The lessons learned within the cell were indelible.
19. **Crucible** - A severe test or trial that leads to transformation.
The cell was a crucible of transformation for the individual.
20. **Precipice** - A very steep cliff or a situation of great peril.
The individual stood on the precipice of a new beginning.

30. THE SMELL OF MEMORY

Evelyn had spent her life surrounded by the art of fragrance. As a renowned perfumer, she was intimately acquainted with the **nuances** of scent—how a single note could evoke emotions, how complex accords could transport someone to another time or place. To her, fragrance was not just a profession; it was an obsession, a language all its own. She could recall the most intricate details of any perfume she had ever encountered, the way it had made her feel, or the memories it had **conjured**. But even with her expertise, Evelyn had never imagined that a single fragrance could alter the course of her life.

It was a rainy afternoon when she first stumbled upon the elusive perfume that would change everything. She had been working late at her boutique, testing new concoctions, when a stranger walked in. The man was tall, his face obscured by the shadow of his wide-brimmed hat. He moved with a strange, deliberate grace, his presence almost **ethereal** as he approached Evelyn's counter.

"I have something you might be interested in," he said, his voice smooth and low, like velvet. He placed a small, unmarked bottle on the counter, the glass dark and **opaque**, the scent within hidden from view.

Evelyn regarded the bottle with curiosity. "What is it?" she asked, her voice tinged with skepticism.

The man smiled **enigmatically**. "A fragrance unlike any other. It does not merely evoke memories. It brings them back—every detail, every sensation, as if you were reliving them. I trust you will understand its power."

Her interest piqued, Evelyn took the bottle from the counter, feeling a strange pulse of energy **imbuing** it. She unscrewed the cap and brought the bottle to her nose. The fragrance was immediate—an **intoxicating** blend of roses, aged wood, and something faintly metallic, almost like the smell of rain on hot pavement. It was as if the scent had been plucked from a place outside of time, something both familiar and unknown.

For a moment, Evelyn was paralyzed, overwhelmed by a flood of sensations. She was not just smelling the fragrance; she was living it. The air was suddenly thick with **nostalgia**, and before she could stop herself, she was whisked away into a memory she hadn't thought about in years.

She was back in her childhood home, a small cottage tucked away at the edge of a quiet forest. The sun was setting, casting long shadows across the garden where her mother had once grown roses—roses just like the ones in the perfume. She could see her mother now, her soft hands gently tending to the flowers, her laughter ringing through the air as Evelyn played in the yard. She could almost feel the warmth of her mother's embrace, the sweet, comforting scent of her perfume mingling with the smell of earth and flowers.

Evelyn staggered back, her breath shallow as the memory faded. The scent still clung to the air around her, a **haunting** reminder of the past she had left behind. She looked at the bottle, her mind spinning. This was no ordinary fragrance. It had the power to bring memories back in **vivid** detail, to **conjure** not just a fleeting image but an entire experience, as if she were living it all over again.

After the stranger had left, Evelyn became consumed by the

perfume. She could not shake the **compulsion** to relive her memories, to seek out those long-lost moments that she had buried deep within herself. Each time she wore the fragrance, she was transported to another chapter of her life—a birthday from her childhood, the first time she kissed a boy, the night her father had left their family. Each memory was a **vivid**, sensory experience, and Evelyn could not stop herself from diving deeper into the past.

But with each new memory, something shifted. It started with small things: a sense of **disorientation**, a fleeting thought that didn't quite belong. At first, she dismissed them as nothing more than the byproducts of reliving her past. But as the days went by, the memories began to bleed into one another, blurring the line between past and present. The more she used the perfume, the more she uncovered—things she had never known, things she hadn't meant to learn.

One evening, as she applied the fragrance once more, Evelyn found herself transported to her teenage years. She was standing in a dimly lit kitchen, a birthday cake in front of her, candles flickering. Her parents were there, smiling, their faces full of love and joy. But as she observed the scene, something was wrong. She noticed the way her father's smile didn't quite reach his eyes, the tension in her mother's posture, the way her parents spoke in hushed tones when they thought she wasn't listening.

It was then that Evelyn realized something terrifying. The memory was not what it had seemed. Her father hadn't been happy that day; he had been masking something, something that only now, through the lens of the perfume, she could see. Her parents had been arguing, she now understood, and it was in that moment that Evelyn's mind began to **unravel** a truth she had long **repressed**: her father had been having an affair. The realization hit her like a cold slap to the face, and she **recoiled** from the memory, horrified by what she had uncovered.

But the perfume did not release its grip on her. Each time she used it, the memories grew more **intrusive**, more **unsettling**. She was no longer simply revisiting the past—she was uncovering it, unearthing secrets she had never wanted to know. She began to see things that had been hidden from her for years, each discovery more painful than the last.

One night, she found herself reliving the moment her mother had passed away. Evelyn had been just a teenager, standing by her mother's bedside, holding her hand as the life drained from her body. But as the memory unfolded, something new emerged—something Evelyn had never noticed before. As her mother took her final breaths, she saw a faint figure standing in the doorway, watching them. It was a man, his face shadowed and unfamiliar, but Evelyn felt an immediate sense of recognition.

The figure disappeared as quickly as he had appeared, but his presence lingered in Evelyn's mind long after the memory had faded. Who was he? Why had he been there? And why had her mother never mentioned him?

Evelyn could no longer deny it—the perfume had opened a door to the past that she was not prepared to walk through. It was **unraveling** her, piece by piece, exposing truths that she had long buried, truths that perhaps she was never meant to uncover. The line between the past and the present had blurred beyond recognition, and she was no longer sure of who she was or what her life had truly been.

As she sat in her boutique, surrounded by the familiar bottles of perfume she had spent her career crafting, Evelyn realized that she could never go back to the way things were. The fragrance had shown her too much, had taken her to places in her mind she could never unsee. The truth, once revealed, could never be concealed again. And in that moment, Evelyn understood the cost of memory—sometimes, the past was better left forgotten.

Comprehension Questions:

1. **How did the mysterious perfume affect Evelyn, and what realizations did it lead her to uncover?**
   The perfume allowed Evelyn to vividly relive past memories, initially bringing her moments of nostalgia and connection. However, as she delved deeper, it revealed hidden truths about her past, such as her father's affair and the mysterious figure at her mother's deathbed, forcing her to confront unsettling realities she had long repressed.
2. **What impact did the perfume have on Evelyn's perception of memory and reality?**
   The perfume blurred the line between memory and reality for Evelyn, turning her past into a living experience. It made her realize that memories could hold hidden truths, but uncovering them came at the cost of emotional upheaval and an altered understanding of her life.

Vocabulary List (C2 Level):

1. **Nuances** - Subtle distinctions or variations in meaning or expression.
   Evelyn was intimately acquainted with the nuances of scent, knowing how each note affected emotions.
2. **Ethereal** - Extremely delicate and light, as if not of this world.
   The man moved with an ethereal grace, his presence almost otherworldly.

3. **Opaque** - Not transparent or translucent; difficult to see through or understand.
   The perfume bottle was dark and opaque, hiding its contents.
4. **Intoxicating** - Exciting or overwhelming to the senses.
   The fragrance was an intoxicating blend of roses and aged wood.
5. **Nostalgia** - A sentimental longing for the past.
   The scent evoked a wave of nostalgia, bringing Evelyn back to her childhood home.
6. **Intrigue** - Arouse curiosity or interest.
   Evelyn's curiosity was piqued by the enigmatic man and his mysterious perfume.
7. **Enigmatic** - Mysterious and difficult to interpret.
   The man's enigmatic smile left Evelyn with more questions than answers.
8. **Compulsion** - An irresistible urge to act.
   Evelyn felt a compulsion to relive her memories through the perfume.
9. **Disorientation** - A state of confusion about time, place, or identity.
   The memories caused a sense of disorientation, blurring the line between past and present.
10. **Intrusive** - Forcing oneself into a space or situation uninvited.
    The memories became increasingly intrusive, uncovering hidden truths Evelyn wasn't prepared for.
11. **Unsettling** - Causing unease or discomfort.
    The perfume revealed unsettling details about Evelyn's family dynamics.
12. **Recoil** - To draw back in fear, disgust, or shock.
    Evelyn recoiled from the memory of her father's betrayal.
13. **Unravel** - To disentangle or solve; to fall apart.
    The perfume began to unravel long-buried secrets about

Evelyn's past.

14. **Vivid** - Producing powerful feelings or clear images in the mind.
    Each memory the perfume evoked was vivid, as if she were truly living it again.
15. **Haunting** - Unforgettable, often in a way that is troubling or evocative.
    The haunting scent of the perfume lingered long after Evelyn put it away.
16. **Bleed** - To spread into something else, causing a change or blurring of boundaries.
    Her memories began to bleed into her present, making it hard to distinguish reality.
17. **Imbue** - To inspire or permeate with a feeling or quality.
    The scent was imbued with an inexplicable sense of nostalgia and melancholy.
18. **Repress** - To suppress or hold back emotions or memories.
    Evelyn realized she had repressed certain truths about her family.
19. **Uncanny** - Strange or mysterious, especially in an unsettling way.
    There was an uncanny familiarity to the figure at her mother's deathbed.
20. **Conjure** - To call forth or bring to mind.
    The fragrance seemed to conjure memories from the depths of her subconscious.

31. THE HEARTLESS DREAM

In the **ethereal** town of Atheris, where **peculiarity** reigned supreme, hearts existed not within chests but hovered beside their owners, pulsating with an **incandescent** luminescence. These **ethereal** entities, both **palpable** and spectral, were not mere symbols of life but tangible vessels of emotion and vitality. The inhabitants of Atheris, accustomed to this reality, walked with their hearts visible, like eternal companions that mirrored their innermost sentiments.

Among these denizens was Elara, a young woman whose heart was a radiant orb of **cerulean** hue, casting an azure glow that reflected her **introspective** and serene nature. Elara was known for her compassionate spirit and her propensity for dreaming about the realms beyond the tangible. Her life, though **labyrinthine** with the intricate **nuances** of daily existence, was one of contentment, until the day her heart inexplicably vanished.

The morning it disappeared, Elara awoke to an unsettling void. Her heart, which usually floated with an **unwavering** loyalty by her side, was nowhere to be seen. Panic unfurled within her, a **cacophony** of dread amplifying with each passing moment. The absence was not merely physical; it was as if her essence had begun to dissipate, her corporeal form becoming **nebulous** and tenuous.

Desperate to reclaim what was lost, Elara resolved to embark on a surreal **odyssey**, a journey both literal and metaphysical, into the depths of the Dreamscape—a mystical realm where reality intertwined with the fantastical. It was said that the Dreamscape held the power to manifest one's innermost desires and fears, a place where the **intangible** could become tangible once more.

With a heart-shaped **amulet** as her only guide, Elara traversed the border between worlds. The Dreamscape unfurled before her like an **enigmatic tapestry**, its landscapes shifting with the fluidity of a painter's brushstroke. The sky was a **kaleidoscope** of shifting hues, and the ground pulsated with an otherworldly energy, a testament to the surreal nature of the realm.

Elara encountered myriad beings on her journey—whimsical creatures with eyes like liquid galaxies, their voices a **symphony** of whispers. They spoke in riddles and rhymes, offering **esoteric** guidance. "Seek the Heartless Dream," they intoned, their words imbued with an **enigmatic** weight. "There, you shall find what you seek."

The Heartless Dream, a place of **paradox** where dreams **coalesced** with nightmares, was said to reside at the heart of the Dreamscape. It was a place of profound **introspection**, where one's innermost truths were laid bare. Elara knew she must confront this **enigmatic** domain to retrieve her heart and restore her fading existence.

As she journeyed deeper into the Dreamscape, Elara encountered a river of memories, its waters shimmering with the reflections of her past. She saw herself as a child, her heart a vibrant beacon of innocence and wonder. She saw moments of joy and sorrow, love and loss, each memory a thread in the intricate **tapestry** of her life.

The river whispered to her, its voice a gentle caress. "To find what is lost, you must relinquish what you hold dear," it murmured. The words lingered in the air, **enigmatic** and foreboding. Elara continued, her resolve **unwavering**, though uncertainty gnawed at her spirit.

Finally, she arrived at the Heartless Dream, a place **shrouded** in an **ethereal** mist. The air was thick with anticipation, and a profound silence enveloped the landscape. Before her stood a colossal mirror, its surface as smooth as still water. Elara approached, her reflection distorted and fragmented, a mosaic of her soul.

As she gazed into the mirror, the truth of her heart's

absence unfurled before her. She saw the myriad facets of her existence—her dreams, her fears, her loves, and her regrets. Each fragment was a piece of the puzzle, a revelation of the complexities that defined her.

In that moment of **introspection**, Elara understood the river's cryptic message. To reclaim her heart, she must confront the truth of her existence, embracing both the light and the shadows that dwelled within her. It was a **cathartic** moment, a release of the burdens she had carried, and a **reconciliation** with her true self.

With newfound clarity, Elara reached out, her hand touching the mirror's surface. The glass rippled like water, and from its depths emerged her heart, its **cerulean** glow restored to its former brilliance. The heart hovered before her, a testament to her journey and her **resilience**.

As Elara reclaimed her heart, the Dreamscape began to dissolve, its **ephemeral** landscapes fading into the ether. She found herself back in Atheris, her heart once again by her side, its presence a comforting weight. The experience had transformed her, **imbuing** her with a profound understanding of herself and the world around her.

In the days that followed, Elara's life resumed its course, yet she carried within her the wisdom gleaned from her journey. She had confronted the Heartless Dream, navigated the **labyrinth** of her soul, and emerged whole. Her heart, once lost, now pulsed with a renewed vigor, a beacon of hope and **resilience** in a world where dreams and reality intertwined.

Comprehension Questions:

1. **What was the significance of Elara's journey through the Dreamscape, and how did it help her reclaim her heart?**
   Elara's journey through the Dreamscape was both a literal and metaphorical quest to confront her innermost fears, truths, and emotions. By navigating this surreal realm and facing the Heartless Dream, she gained profound self-awareness, embraced the complexities of her existence, and ultimately reclaimed her heart, which symbolized her emotional vitality and identity.
2. **How did the Heartless Dream and the mirror play a pivotal role in Elara's transformation?**
   The Heartless Dream, with its enigmatic mirror, served as a place of profound introspection. The mirror reflected Elara's fragmented soul, forcing her to confront her dreams, fears, and regrets. By accepting and reconciling with these facets of herself, she was able to restore her heart and

achieve a renewed sense of wholeness.

Vocabulary List (C2 Level):

1. **Ethereal** - Extremely delicate and light, almost otherworldly.
   The town of Atheris had an ethereal quality, with hearts glowing beside their owners.
2. **Incandescent** - Emitting light as a result of being heated or glowing brightly.
   Elara's heart pulsed with an incandescent cerulean light.
3. **Peculiarity** - A distinctive or unusual feature or characteristic.
   The peculiarity of Atheris lay in its visible, floating hearts.
4. **Labyrinthine** - Complicated and intricate, like a labyrinth.
   Elara's life was labyrinthine, full of twists and turns.
5. **Nebulous** - Vague, indistinct, or ill-defined.
   Without her heart, Elara felt her physical form becoming nebulous.
6. **Odyssey** - A long, adventurous journey.
   Elara embarked on an odyssey through the Dreamscape to retrieve her heart.
7. **Esoteric** - Understood by or meant for only a small number of people with specialized

knowledge.
The Dreamscape was filled with beings speaking in esoteric riddles.

8. **Metamorphosis** - A profound transformation or change.
The Dreamscape constantly shifted, undergoing a metamorphosis with every step.

9. **Amulet** - An ornament or small piece of jewelry thought to give protection.
Elara carried a heart-shaped amulet to guide her through the Dreamscape.

10. **Introspective** - Reflective and inward-looking.
Elara's cerulean heart reflected her introspective and serene nature.

11. **Cerulean** - A deep blue resembling the sky.
The cerulean hue of her heart symbolized her calm and thoughtful personality.

12. **Symphony** - A harmonious combination of sounds or elements.
The creatures' voices in the Dreamscape were like a symphony of whispers.

13. **Kaleidoscope** - A constantly changing pattern or scene.
The Dreamscape was a kaleidoscope of shifting colors and forms.

14. **Paradox** - A seemingly self-contradictory statement or situation that holds truth.
The Heartless Dream was a paradox where dreams

and nightmares coalesced.

15. **Shrouded** - Covered or concealed.
    The Heartless Dream was shrouded in an ethereal mist.
16. **Cathartic** - Providing relief through the expression of strong emotions.
    Facing her truths in the mirror was a cathartic moment for Elara.
17. **Reconciliation** - The restoration of friendly relations or harmony.
    Elara's journey led to a reconciliation with her true self.
18. **Resilience** - The capacity to recover quickly from difficulties.
    Elara's reclaimed heart pulsed with resilience and hope.
19. **Ephemeral** - Lasting for a very short time.
    The Dreamscape's ephemeral landscapes faded as Elara's journey concluded.
20. **Intangible** - Unable to be touched or grasped; not having physical presence.
    The Dreamscape made the intangible aspects of Elara's soul manifest.

32. THE FORGOTTEN OCEAN

The seabed was strewn with fragments of antiquity, relics **enshrouded** in centuries of sediment. Dr. Eliza Maynard adjusted her oxygen tank and descended deeper into the **abyss**, the rhythmic hum of her rebreather the only sound accompanying her. A marine archaeologist of renown, Eliza had spent her career unearthing secrets that history had relegated to the depths. But this expedition was unlike any other. She wasn't searching for shipwrecks or ancient pottery—she was pursuing a myth.

"Eliza, the readings are spiking," crackled a voice through her earpiece. It was her colleague, Dr. Jonas Reed, monitoring her progress from the surface. "We're detecting **anomalous** salinity levels and strange acoustic signatures. Be careful."

"Acknowledged," she replied, her voice steady despite the thrill coursing through her veins. For centuries, sailors' tales spoke of an ocean within the ocean, a vast hidden expanse shielded by treacherous currents and uncharted trenches. The "Forgotten Ocean," they called it, dismissed as nothing more than maritime lore. Yet here she was, on the **precipice** of discovery, armed with cutting-edge technology and an unyielding determination.

As she descended, the water grew colder, the light dimmer. Her flashlight pierced the darkness, revealing an **ethereal** landscape below. The seafloor suddenly dropped away, plunging into an enormous chasm. Her sonar beeped furiously, the screen displaying an impossible void that seemed to stretch infinitely. She activated her thrusters and crossed the threshold, her breath hitching as she entered an uncharted realm.

The water here was different, thicker, almost gelatinous. It shimmered with an **iridescent** glow, as if infused with **bioluminescent** particles. "Jonas, I think I've found it," she whispered, unable to mask the awe in her voice.

"Found what?" he asked, his tone **incredulous**.

"The Forgotten Ocean."

Her light revealed towering coral structures, their colors vivid and otherworldly. Schools of fish, unlike any she had seen, darted past her. They were **translucent**, their organs visible, glowing faintly in hues of green and blue. Larger shapes loomed in the distance, their silhouettes hinting at creatures far removed from earthly biology.

"You're not going to believe this," Eliza said, angling her camera to capture the scene. "These organisms… they defy categorization. It's as if evolution took an entirely different path here."

"Be cautious," Jonas urged. "We have no idea what's down there. And the radiation levels are… **peculiar**."

Ignoring his warning, Eliza swam deeper into the glowing expanse. A **colossal** structure came into view, a **monolithic** spire rising from the seabed. It appeared to be made of crystal, its surface etched with patterns that bore an **uncanny** resemblance to writing. She hovered closer, her fingers brushing the surface. It was warm to the touch, pulsing faintly as if alive.

"Jonas, there's something inscribed here. It looks like… glyphs? No, more like **fractals**," she said, her voice tinged with fascination. "It's... communicating, I think."

Suddenly, a deep vibration resonated through the water, a low-frequency hum that reverberated in her chest. The spire lit up, casting intricate patterns of light across the ocean floor. Her equipment flickered, overwhelmed by the electromagnetic interference.

"Eliza, get out of there!" Jonas shouted, his voice distorted by static.

But Eliza couldn't move. Her eyes were locked on the spire, transfixed by the intricate play of light and sound. Images flooded her mind—visions of a civilization that had thrived beneath the waves, their technology merging seamlessly with the marine environment. She saw towering cities made of coral and crystal, creatures **symbiotic** with their surroundings, and a vast network of energy that sustained them.

And then she saw their end.

A **cataclysm**, triggered by forces they could neither control nor understand, had swallowed their world. The spire was a **remnant** of their legacy, a beacon of warning and remembrance.

Eliza snapped back to reality, her breath ragged. She activated her thrusters, propelling herself away from the spire. The water around her churned violently, as if the ocean itself was resisting her departure.

"Jonas, I'm coming back," she said, her voice trembling.

The ascent felt interminable. The water grew lighter, the temperature warmer, but the sense of unease lingered. When she finally breached the surface, Jonas was there to pull her aboard the research vessel.

"What happened down there?" he demanded, his eyes wide

with concern.

Eliza removed her helmet, her face pale. "I... I saw them," she murmured. "They weren't just creatures. They were... people. Intelligent, advanced. And they left something behind. Something we're not meant to understand."

Jonas frowned. "You're saying the myths were true? That there was an entire civilization down there?"

"Yes," she replied, her voice firm despite the weight of her discovery. "And whatever destroyed them... it's still down there."

For a moment, neither spoke, the gravity of her words hanging in the air. Then Jonas glanced at the monitors, their screens filled with erratic readings. "We need to report this. The world needs to know."

Eliza shook her head. "No. If we reveal this, it'll lead to **exploitation**. They've been forgotten for a reason. We have to protect their legacy."

Jonas hesitated but eventually nodded. "Alright. But this isn't over. Whatever you found down there, it's only the beginning."

Eliza gazed at the horizon, the sun setting in a blaze of orange and gold. The ocean—vast, mysterious, and **unfathomable**—held secrets that humanity was not ready to confront. And she vowed to ensure that some secrets remained hidden, for the sake of the world above.

Comprehension Questions:

1. **What discovery did Dr. Eliza Maynard make in the depths of the ocean, and how did it challenge conventional understanding of marine life and history?**

Dr. Eliza Maynard discovered the mythical "Forgotten Ocean," a hidden marine expanse containing unique organisms and evidence of an advanced underwater civilization. The lifeforms defied biological categorization, and the crystal spire she found revealed insights into a lost, symbiotic civilization destroyed by forces beyond their control.

2. **Why did Eliza choose to keep her discovery a secret, and what implications did this decision carry?**

   Eliza decided to protect the legacy of the forgotten civilization, fearing exploitation and harm to their remnants. This decision reflects her moral responsibility and recognition of humanity's tendency to exploit rather than preserve, emphasizing the importance of safeguarding such secrets for the greater good.

Vocabulary List (C2 Level):

1. **Abyss** - A deep or seemingly bottomless chasm.
   Eliza descended into the abyss, where light barely penetrated the water.
2. **Enshrouded** - To cover or envelop completely and obscure from view.
   The relics were enshrouded in centuries of sediment.
3. **Precipice** - A very steep rock face or cliff, typically a tall one; a dangerous situation.
   She was on the precipice of a groundbreaking discovery.
4. **Luminescence** - The emission of light by a substance not resulting from heat.
   The water shimmered with an iridescent luminescence.
5. **Iridescent** - Showing luminous colors that seem to change when seen from different angles.
   The fish were iridescent, glowing faintly with hues of green and blue.

6. **Bioluminescent** - The production and emission of light by living organisms.
   Bioluminescent particles illuminated the Forgotten Ocean's depths.
7. **Translucent** - Allowing light to pass through but diffusing it so that objects beyond are not clearly visible.
   The creatures in the ocean were translucent, revealing their glowing organs.
8. **Colossal** - Extremely large or massive.
   A colossal crystal spire rose from the seabed, towering over the surroundings.
9. **Fractals** - Complex geometric patterns that are self-similar across different scales.
   The spire's surface was etched with fractals resembling ancient symbols.
10. **Symbiotic** - Involving interaction between two different organisms living in close physical association.
    The underwater civilization had a symbiotic relationship with its environment.
11. **Cataclysm** - A large-scale and violent event in the natural world.
    The civilization's end was brought about by a catastrophic cataclysm.
12. **Anomalous** - Deviating from what is standard, normal, or expected.
    The sonar detected anomalous salinity levels and strange acoustic signatures.
13. **Incredulous** - Unwilling or unable to believe something.
    Jonas sounded incredulous when Eliza described the Forgotten Ocean.
14. **Peculiar** - Strange or unusual.
    The radiation levels in the Forgotten Ocean were peculiar and unexplained.

15. **Ethereal** - Extremely delicate and light in a way that seems not of this world.
The landscape of the Forgotten Ocean had an ethereal beauty.
16. **Symphony** - A harmonious combination of elements.
The creatures' movements created a symphony of life and light.
17. **Monolithic** - Massive, uniform, and unyielding.
The monolithic spire stood as a testament to the lost civilization's legacy.
18. **Unfathomable** - Incapable of being fully understood or explored.
The vastness of the ocean and its secrets seemed unfathomable.
19. **Remnant** - A small remaining quantity of something.
The spire was a remnant of the underwater civilization's achievements.
20. **Exploitation** - The action of making use of and benefiting from resources unfairly or unethically.
Eliza feared the discovery would lead to exploitation of the ancient site.

33. THE MAPMAKER'S CURSE

The workshop was dim, **illuminated** only by the flickering light of a single oil lamp. Marcus, the **renowned** mapmaker, hunched over his latest creation, his quill gliding effortlessly across the **parchment**. His maps were unlike any others, alive with an **eerie** vibrancy. His talent was whispered about in hushed tones, some hailing him as a genius, others muttering of dark arts. But Marcus's secret was simple—or so he told himself. His maps changed when touched, revealing paths, territories, and secrets unseen by the naked eye.

"This one feels different," Marcus murmured, leaning closer to inspect the **intricate** lines and flourishes. The map began to shimmer under his fingertips, and the faint outline of a city appeared, its name forming in ornate script: Aeterna.

"Aeterna?" he whispered aloud. He had never heard of such a place. The name resonated, almost as if the map itself wanted him to acknowledge its significance. "It must be a trick of the mind. Perhaps too many late nights."

But as he reached for a sip of tea, the map pulsed faintly, the glowing lines drawing his attention back. He pressed his hand against it **instinctively**, and in an instant, the room shifted. The air grew dense, tinged with a metallic tang. Marcus pulled his hand back in alarm, but the map clung to his skin like a second layer. He stumbled backward, knocking over the lamp, which sputtered out, plunging the room into darkness.

A voice—soft yet commanding—whispered from nowhere and everywhere. "You have found Aeterna, but do you deserve its secrets?"

"Who's there?" Marcus demanded, his voice trembling. He fumbled for the lamp, but the room remained unnaturally still. The map on his desk began to emit a faint golden glow, and the outlines of Aeterna grew sharper, more vivid. Buildings towered, waterways shimmered, and streets seemed to beckon him.

"This is madness," he muttered, but curiosity gnawed at him. Marcus had spent his life charting territories, decoding ancient riddles, and unveiling forgotten lands. Aeterna was unlike anything he had ever encountered. He could not turn away.

"Reveal yourself!" Marcus commanded, his voice stronger now.

The whisper returned, this time more insistent. "Touch the map, Marcus. Become part of its story."

His fingers hesitated above the glowing **parchment**. He wanted to resist, but the allure was undeniable. With a deep breath, he pressed his hand against the map again. The world spun violently, and when it steadied, he was no longer in his workshop.

The streets of Aeterna stretched before him, impossibly **pristine** and vibrant. The sky above was a swirling canvas of colors he could not name. The air was thick with the scent of blooming flowers and ancient stone. Yet, something was amiss. The city was silent, devoid of the bustling life such grandeur should host.

"Am I dreaming?" he murmured. He turned a corner and found himself in a grand plaza. At its center stood a towering obelisk, its surface inscribed with unfamiliar symbols that seemed to shift when he looked too closely. Around it were statues of figures in flowing robes, their expressions **inscrutable**.

A voice—no longer disembodied but belonging to a figure cloaked in shimmering gold—spoke. "You have entered Aeterna, the city of infinite knowledge and **unyielding** power. Few have found it; fewer still have left."

Marcus stepped back, wary. "Who are you? What is this place?"

The figure tilted its head. "I am the **Custodian**. And you, Marcus, are the Mapmaker. Your talent has brought you here, but your purpose remains unclear."

"I don't understand. I only make maps. I—"

"Your maps shape reality, Marcus," the **Custodian** interrupted, their voice calm yet heavy with significance. "Every stroke of your quill bends the fabric of the world. Aeterna exists because you willed it so. But with great creation comes responsibility."

"This is absurd!" Marcus protested. "Maps are tools, nothing more. They document what already exists."

The **Custodian**'s gaze seemed to pierce through him. "Then why does Aeterna exist on no other map but yours? Why does it grow more vivid with every line you draw?"

Marcus had no answer. The thought terrified him. Was it possible? Could his work have such power?

"What do you want from me?" he asked, his voice barely above a whisper.

The **Custodian** extended a hand, and a new map appeared in its grasp. It was blank, save for a single instruction written in bold, flowing script: "Choose."

"Choose what?" Marcus demanded, his frustration mounting.

"Aeterna's fate," the **Custodian** replied simply. "It is a city of boundless potential, but potential untamed leads to **stagnation**. Will you preserve it, binding it forever within the confines of your map? Or will you set it free, allowing it to exist in the real world, with all the unpredictability that entails?"

Marcus stared at the map, his mind racing. To preserve Aeterna meant safeguarding its beauty and secrets but condemning it to eternal **stagnation**. To release it meant **relinquishing** control, risking that it could wreak havoc or fade into oblivion.

"Why must I decide?" he asked, desperation creeping into his voice. "This isn't my responsibility."

"Creation always bears responsibility," the **Custodian** replied. "The power to shape the world is not given lightly. Choose, Marcus. The map awaits."

He hesitated, his hand hovering over the **parchment**. The weight of the decision pressed down on him. Finally, he spoke.

"I will..." His voice faltered, but he steadied himself. "I will set it free."

The **Custodian** nodded, and the map began to glow with an intense, blinding light. The city around him shimmered, its colors bleeding into reality. Marcus shielded his eyes, and when he opened them again, he was back in his workshop. The map of Aeterna lay before him, but it was blank now, its secrets gone.

Outside his window, the world seemed unchanged. Yet, deep within him, Marcus knew Aeterna was out there, somewhere, waiting to reveal itself to those brave enough to seek it. And he, the Mapmaker, would carry the memory of its curse and its wonder forever.

Comprehension Questions:

1. **What was unique about Marcus's maps, and how did his latest creation lead him to Aeterna?**

Marcus's maps were extraordinary because they revealed hidden paths and secrets when touched. His latest creation, a map of Aeterna, drew him into the mystical city when he interacted with it, transporting him to a realm of infinite knowledge and power.

2. **What moral dilemma did Marcus face in Aeterna, and what choice did he ultimately make?**

Marcus had to decide whether to preserve Aeterna as a perfect, static creation within the confines of the map or to set it free, allowing it to exist in the real world with all the risks and unpredictability that entailed. Ultimately, he chose to set it free, releasing its potential into reality.

Vocabulary List (C2 Level):

1. **Illuminate** - To light up or make clear.
   The workshop was dim, illuminated only by the flickering light of a single oil lamp.
2. **Renowned** - Famous or well-regarded for a particular quality or skill.
   Marcus, the renowned mapmaker, was whispered about in both awe and suspicion.
3. **Eerie** - Strange and frightening.
   His maps were alive with an eerie vibrancy, unlike anything others had seen.
4. **Intricate** - Very complicated or detailed.
   Marcus inspected the intricate lines and flourishes of the map.
5. **Parchment** - A stiff, flat material used for writing, often made from animal skin.
   His quill glided effortlessly across the parchment as he worked.
6. **Instinctively** - Acting on natural impulse without

conscious thought.
He pressed his hand against the map instinctively, unable to resist its pull.

7. **Abyss** - A deep, immeasurable space or chasm.
   The room shifted, and Marcus felt as though he was staring into an abyss.
8. **Palpable** - So intense as to seem almost tangible.
   The air grew dense, tinged with a palpable tension.
9. **Inscrutable** - Impossible to understand or interpret.
   The statues' expressions were inscrutable, adding to the enigma of Aeterna.
10. **Esoteric** - Intended for or understood by only a small number of people with specialized knowledge.
    The Custodian's words were imbued with an esoteric weight.
11. **Manifest** - To show or display through actions or appearance.
    The Dreamscape could manifest one's innermost fears and desires.
12. **Pristine** - Clean and fresh, untouched by human influence.
    The streets of Aeterna were impossibly pristine, as if untouched by time.
13. **Symmetry** - Balanced and harmonious arrangement of parts.
    The obelisk's symmetry added to its ethereal allure.
14. **Stagnation** - The state of not flowing or moving, often leading to a lack of progress.
    Preserving Aeterna meant condemning it to eternal stagnation.
15. **Relinquish** - To voluntarily let go of or release.
    To release Aeterna meant relinquishing control and accepting unpredictability.
16. **Unyielding** - Unwilling to bend or give way under pressure.
    The Custodian's gaze was unyielding, demanding a

decision.

17. **Transfix** - To captivate or make someone unable to move due to awe or fear.
    Marcus was transfixed by the glowing patterns of light on the spire.
18. **Reverberate** - To echo or resound repeatedly.
    The low hum of the spire seemed to reverberate through Marcus's chest.
19. **Ephemeral** - Lasting for a very short time.
    The city seemed ephemeral, as if it might vanish at any moment.
20. **Custodian** - A person who is responsible for taking care of something.
    The Custodian declared Marcus responsible for Aeterna's fate.

34. THE WEIGHT OF SOUND

In the heart of **Sonorous** City, where every sound bore physical weight, silence was considered an elusive luxury. The streets pulsed with vibrations—the rhythmic thuds of horse hooves, the lilting chatter of merchants, and the ceaseless **clamor** of machinery. To live here meant to carry sound, both metaphorically and quite literally. The populace had adapted, wearing belts with hooks to hang their auditory burdens. Some sounds were light, like whispers that hovered around one's shoulders, while others, like the resonating clang of a blacksmith's hammer, pressed heavily on the chest.

Among this **cacophony** lived Alden, a musician of unparalleled talent. His nimble fingers coaxed **ethereal** melodies from his violin, and his voice could soothe even the most **tumultuous** of hearts. Yet Alden was restless, yearning for more than the applause of crowds and the fleeting weight of admiration. He desired to create something indelible—a sound so profound it would shift the very fabric of their existence.

One evening, as the sun dipped below the horizon and painted the sky with molten hues, Alden's wanderings led him to the outskirts of the city. There, nestled among the rolling hills, stood an ancient **amphitheater**. Overgrown with ivy and worn by time, it **exuded** an air of forgotten grandeur. Intrigued, Alden ventured inside. The acoustics of the place were unlike anything he'd encountered. Even the faintest whisper echoed with a strange, **resonant** clarity, as though the air itself yearned to hold onto the sound.

As Alden played his violin, the **amphitheater** responded. The notes grew heavier, pressing against his skin and pooling at his feet. Suddenly, the earth beneath him quivered, and a low, **sonorous** hum emanated from the ground. Startled, Alden stopped playing. The hum ceased instantly, leaving a **tangible** void in its wake. "What is this place?" he murmured, his voice carrying the weight of his confusion.

"It is the cradle of **resonance**," a voice replied, startling Alden. He spun around to see an elderly man cloaked in tattered robes, his eyes glinting with an otherworldly light. "You have awakened it," the man continued, his voice heavy with significance. "This **amphitheater** amplifies sound, giving it mass and form. But beware, for sound with mass has the power to shape reality itself."

Alden's curiosity was piqued. "Shape reality? How?"

The old man gestured to a nearby wall, where a mural depicted scenes of creation and destruction—mountains rising from plains, rivers carving through valleys, and cities crumbling to dust. "Sound is the essence of this world," he explained. "Wield it wisely, and you can sculpt wonders. Use it recklessly, and you may invite ruin."

Alden's mind raced with possibilities. Could he compose a **melody** that lightened the burdens of the people? A **symphony** that reshaped the oppressive streets of **Sonorous** City into open fields? "Teach me," he implored the old man.

For weeks, Alden trained under the sage's watchful eye, learning to manipulate sound's weight and impact. He discovered how to infuse his music with **intention**, crafting notes that could lift, push, and pull. Each lesson brought him closer to mastering this enigmatic art, but the weight of responsibility grew heavier with each passing day.

One fateful morning, Alden returned to the city, his violin slung over his shoulder and his heart brimming with resolve. He began by playing in the marketplace, where the din of haggling voices and clinking coins made movement cumbersome. His **melody** was light and playful, and as it resonated through the air, the burdens of sound lifted. The crowd paused, their eyes widening as they felt the newfound ease. Laughter and cheers erupted, and Alden knew he had made a difference.

Encouraged, he took his music to the city's industrial district, where the relentless clanging of machinery weighed heaviest. Here, he played a composition that mimicked the rhythm of the workers' toil, harmonizing with their labor. The oppressive weight of the machines lessened, and the workers moved with renewed vigor. Word of Alden's miraculous music spread like wildfire, and soon he was summoned to perform before the city council.

The council chamber was a grand hall, its vaulted ceiling adorned with murals depicting the city's history. The weight of governance was palpable, the air thick with the **resonant** echoes of heated debates and decisions. Alden stood before the council, his violin in hand, and spoke with quiet **conviction**. "I can lighten the burdens of our people, reshape our city into a haven of **harmony**. But I need your support."

The council members exchanged wary glances. Finally, the mayor, a stern woman with piercing eyes, addressed him. "Your intentions are noble, but tampering with the fabric of our reality is a dangerous game. What if your music unravels more than it mends?"

Alden's grip on his violin tightened. "I understand the risks, but I believe the potential for good outweighs the dangers. Let me show you."

Reluctantly, the council agreed. Alden stepped into the center of the chamber and began to play. His composition was unlike anything he had performed before, a masterful blend of light and heavy notes that wove together into a tapestry of sound. The air shimmered, and the oppressive weight of the chamber lifted. The murals on the ceiling came to life, their colors vibrant and dynamic. The council members gasped as the room transformed into a space of balance and clarity.

But as the final note hung in the air, a tremor rippled through the city. Alden's heart sank as he realized he had underestimated the **amphitheater**'s power. Outside, the streets began to shift, buildings swaying and reshaping themselves. The people's initial joy turned to panic as the city's very foundations seemed to liquefy.

Alden rushed to the **amphitheater**, the old man's warning echoing in his mind. "Sound with mass has the power to shape reality itself." He needed to restore balance before the city collapsed entirely. Taking his place in the **amphitheater**'s center, he played a **melody** of **restoration**. The notes were heavy and deliberate, anchoring the shifting structures and calming the trembling ground. Slowly, the city settled, its streets and buildings solidifying once more.

Exhausted but triumphant, Alden returned to the council. "I have learned my lesson," he admitted, his voice heavy with remorse. "Sound is a double-edged sword. It can heal, but it can also harm. We must use it with care."

The mayor nodded solemnly. "You have shown us the power of sound and the responsibility that comes with it. Let us work together to harness this gift for the betterment of our city."

From that day forward, **Sonorous** City embraced a new era of **harmony**. Alden continued to compose, his music a beacon of hope and unity. The people learned to listen—not just to the sounds around them, but to the intentions behind them. And in the cradle of **resonance**, the weight of sound became a force for balance, shaping a world where even the heaviest burdens could be carried together.

Comprehension Questions:

1. **How did Alden's music impact the people of Sonorous City, and what challenges did it eventually create?**
   Alden's music initially alleviated the physical and metaphorical burdens of the city's sounds, bringing joy and relief to the people. However, when his powerful composition unintentionally disrupted the city's foundation, it caused panic and instability, forcing Alden to use his music to restore balance.
2. **What lesson did Alden learn about the power of sound, and how did he apply it moving forward?**
   Alden learned that sound, while capable of creating harmony, could also cause harm if misused. He realized the importance of responsibility when wielding such power and dedicated himself to using his music thoughtfully to benefit the city and its people.

Vocabulary List (C2 Level):

1. **Sonorous** - Producing a deep, resonant sound.
   The streets of Sonorous City pulsed with sonorous vibrations that carried weight.
2. **Ethereal** - Delicate and light in a way that seems not of this world.
   Alden's violin produced ethereal melodies that enchanted his audience.
3. **Tumultuous** - Full of confusion or commotion;

emotionally intense.
His music soothed even the most tumultuous of hearts.
4. **Amphitheater** - A round or oval open-air venue with rising tiers of seats.
The ancient amphitheater responded to Alden's music with an otherworldly resonance.
5. **Resonance** - The quality of a sound that stays loud, clear, and deep for a long time.
The amphitheater's resonance amplified even the faintest whispers.
6. **Vibrant** - Full of energy and life; bright and striking.
The murals in the council chamber came to life with vibrant colors as Alden played.
7. **Tangible** - Perceptible by touch; clear and definite.
In Sonorous City, sound had tangible weight, affecting daily life.
8. **Clamor** - A loud and confused noise, especially from a crowd.
The clamor of the marketplace filled the air with a cacophony of sounds.
9. **Cacophony** - A harsh, discordant mixture of sounds.
The industrial district was overwhelmed by the cacophony of clanging machinery.
10. **Melody** - A sequence of notes that is musically satisfying.
Alden played a melody that lightened the burdens of the workers.
11. **Intention** - A plan or purpose behind an action.
Alden learned to infuse his music with intention, shaping its effects.
12. **Amplify** - To increase the strength or magnitude of something.
The amphitheater amplified sound, giving it mass and form.
13. **Exude** - To display a strong quality openly and clearly.
The amphitheater exuded an air of forgotten grandeur,

drawing Alden in.

14. **Symphony** - A complex, harmonious composition, often involving multiple elements.
    Alden's symphony reshaped the streets into a harmonious environment.
15. **Harmony** - A pleasing combination of different elements, especially sounds.
    The council chamber transformed into a haven of balance and harmony.
16. **Unyielding** - Unable to be changed or persuaded; steadfast.
    The old man's warning about sound's power was unyielding.
17. **Conviction** - A strong belief or certainty.
    Alden spoke with quiet conviction about his ability to help the city.
18. **Tumult** - A loud, confused noise or commotion.
    The shifting streets caused tumult among the citizens of Sonorous City.
19. **Restoration** - The act of returning something to its original state.
    Alden's final melody was one of restoration, calming the city's chaos.
20. **Equilibrium** - A state of balance or stability.
    Alden sought to restore equilibrium to Sonorous City with his music.

35. THE MIRROR OF YESTERDAY

The antique store was a **labyrinth** of forgotten artifacts and shadowy corners, filled with the musty scent of time. Joanna had wandered in by accident, her original intent to escape the biting wind that whipped down the narrow alley. Her eyes darted from one peculiar item to the next: an **ornate** music box, a tarnished brass telescope, a collection of mismatched porcelain figurines. None of it held her attention for long until she saw it.

The mirror stood propped against the far wall, its **gilded** frame adorned with intricate carvings of vines and cherubs. The glass was unusually clear for something that appeared centuries old, almost as if it had been polished obsessively. Joanna felt an **inexplicable** pull toward it, as though the mirror were calling her name in a voice she couldn't quite hear.

"Beautiful, isn't it?" The voice startled her, and she turned to see the shopkeeper, an elderly man with sharp eyes and a smile that didn't reach them. His hands were clasped behind his back, giving him the air of a museum curator.

"Yes," Joanna replied, hesitating. "It's unusual. Do you know its history?"

The shopkeeper tilted his head as if considering her question. "They say it's **enchanted**. Legends surround its origins, though none can be verified. Some claim it was crafted by an alchemist who wished to preserve the **essence** of time itself. Others insist it belonged to a noblewoman whose secrets were too heavy to bear. What is certain, however, is that this mirror does not show the present."

"What do you mean?" Joanna's brow furrowed.

"It reflects the past," he said simply. "Your past."

Joanna chuckled nervously, assuming the man was indulging in the kind of sales pitch designed to intrigue gullible customers. But his expression didn't waver, and his eyes seemed to peer into her soul, unsettling her.

"How much is it?" she asked, almost against her will.

"For you, my dear, a mere pittance," he said with a wave of his hand. "Take it and see for yourself."

Joanna hesitated but found herself unable to resist. The mirror was heavier than it looked, and she struggled to carry it back to her small apartment. Once home, she propped it against the wall in her bedroom, its golden frame gleaming in the dim light. She sat on the edge of her bed, staring at her own reflection, which seemed ordinary enough.

"What nonsense," she muttered, shaking her head. Yet, as she stood to leave the room, something caught her eye. The reflection had shifted. Her heart leapt into her throat as she turned back to face the mirror.

Instead of her modern apartment, the background was now that of a familiar room. It was her childhood bedroom, the pale pink walls adorned with posters of pop stars and fairy lights. And there, seated on the floor, was a younger version of herself, no more than ten years old, scribbling furiously in a diary.

"This can't be real," Joanna whispered, her voice **trembling**. Yet the scene continued to unfold as though she were watching a movie. Her younger self paused, glancing toward the door as if anticipating someone's arrival. A moment later, her mother entered the room, her expression strained.

Joanna's breath caught. It had been years since she'd thought about this day, but now the memories flooded back with **vivid** clarity. Her mother had come to deliver news that their family was moving—a decision that had uprooted Joanna's life and severed her friendships. She remembered the anger and betrayal she had felt, emotions she had long buried.

"No," she said aloud, shaking her head. "I don't want to see this."

But the mirror did not obey. The scene dissolved into another memory, this one from her teenage years. Joanna was at a party, laughing with friends, a red solo cup in hand. The carefree moment shifted abruptly when an argument broke out in the corner of the room. She watched as her younger self stepped in to mediate, only to become the target of harsh words that had left her feeling humiliated.

"Stop," Joanna pleaded, her voice cracking. She reached out to touch the mirror, but the surface was cold and **unyielding**. The memories continued to play out, each one dredging up feelings she had tried to forget: the time she had failed an important exam despite her best efforts, the day her first boyfriend broke her heart, the argument with her father that had led to years of **estrangement**.

By the time the mirror went dark, Joanna was **trembling**. She sank to the floor, her head in her hands, overwhelmed by the weight of what she had seen. It wasn't just the memories themselves but the realization that she had never truly confronted them. Instead, she had buried them deep, allowing them to **fester** and shape her life in ways she hadn't understood until now.

Over the following days, Joanna found herself unable to stay away from the mirror. Each time she looked into it, it revealed another fragment of her past, some **bittersweet**, others unbearably painful. Yet she couldn't deny the **catharsis** that came with it. The mirror forced her to confront truths she had avoided for years, peeling back the layers of her carefully constructed **persona**.

One evening, as she stared into the mirror, it showed her something different. The image was of a moment she had almost forgotten, a day when she had helped an elderly neighbor carry groceries up several flights of stairs. The woman's gratitude had been **profound**, and Joanna had felt an unshakable sense of fulfillment. The memory brought tears to her eyes, not from sadness but from a sense of lost purpose.

"What are you trying to show me?" she whispered to the mirror.

The reflection did not answer, but Joanna felt as though the answer was within her all along. The mirror was not a curse but a gift, a tool to help her understand herself. It reflected the good and the bad, the triumphs and the failures, the moments that had shaped her into the person she was today.

The next morning, Joanna made a decision. She contacted her father for the first time in years, initiating a conversation that was both awkward and healing. She dug out her childhood diary from a dusty box and began to reread the thoughts and dreams of her younger self. She even revisited the neighborhood she had left behind, reconnecting with old friends she had thought were lost to time.

The mirror remained in her room, its surface now quiet and still. Joanna no longer needed its guidance, for she had found the courage to face her past on her own. Yet she couldn't bring herself to part with it, knowing that its magic had changed her life.

One day, the shopkeeper appeared at her door, as though summoned by some invisible force. He smiled that same

inscrutable smile and asked if she was ready to return the mirror.

"I think I am," Joanna said, her voice steady. "Thank you."

The shopkeeper nodded and took the mirror without another word, disappearing down the hallway. Joanna watched him go, a sense of peace washing over her. She didn't know where the mirror would go next or who would find it, but she hoped it would help them as it had helped her.

As the door closed behind him, Joanna turned back to her reflection in the ordinary mirror above her dresser. For the first time in years, she liked what she saw.

Comprehension Questions:

1. **What is the significance of the mirror in Joanna's journey, and how does it help her transform?**
   The mirror forces Joanna to confront buried memories and emotions, showing her both painful and joyful moments from her past. By reliving these experiences, she gains insight into herself, understands the unresolved aspects of her life, and finds the courage to heal relationships and rediscover her sense of purpose.
2. **Why does Joanna decide to return the mirror to the shopkeeper, and what does this indicate about her personal growth?**
   Joanna returns the mirror because she no longer needs its guidance, having faced her past and gained the strength to move forward. This decision reflects her personal growth and newfound ability to confront life's challenges without relying on external tools.

Vocabulary List (C2 Level):

1. **Labyrinth** - A complicated and confusing network of paths or passages.
   The antique store was a labyrinth of forgotten artifacts and shadowy corners.
2. **Gilded** - Covered thinly with gold leaf or gold paint.
   The mirror stood propped against the far wall, its gilded frame gleaming.
3. **Inexplicable** - Unable to be explained or accounted for.
   Joanna felt an inexplicable pull toward the mirror.
4. **Essence** - The intrinsic nature or indispensable quality of something.
   The alchemist wished to preserve the essence of time itself.
5. **Enchanted** - Filled with delight or magically charmed.
   The shopkeeper claimed the mirror was enchanted, reflecting the past.
6. **Trembling** - Shaking slightly, typically as a result of fear or anxiety.
   Her voice was trembling as she whispered to herself.
7. **Profound** - Very great or intense; having deep meaning.
   The woman's gratitude left Joanna with a profound sense of fulfillment.
8. **Estrangement** - The state of being alienated or separated from someone.
   The argument with her father had led to years of estrangement.
9. **Catharsis** - The process of releasing, and thereby providing relief from, strong emotions.
   The mirror brought Joanna a catharsis she didn't know

she needed.

10. **Persona** - The aspect of someone's character presented to others.
    The mirror peeled back the layers of her carefully constructed persona.
11. **Bittersweet** - Both pleasant and painful or regretful.
    The mirror revealed bittersweet memories from her teenage years.
12. **Unyielding** - Not giving way to pressure; inflexible.
    The mirror's surface was cold and unyielding to her touch.
13. **Inscrutable** - Impossible to understand or interpret.
    The shopkeeper offered an inscrutable smile as he handed her the mirror.
14. **Fester** - To become worse or more intense, especially through neglect.
    Joanna realized she had allowed unresolved emotions to fester.
15. **Tapestry** - A rich and complex combination of events or elements.
    Her memories formed an intricate tapestry of her life.
16. **Ornate** - Elaborately or highly decorated.
    The mirror's ornate carvings of vines and cherubs drew her attention.
17. **Reconcile** - To restore friendly relations between.
    Joanna reconciled with her father after years of silence.
18. **Luminescence** - Emission of light by a substance not resulting from heat.
    The mirror seemed to glow with an otherworldly luminescence.
19. **Burden** - A heavy load, typically of a physical or emotional nature.
    She realized the burden of her past had shaped her present.
20. **Resolve** - Firm determination to do something.
    Joanna's resolve to reconnect with her old friends grew

stronger.

36. THE TASTE OF STARS

In a quiet corner of the bustling city, where narrow streets **meandered** between tightly packed buildings, there stood an unassuming restaurant named Celeste. The chef, Emilio, was known for his enigmatic dishes that defied conventional culinary wisdom. But even his most devoted patrons had no idea about the secret ingredient that had **catapulted** his fame to **celestial** heights.

One fateful night, while walking through a meteorite shower in a secluded field, Emilio stumbled upon a fragment of something extraordinary—a shard of shimmering stardust, glowing faintly with an otherworldly **luminescence**. Intrigued, he pocketed it, not knowing that this discovery would transform his craft and his life forever.

Back in his modest kitchen, Emilio examined the dust under the dim light. Its texture was finer than powdered sugar, its aroma subtle yet **intoxicating**, reminiscent of an undefined sweetness that lingered like a forgotten memory. Against his better judgment, he added a pinch of the stardust to a simple soufflé batter.

As the soufflé baked, a peculiar warmth filled the room, as though the air itself had come alive. When Emilio tasted the final product, his senses erupted into a **kaleidoscope** of sensations: vivid images of a desert at dawn, the sound of an ancient lullaby, the ghostly caress of a breeze that seemed to come from another world. He was entranced.

The next evening, Emilio cautiously served the stardust soufflé to a trusted regular, a poet named Margot. Her reaction was immediate and **visceral**. Tears welled in her eyes as she recounted a vivid dream of standing beneath a sky with two suns, her long-deceased mother whispering forgotten words of comfort.

"What have you done to me?" Margot asked, her voice trembling.

"I don't know," Emilio admitted, "but I think it's the stars."

From that night onward, Emilio began experimenting, infusing stardust into his creations in minute quantities. Each dish evoked something unique in its consumer. A businessman claimed to have seen his unborn child; a widow relived her wedding day in a field of wildflowers. Word spread, and soon, Celeste became the **nexus** of the city's most inexplicable and intimate experiences.

Yet, as demand for Emilio's **celestial** cuisine grew, so too did the complexity of the visions it provoked. Some customers left transformed, their lives enriched by newfound purpose. Others, however, departed haunted, their forgotten desires and regrets gnawing at their souls. A young artist destroyed all his paintings after consuming a stardust-infused tart, claiming they paled in comparison to the vistas he had witnessed in his mind. A scholar abandoned her lifelong research, obsessed with deciphering a language she had heard in a dream after eating Emilio's stardust risotto.

"You're playing with something you don't understand," Margot warned one evening as she lingered after closing time. Her tone was soft but firm, her poetic sensibility attuned to the dangerous **allure** of Emilio's craft.

"Do you think I don't know that?" Emilio retorted, his voice tinged with frustration. "But how can I stop now? Every pinch, every granule reveals something new—something beautiful, something terrifying. It's as if I'm unlocking the universe."

Margot sighed, her gaze fixed on the flickering candle between them. "The universe doesn't give without taking, Emilio."

Her words weighed heavily on him, but he continued nonetheless, driven by an **insatiable** curiosity. The stardust seemed inexhaustible, as if it **replenished** itself in the small jar he had brought back from the field. Yet, Emilio couldn't shake the feeling that it was watching him, its faint glow pulsating in time with his own heartbeat.

One night, an unfamiliar patron arrived—a **gaunt** figure with piercing, otherworldly eyes. He ordered the Celestial Degustation, Emilio's signature multi-course meal infused with stardust. As the stranger consumed each dish, his expression remained inscrutable, but a **palpable** tension filled the room.

When the final course was served—a dessert Emilio had named Nebula's Embrace—the man finally spoke. "You've meddled with forces you cannot comprehend," he said, his voice resonating like a distant echo.

"Who are you?" Emilio demanded, his hands trembling.

"I am merely a messenger," the man replied, "sent to warn you. The stars do not belong to you, and neither does their essence. What you have taken must be returned, or the balance will **unravel**."

Emilio's mind raced. Was this stranger merely a delusional eccentric, or had he truly been sent by the very cosmos he had dared to harness? Torn between defiance and fear, Emilio decided to test the man's authenticity.

"If the stars demand their due," he said, his voice steadying, "then why do they let me use their gift? Why have they not stopped me?"

The man's lips curled into a faint, **enigmatic** smile. "The stars are patient, Chef. They watch, they wait, and when the time comes, they reclaim."

After the stranger left, Emilio found himself plagued by doubt. For the first time, he hesitated as he reached for the jar of stardust. Its glow seemed dimmer, its weight heavier. That night, he dreamed of an infinite void, a **kaleidoscope** of constellations collapsing into darkness. The stars, once brilliant and eternal, were fading, their light consumed by a shadow that whispered his name.

Determined to understand the truth, Emilio returned to the field where he had found the stardust. But the meteorite shower was gone, and the landscape was eerily silent, as if holding its breath. He knelt on the ground, pouring the remaining stardust from the jar onto the soil. The particles floated momentarily before dissolving into the earth, their glow extinguished.

As he stood, a strange calm washed over him. The weight that had burdened his soul was lifted, but so too was the spark of inspiration that had driven his culinary genius. Back at Celeste, his dishes returned to their earthly origins—artful but ordinary. The patrons dwindled, seeking the **ethereal** experiences they could no longer find.

Margot visited one last time, ordering a simple soup. "You did the right thing," she said, her voice tinged with sadness.

"Did I?" Emilio asked, staring into the steam rising from her bowl. "Or did I just give up the only thing that made me extraordinary?"

Margot smiled faintly. "Sometimes, the extraordinary is too much for this world."

As the restaurant's lights dimmed for the final time, Emilio realized he was free—not from the stars, but from the **insatiable** hunger they had awoken in him. And though the stars no longer graced his dishes, their taste lingered in his memory, a **bittersweet** reminder of the infinite possibilities—and perils—that lay beyond the reach of human hands.

Comprehension Questions:

1. **How did the stardust transform Emilio's cooking, and what effects did it have on his patrons?**
   Emilio's discovery of stardust infused his dishes with the ability to evoke vivid, otherworldly experiences in those who consumed them. Patrons experienced profound visions of their past, future, or unfulfilled desires, which sometimes enriched their lives and other times left them haunted or obsessed.
2. **Why did Emilio ultimately decide to return the stardust, and what was the result of his decision?**
   After a mysterious stranger warned Emilio of the cosmic balance he was disrupting, he returned the stardust to the field where he had found it. This act restored balance and freed Emilio from the stardust's burden but also ended the celestial magic of his cooking, returning his dishes to ordinary creations and leading to the decline of his restaurant.

Vocabulary List (C2 Level):

1. **Meander** - To wander aimlessly or casually without urgency.
   The narrow streets meandered between tightly packed buildings, leading Emilio to the field.
2. **Luminescence** - The emission of light by a substance

not caused by heat.
The stardust shimmered with an otherworldly luminescence, captivating Emilio.

3. **Ethereal** - Extremely delicate and light, seeming otherworldly.
The soufflé emitted an ethereal warmth that filled the room.

4. **Visceral** - Relating to deep inward feelings rather than intellect.
Margot's reaction to the dish was visceral, bringing tears to her eyes.

5. **Catapult** - To hurl or launch something suddenly; to propel to fame or success.
The stardust catapulted Emilio's reputation to celestial heights.

6. **Intoxicating** - Exhilarating or overwhelming, often in an addictive way.
The stardust's aroma was intoxicating, drawing Emilio deeper into its allure.

7. **Nexus** - A central or focal point linking multiple elements.
Celeste became the nexus of the city's most inexplicable experiences.

8. **Unfathomable** - Impossible to fully understand.
The stardust carried an unfathomable power that Emilio couldn't resist.

9. **Allure** - The quality of being powerfully attractive or fascinating.
Margot warned Emilio of the dangerous allure of his stardust creations.

10. **Gaunt** - Lean and haggard, often due to suffering or hunger.
The gaunt stranger with piercing eyes issued a dire warning to Emilio.

11. **Enigmatic** - Difficult to interpret or understand; mysterious.

The stranger offered an enigmatic smile before departing.

12. **Palpable** - Able to be felt or touched; easily perceived.
    A palpable tension filled the restaurant when the stranger dined there.
13. **Insatiable** - Impossible to satisfy.
    The stardust awakened an insatiable curiosity in Emilio.
14. **Replenish** - To restore or refill to its previous level.
    The jar of stardust seemed to replenish itself mysteriously.
15. **Unravel** - To solve or untangle something complex or mysterious.
    The stranger warned Emilio that meddling with the stars might unravel the balance.
16. **Kaleidoscope** - A constantly changing pattern or sequence of elements.
    Emilio dreamed of a kaleidoscope of constellations collapsing into darkness.
17. **Ephemeral** - Lasting for a very short time.
    The stardust's glow was ephemeral, fading as it dissolved into the earth.
18. **Celestial** - Pertaining to the heavens or the sky; divine.
    The celestial magic of the dishes drew patrons from far and wide.
19. **Bitter** - Having a sharp, unpleasant taste or experience; metaphorically painful.
    The decision to return the stardust left a bitter yet freeing taste in Emilio's soul.
20. **Resonance** - The quality of a sound being deep and full, or the impact of something profound.
    The stranger's warning carried a resonance that Emilio could not ignore.

37. THE CLOCK THAT STOPPED

In the heart of the city, amidst the forgotten alleyways and crumbling **façades** of an old district, stood the Museum of Oddities. It was a peculiar place, visited mostly by those who thrived on tales of the strange and inexplicable. The most **inconspicuous** exhibit, tucked away in a dimly lit corner, was a dusty, brass clock with a cracked glass face. It bore no name, no description, merely a plaque that read, "Do not stare directly at the clock."

Few paid it much attention, save for Elena, the museum's night custodian. She had passed by the clock countless times, its silent, frozen hands stuck at 11:57, as if perpetually awaiting an event that never came. She would sometimes pause, curious but cautious, wondering what power it held to warrant such a **cryptic** warning.

One evening, during a particularly quiet shift, Elena's curiosity got the better of her. Alone in the dim halls, she stepped closer to the clock, its brass frame glinting faintly under the flickering museum lights. Her reflection distorted in the cracked glass, her eyes locked onto the unmoving hands.

And then, everything stopped.

The air around her grew heavy, as though the world itself had been drained of **momentum**. The faint hum of the museum's electricity ceased, her breath hung visible in the stillness, and the light froze mid-flicker. But Elena herself was unharmed, untouched by the inexplicable stillness. As she turned, she realized she was no longer in the museum.

She stood in the middle of a cobblestone street, bustling with people dressed in the fashion of centuries past. Carriages rattled by, horses' hooves striking the stones in rhythm, yet none of them moved. It was as though the world had been turned into a living **tableau**. She walked among the figures, her footsteps echoing eerily. She approached a flower vendor, the petals of a rose captured mid-breeze, its delicate movement halted like a photograph come to life.

"What is this?" she whispered, her voice oddly amplified in the silence.

From behind her, a voice answered. "It is a moment."

Elena spun around to find a man dressed in a tailored waistcoat and top hat, his appearance as **anachronistic** as the scene around her. His eyes, however, gleamed with an unsettling familiarity, as if he had been expecting her.

"A moment?" she echoed.

He nodded. "You have gazed into the clock. It does not merely stop time; it transports you into moments **preserved** by its gaze."

"Preserved?" she asked, her voice trembling. "Why? How?"

The man tilted his head, considering her. "The clock captures fragments of time, memories too powerful to fade but too dangerous to remain. Every moment you see here is something the world wished to forget."

Elena frowned, her heart pounding. "But this—this is just a street. It seems ordinary."

The man smiled faintly. "Does it? Look closer."

She turned her gaze back to the scene, her eyes scanning the frozen faces. At first, nothing seemed amiss. But then she noticed it—the fear etched into the features of the passersby. The flower vendor's hand, trembling as it extended the rose. The carriage driver, his mouth open mid-shout, his eyes wide with alarm.

"What happened here?" she whispered.

"A riot," the man said softly. "A moment of chaos, captured and hidden away. The clock keeps it safe, so it cannot bleed into the present."

Elena stepped back, her unease growing. "How do I leave?"

The man's expression darkened. "The clock will release you—eventually. But beware, each time you look into it, it will take you deeper, to moments more dangerous, more **profound**. And each time, it will be harder to return."

With a sudden jolt, Elena found herself back in the museum, the hum of electricity resuming, the lights flickering as though nothing had happened. Her knees buckled, and she gripped the nearest wall for support. She glanced back at the clock, its brass surface dull and unremarkable once more. But her reflection in the cracked glass seemed different—older, perhaps, or simply more burdened.

For weeks, Elena avoided the clock, her mind plagued by dreams of frozen moments and the man's **cryptic** warnings. But the pull of the unknown gnawed at her. She couldn't shake the feeling that the clock held answers to questions she hadn't yet dared to ask.

One night, unable to resist, she returned to the museum's corner. Her pulse quickened as she stepped closer, her eyes drawn once more to the clock's cracked face. This time, she saw not her reflection but a flicker of movement—a soldier in a tattered uniform, clutching a letter as flames consumed the edges of his world.

Before she could look away, the stillness claimed her again.

She stood on a battlefield, the air thick with smoke and the acrid scent of gunpowder. Soldiers lay frozen mid-charge, their faces contorted with pain and determination. Nearby, a young man held a letter close to his chest, his eyes filled with tears that had yet to fall.

"Elena," the familiar voice called.

She turned to find the man in the waistcoat, his presence as unnerving as before. "Why am I here?" she demanded. "What does the clock want from me?"

"It shows you what the world has buried," he replied. "Moments of triumph, despair, **revelation**. But these fragments are not without consequence. Each one holds a piece of truth, and truth is not always kind."

She knelt beside the soldier, her hand trembling as she reached for the letter. As her fingers brushed the paper, a surge of emotion flooded her—love, regret, hope. She saw flashes of a life lived and lost, the soldier's final thoughts etched into the letter's ink.

"Do you understand now?" the man asked, his tone softer. "The clock is not a tool. It is a **guardian**, a keeper of what humanity cannot bear to remember."

Elena stood, her heart heavy. "But why show me?"

The man's gaze bore into hers. "Perhaps it sees in you a willingness to bear what others cannot."

When she returned to the museum this time, the weight of the soldier's story lingered in her chest. She could feel it, a **tangible** ache that refused to fade. She avoided the clock for as long as she could, but its silent presence beckoned her.

Eventually, she gave in. Time after time, she returned to its frozen moments, each one more harrowing than the last—a burning library filled with the cries of those trapped inside, a celebration turned to tragedy as the ground beneath a village crumbled, a child's desperate plea for help in a storm that swallowed their world.

Each journey left her more drained, more **fragmented**. Yet, she couldn't stop. The clock had become a part of her, its cracked glass reflecting not just moments of history but pieces of her own soul.

One final night, as she stared into the clock, she saw her own reflection staring back—not frozen, but alive, pleading. And she understood. The clock had not chosen her; she had chosen it. And now, she was as much a part of its story as the moments it **preserved**.

Comprehension Questions:

1. **What does the clock in the Museum of Oddities do, and why is it considered dangerous?**
   The clock captures and preserves powerful moments from history—fragments of time that the world cannot bear to remember. These moments are often dangerous or traumatic, and staring into the clock pulls individuals into these frozen memories, making it increasingly difficult to return to the present.
2. **Why does Elena keep returning to the clock despite its warnings and dangers?**
   Elena is drawn to the clock by an insatiable curiosity and a growing sense of responsibility. She feels compelled to explore the frozen moments and uncover their truths, even as the experiences leave her increasingly fragmented and burdened.

Vocabulary List (C2 Level):

1. **Inconspicuous** - Not easily seen or noticed; subtle.
   The clock was inconspicuous, tucked away in the corner of the museum.
2. **Facade** - The outward appearance, especially a deceptive one.
   The crumbling facades of the old district concealed a rich history.
3. **Momentum** - The force or speed of movement.
   The air around her grew heavy, as though the world had been drained of momentum.
4. **Tableau** - A striking or artistic arrangement of objects or figures, often motionless.
   The bustling street was frozen into a living tableau.
5. **Anachronistic** - Belonging to a different time period; out of place in history.
   The man's tailored waistcoat gave him an anachronistic appearance.
6. **Preserve** - To maintain or keep something in its original state.
   The clock preserves moments too powerful to fade but too dangerous to remain.
7. **Profound** - Deep, intense, and meaningful.
   Each journey into the clock revealed a profound truth about humanity's past.
8. **Cryptic** - Mysterious and obscure in meaning.
   The man's cryptic warnings left Elena both curious and uneasy.
9. **Ethereal** - Extremely delicate and light, seeming otherworldly.
   The petals of the rose floated mid-air with an ethereal grace.
10. **Tangible** - Perceptible by touch; something real and

concrete.
The weight of the soldier's story felt tangible in her chest.

11. **Harbor** - To keep something in one's mind, especially secretly.
The clock harbored fragments of history too painful to be remembered.

12. **Revelation** - A surprising and previously unknown fact, often dramatic.
Each frozen moment held a revelation about forgotten truths.

13. **Fragmented** - Broken into pieces; disconnected.
Each journey into the clock left Elena feeling more fragmented.

14. **Unyielding** - Not giving way under pressure; resolute.
The cracked glass of the clock remained unyielding under Elena's touch.

15. **Resonance** - The quality of evoking a strong emotional response.
The soldier's letter carried a resonance that lingered in her heart.

16. **Perpetual** - Never-ending or changing; continuous.
The clock's hands were stuck in a perpetual state of waiting.

17. **Futility** - Pointlessness or uselessness.
Elena fought against the futility of trying to escape the clock's grip.

18. **Invoke** - To call upon or summon, often with authority.
The clock seemed to invoke forgotten moments from time itself.

19. **Burden** - A heavy responsibility or emotional weight.
The clock's frozen memories became an emotional burden for Elena.

20. **Guardian** - A protector or keeper of something valuable.
The clock served as a guardian of forgotten histories.

38. THE SMOLDERING SKY

The first time the sky turned red, the world watched in silence. It was unlike any sunset humanity had ever known. The deep **cerulean** of the afternoon was consumed by fiery hues that roared across the heavens, turning clouds into embers and the horizon into a smoldering **inferno**. At first, people thought it was a trick of the atmosphere, a rare celestial phenomenon, but as the nights grew longer and the days shorter, the fiery sky became a **harbinger** of something far worse.

Elliot stood at the edge of the cliffs, staring at the horizon as the sky shifted from crimson to black. His hand tightened around the compass dangling from his neck—a relic his mother had given him before she disappeared into the night like so many others. She had whispered only one **cryptic** phrase before vanishing: "Find the heart of the sky."

"What does it even mean?" Elliot muttered, his voice barely audible above the howling wind. The compass's needle spun **erratically**, as though mocking him.

"You still don't know?" came a voice from behind.

Startled, Elliot spun around to see Mira, her sharp eyes glinting in the fading light. She had an uncanny ability to appear out of nowhere, a trait that annoyed and unsettled him in equal measure.

"Shouldn't you be skulking around the village, stealing bread or whatever it is you do?" he retorted.

Mira smirked, brushing a lock of raven-black hair out of her face. "And leave you to decipher the apocalypse alone? Tempting, but no. Besides," she added, stepping closer, "I think you're onto something."

Elliot sighed, turning his gaze back to the horizon. "If you're here to criticize, spare me. I've got enough on my plate trying to figure out what 'heart of the sky' even means. It's not like the sky has a map."

"Maybe it does," Mira said softly.

Elliot frowned, looking at her. "What are you talking about?"

She reached into her satchel and pulled out a weathered piece of parchment. Its edges were singed, the ink faded, but the outlines of constellations and **cryptic** symbols were still discernible. "I found this in the archives," she said, handing it to him. "It's old—older than anything else in the village. It talks about the 'heart of the sky' as if it's an actual place."

Elliot studied the map, his pulse quickening. "This… this can't be real."

Mira shrugged. "Real enough for me to risk getting caught by the guards for it. Look," she pointed to a symbol etched near the bottom corner, "this matches the carving on your compass."

Elliot stared at the symbol, a swirling vortex that seemed to draw his gaze deeper with every second. His mother's words echoed in his mind: "Follow the compass. It knows the way."

"So, what's the plan, hero?" Mira asked, her tone dripping with sarcasm. "You going to march into the sky and demand it give back its heart?"

Elliot ignored her, his mind racing. The map indicated a location deep within the mountains—a place shrouded in myth and unreachable by most. He traced the route with his finger, his determination hardening. "We go here," he said, pointing to the mark on the map.

Mira raised an eyebrow. "The Blazing Peaks? You do realize no one comes back from there, right?"

"Then it's a good thing I wasn't planning on coming back," Elliot said, pocketing the map and compass.

Mira's smirk faltered, replaced by a rare moment of sincerity. "You're serious about this?"

"If I'm wrong," Elliot said, his voice steady, "then the sky burns and takes us all with it. If I'm right… we might have a chance."

The journey to the Blazing Peaks was **treacherous**, each step more grueling than the last. The landscape grew increasingly **desolate**, the air thinner, the ground hotter as though the earth itself mirrored the **inferno** above. By the time they reached the base of the mountains, the sky had become a perpetual shade of ember, casting everything in an eerie, otherworldly glow.

"Are we sure this is a good idea?" Mira asked, wiping sweat from her brow. "I mean, sure, the apocalypse is bad, but this? This feels worse."

"You can turn back if you want," Elliot said, not breaking stride. He knew she wouldn't. Despite her **caustic** demeanor, Mira had a knack for staying where she wasn't wanted—usually because she was needed.

The climb was relentless, the path narrow and fraught with danger. The compass's needle continued its **erratic** dance, but as they ascended, it began to settle, pointing toward the summit with unwavering precision.

At the peak, they found a cavern, its entrance marked by ancient runes that glowed faintly in the dim light. Elliot hesitated, his hand hovering over the hilt of his knife.

"Do you feel that?" Mira asked, her voice barely a whisper.

Elliot nodded. The air was charged, vibrating with an energy that seemed to **resonate** deep within their bones. He stepped forward, the compass growing warmer in his hand as they entered the cavern.

Inside, the walls shimmered with veins of crystal, each one **pulsating** with a rhythm that mimicked a heartbeat. At the center of the chamber lay an altar, and atop it floated an orb of pure light. It **pulsated** in sync with the crystals, a **beacon** of raw, **unbridled** power.

"The heart of the sky," Mira breathed, her voice filled with awe.

Elliot approached the altar, the compass now glowing brightly. As he reached for the orb, a deafening roar echoed through the chamber. From the shadows emerged a figure cloaked in flames, its eyes burning with an intensity that made Elliot stagger.

"Who dares disturb the heart?" the figure boomed, its voice **resonating** like thunder.

Elliot swallowed his fear, stepping forward. "We mean no harm. The sky—it's dying. We need the heart to save it."

The figure laughed, a sound that sent shivers down their spines. "The sky does not die, mortal. It is you who are killing it with your greed, your wars, your ceaseless consumption. The heart is not yours to take."

"Then what do we do?" Mira shouted. "We can't just let the world burn!"

The figure's flames flickered, its gaze softening. "The heart must choose. Only one with a soul untainted by selfishness can wield its power."

Elliot looked at Mira, then back at the heart. He thought of his mother, of her sacrifice, of the countless people who had disappeared, leaving only fragments of hope behind. Taking a deep breath, he placed his hand on the orb.

A searing pain shot through him, and for a moment, he felt as though he were being torn apart. Memories flashed before his eyes—his mother's smile, Mira's **unyielding** loyalty, the faces of strangers he had passed in the village. And then, he felt it: the heartbeat of the sky, **resonating** within him.

The orb's light **enveloped** him, and the cavern was filled with a deafening silence. When the light faded, the figure was gone, and the heart had merged with the compass, its glow subdued but steady.

Elliot turned to Mira, his voice firm. "We have to return. The sky isn't going to fix itself."

As they descended the mountain, the fiery red of the heavens began to fade, replaced by the cool blues and purples of dawn. The apocalypse had been averted, but Elliot knew the heart had not saved the sky for humanity's sake. It had given them another chance—a fragile, **fleeting reprieve**.

Comprehension Questions:

1. **What is the significance of the "heart of the sky," and why is it essential to Elliot's quest?**
   The "heart of the sky" is a powerful orb that holds the essence of the sky's vitality. It is essential to Elliot's quest because the fiery sky signals a world-ending imbalance, and the heart is the only way to restore harmony. Elliot's mother directed him to find it before she disappeared, knowing its importance.
2. **How does Elliot's journey to the Blazing Peaks reflect themes of sacrifice and responsibility?**

Elliot's journey to the Blazing Peaks represents a willingness to confront danger and sacrifice personal safety for the greater good. His determination to save the sky, even at the cost of not returning, highlights his sense of responsibility for humanity's survival and his connection to his mother's legacy.

Vocabulary List (C2 Level):

1. **Harbinger** - A sign or omen of something to come, especially something bad.
   The fiery sky became a harbinger of impending doom.
2. **Cerulean** - A deep shade of blue resembling the sky.
   The deep cerulean of the afternoon was consumed by fiery hues.
3. **Cryptic** - Mysterious and difficult to interpret.
   Her mother had whispered only one cryptic phrase before disappearing.
4. **Erratic** - Unpredictable and irregular in movement or behavior.
   The compass's needle spun erratically, as though mocking him.
5. **Anachronistic** - Out of place in time or chronology.
   Mira's sharp eyes glinted with an almost anachronistic wisdom.
6. **Treacherous** - Extremely dangerous and difficult to navigate.
   The journey to the Blazing Peaks was treacherous, each step more grueling.
7. **Desolate** - Barren, empty, and devoid of life.
   The landscape grew increasingly desolate as they approached the mountains.
8. **Unyielding** - Refusing to give way or change; resolute.
   The air around them carried an unyielding tension.

9. **Resonate** - To produce or evoke a strong emotional or physical response.
   The cavern resonated with an energy that mirrored a heartbeat.
10. **Pulsate** - To expand and contract rhythmically, like a heartbeat.
    The veins of crystal pulsated with a rhythm that matched the heart.
11. **Beacon** - A guiding or warning signal, often of light.
    The orb of light on the altar served as a beacon of raw power.
12. **Unbridled** - Unrestrained or uncontrolled.
    The orb glowed with unbridled energy, filling the cavern with light.
13. **Caustic** - Sharp, biting, or sarcastic in tone.
    Mira's caustic demeanor often masked her genuine concern.
14. **Profound** - Deep, intense, and meaningful.
    The air in the cavern held a profound stillness, heavy with anticipation.
15. **Reprieve** - A temporary relief or delay from something unpleasant.
    The heart had given humanity a fragile, fleeting reprieve.
16. **Inferno** - A large, intense, and dangerous fire.
    The horizon turned into a smoldering inferno under the fiery sky.
17. **Envelop** - To wrap or surround completely.
    The orb's light enveloped him, filling the cavern with brilliance.
18. **Inscrutable** - Difficult to understand or interpret.
    The figure's inscrutable gaze unnerved Elliot.
19. **Imbue** - To fill something with a particular quality or feeling.
    The compass seemed imbued with the heart's power.
20. **Fleeting** - Lasting for a very short time.

The sky's reprieve was fleeting, a reminder of humanity's fragile balance.

39. THE FOREST OF STOLEN VOICES

The forest was an **abyss** of shadows, its **canopy** so thick that the sunlight barely pierced through. A dense mist clung to the undergrowth, **muffling** every sound and shrouding the hunter in an **eerie** silence. Dressed in leather armor and carrying a bow strapped to his back, Ronan ventured deeper into the Forest of Stolen Voices—a place spoken of only in hushed tones, a place where few who entered ever returned.

He had heard the tales countless times at the taverns: travelers who wandered into the forest and emerged as **hollowed** versions of themselves, their eyes wide with terror, their voices forever stolen. But Ronan wasn't one for myths. His quarry had fled into the forest, and he was determined not to let it escape, even if it meant stepping into the realm of legend.

As he trudged through the thick, moss-covered terrain, he felt a chill crawl up his spine. The air was heavier here, as though the forest itself pressed down on him. His boots crunched against the twigs and leaves, but the sound seemed to die almost instantly, swallowed by the **oppressive** quiet.

"Strange," he muttered to himself, his voice barely above a whisper. Yet even that faint sound echoed unnaturally, bouncing between the **gnarled** trunks as though the forest were mocking him.

The first sign of something amiss came when he reached a clearing. At the center stood a tree unlike any he had seen before. Its bark was pale, almost skeletal, and its branches twisted upward like skeletal fingers clawing at the sky. But what struck him most were the faces. Dozens—no, hundreds—of faces carved into the bark, their expressions frozen in silent screams.

"What in the gods' name…" Ronan stepped closer, his instincts urging him to flee, yet his curiosity holding him in place. He reached out to touch the bark, and as his fingers brushed against it, he **recoiled**. The surface was warm, pulsing faintly, as though the tree were alive.

"Leave," came a voice, soft and breathy, like the rustling of leaves in a dying breeze.

Ronan spun around, his hand instinctively reaching for the hilt of his knife. But there was no one there. The clearing was empty save for the tree and the **oppressive** weight of the mist.

"Who's there?" he demanded, his voice steadier than he felt.

"Leave," the voice repeated, this time more insistent. It seemed to **resonate** from the very air, surrounding him, pressing into his ears. "Or you will lose what you came with."

"I've come for my prey," Ronan said, his **defiance** masking his growing unease. "Not for your games."

The voice fell silent, but the stillness that followed was even more unnerving. Ronan tightened his grip on his knife and turned to leave the clearing, but as he took his first step, he felt it—a sharp, almost imperceptible tug at his throat. He froze, his breath hitching.

"What was that?" he whispered, but the words felt… wrong. Fainter. As if the forest itself were **siphoning** them away.

He shook his head, forcing himself to move forward. But with every step, the tugging sensation grew stronger, and his voice grew weaker. By the time he reached the edge of the clearing, he realized with dawning horror that he couldn't speak at all. His throat moved, his lips formed the shapes of words, but no sound emerged.

Panic surged through him. He turned back toward the clearing, his eyes scanning for the pale tree, but the mist had thickened, obscuring everything. He tried to cry out, to demand his voice back, but the silence was absolute.

And then came the whispers.

They were faint at first, like the distant murmur of a stream, but they grew louder, converging into a **cacophony** of disembodied voices. They surrounded him, filled him, each one overlapping the next:

"Help me."

"Why did I come here?"

"I can't leave. I can't leave."

Ronan clapped his hands over his ears, but the voices persisted, not heard so much as felt. He stumbled forward, desperate to escape the **oppressive** noise. His vision blurred, the forest spinning around him, until he tripped over a root and fell hard onto the ground.

When he looked up, he was no longer alone.

A figure stood before him, cloaked in shadows, their features obscured save for their glowing eyes—pale, cold, and **unyielding**. The figure tilted its head, observing him with an unsettling stillness.

"You seek to reclaim your voice," the figure said, its tone neither malevolent nor kind. "But what will you give in return?"

Ronan scrambled to his feet, his knife raised defensively. But the figure merely laughed, a hollow sound that echoed through the forest.

"You think steel can harm me? You think **defiance** will save you?" The figure stepped closer, and Ronan felt the temperature drop, his breath visible in the **frigid** air. "This forest is alive, Hunter. It breathes. It listens. It takes."

Ronan tried to speak, to demand answers, but his silence was total. He glared at the figure, his frustration boiling over.

The figure seemed to sense his thoughts. "You were warned, yet you came. Do you know why the forest steals voices? It is because words hold power. They shape reality, bind memories, create meaning. Without your voice, you are nothing but a shadow—a memory waiting to fade."

Ronan's grip on his knife tightened. He pointed to his throat, his eyes blazing with determination.

"You wish to bargain?" the figure asked, amusement lacing its voice. "Very well. The forest can be generous, but its price is steep."

The figure extended a hand, and the whispers grew louder, their chaotic **symphony** threatening to drown Ronan's thoughts. "To reclaim your voice, you must leave something behind. Your name, your memories, your very essence—choose wisely, for once it is given, it cannot be undone."

Ronan hesitated, his mind racing. His name? His memories? What was a voice without identity? What was identity without memory? The weight of the choice pressed down on him, suffocating.

Finally, he lowered his knife, his shoulders slumping. He touched the compass around his neck—a token from his father, the only connection to a past he barely remembered. He held it out to the figure, his gesture clear.

The figure stared at the compass for a long moment before

nodding. "Very well. The forest accepts your offering."

As the compass left his hand, Ronan felt a sharp pain in his chest, as though a piece of his soul had been torn away. The whispers subsided, replaced by a deafening silence. And then, like the first breath after drowning, his voice returned.

"Where am I?" he rasped, his voice hoarse but whole.

The figure smiled faintly. "You are in the Forest of Stolen Voices, Hunter. But you are no longer lost."

The mist began to recede, the **oppressive** weight lifting. Ronan looked around, the forest transforming before his eyes. The faces on the trees faded, the whispers dissipated, and the air grew lighter. But when he looked down, the compass was gone, and with it, any memory of his father's face.

He walked out of the forest, his steps slow and measured. His voice was his once more, but he knew he had left a part of himself behind, a piece he could never reclaim. The forest had taken its due, as it always did.

Comprehension Questions:

1. **What happens to Ronan when he ignores the warning and ventures deeper into the Forest of Stolen Voices?**
Ronan begins to lose his voice as the forest drains it, leaving him unable to speak. He encounters a mysterious figure who reveals that the forest steals voices because they hold power, and to reclaim his voice, Ronan must offer something valuable in exchange.
2. **Why does Ronan ultimately offer the compass to reclaim his voice, and what does the exchange symbolize?**

Ronan offers the compass, a token from his father, because it is his most meaningful possession. The exchange symbolizes the deep cost of reclaiming what was lost and highlights the forest's demand for a personal sacrifice, leaving Ronan with his voice but stripped of part of his identity.

Vocabulary List (C2 Level):

1. **Abyss** - A deep or seemingly bottomless space.
   The forest was an abyss of shadows, its canopy thick and unyielding.
2. **Canopy** - A covering, often of leaves, that forms a roof-like layer.
   The forest canopy was so dense that sunlight barely pierced through.
3. **Oppressive** - Uncomfortably heavy or stifling.
   The air was heavy and oppressive, pressing down on him as he walked.
4. **Siphon** - To draw off or transfer, often gradually.
   The forest seemed to siphon away his voice with each step.
5. **Eerie** - Strange and frightening.
   The forest was cloaked in an eerie silence that made his footsteps unnerving.
6. **Defiance** - Open resistance or bold disobedience.
   Despite his growing fear, Ronan's defiance masked his unease.
7. **Muffled** - Muted or softened in sound.
   The mist muffled every sound, creating an unsettling quiet.
8. **Unyielding** - Unrelenting or not giving way to pressure.
   The figure's pale, glowing eyes were cold and unyielding.
9. **Cacophony** - A harsh, discordant mixture of sounds.

The whispers grew into a cacophony of voices, overwhelming his senses.

10. **Recoil** - To suddenly spring or flinch back in fear or disgust.
    Ronan recoiled as the tree's pulsing warmth shocked him.
11. **Frigid** - Extremely cold.
    The temperature dropped, and the air became frigid as the figure stepped closer.
12. **Symphony** - A harmonious or structured arrangement of sounds.
    The voices blended into a chaotic symphony that filled the forest.
13. **Anachronistic** - Out of place in time, especially in a historical context.
    The figure's old-fashioned cloak felt anachronistic in Ronan's modern perspective.
14. **Hollowed** - Empty or having lost substance.
    Travelers emerged hollowed, their eyes wide with unspeakable fear.
15. **Gnarled** - Twisted, rough, and knotted, typically with age.
    The gnarled tree trunks seemed to watch him as he passed.
16. **Resonant** - Deep and full of sound, often carrying emotional significance.
    The figure's resonant voice seemed to echo in his very bones.
17. **Ethereal** - Delicate and light in a way that seems too perfect for this world.
    The pale mist gave the forest an ethereal quality, otherworldly and fragile.
18. **Sacrifice** - To give up something valued for the sake of something else.
    Ronan's sacrifice of the compass was necessary to reclaim his voice.
19. **Immutable** - Unchanging over time or unable to be

changed.
The forest's immutable silence swallowed every sound he tried to make.

20. **Ominous** - Giving the impression that something bad is going to happen.
The ominous clearing held an unsettling stillness, forewarning danger.

40. THE GOD WHO FORGOT

The god awoke to silence.

It was not the tranquil stillness of a sleeping world but the kind of silence that **suffocates**. For **eons**, the god had known the hum of creation—the constant thrumming of stars being born, rivers carving new paths, and life unfurling in endless complexity. But now, that hum was gone, replaced by a void that pressed against their mind like a smothering fog.

They opened their eyes to their **celestial** chamber, an expanse of **shimmering** constellations and swirling nebulae, yet something was wrong. The light of the stars seemed dimmer, their glow muted. The god rose, their movements slow and uncertain. Their form was neither male nor female, neither young nor old. They were the embodiment of potential, a being of **infinite** possibilities—or at least, they had been.

"What is this emptiness?" they murmured, their voice echoing faintly in the vastness. "Why do I feel... **hollow**?"

The answer did not come, for there was no one to answer. The god was alone in their domain, the other deities having long since scattered to their own corners of existence. This solitude had never bothered them before. They were the Creator, the Weaver of Realities, the Shaper of Worlds. Their purpose had always been singular and clear. But now, a single, terrifying realization struck them: they had forgotten how to create.

The god wandered through the **celestial** plane, their mind racing. The tools of their craft surrounded them—stars waiting to be shaped, galaxies yearning for form, **fragments** of existence eager to be woven into something greater. But when they reached out to touch them, nothing happened. The **fragments** remained **inert**, lifeless, as if mocking their impotence.

"How can this be?" they whispered. "I am the Creator. This is my domain, my purpose."

Their hands trembled as they attempted to summon a spark of life, but their fingers merely brushed against the void, cold and **unyielding**. Panic gnawed at them. What was a god without their power? What was divinity without creation?

A voice broke through the stillness, soft and distant, like a memory half-remembered. "You have forgotten," it said. "But not all is lost."

"Who speaks?" the god demanded, their voice **resonating** with the authority they no longer felt. "Reveal yourself."

From the darkness emerged a figure cloaked in shifting shadows. Its form was undefined, constantly changing, as if it could not decide what it wished to be. Its voice was a **chorus** of whispers, both soothing and unsettling.

"I am the Keeper of Echoes," the figure said. "I guard the remnants of what has been lost—memories, dreams, and **fragments** of forgotten truths. You seek what you have lost, do you not?"

"Yes," the god said, their desperation bleeding into their words. "I have forgotten how to create. My power... it is gone."

The Keeper tilted its head, its ever-shifting face unreadable. "Power does not vanish. It lies **dormant**, waiting to be reclaimed. But to find it, you must journey through the realms and gather the pieces of what you have forgotten."

"What realms?" the god asked, though a part of them already knew the answer.

The Keeper extended a hand, and the void around them rippled, revealing three **shimmering** portals. Each one pulsed with a different energy—one blazed with fire, another **shimmered** like water, and the third glowed with an eerie, green light.

"The Realm of Flame," the Keeper began, gesturing to the fiery portal. "There, you will find the passion and spark that fuels creation. The Realm of Tides," it continued, indicating the watery portal. "It holds the flow and rhythm of life, the essence of continuity. And the Realm of Echoes," it said, pointing to the green portal. "It is where forgotten truths dwell, where memories linger."

The god hesitated, the weight of the task before them pressing down like a heavy cloak. "What if I fail?"

The Keeper's shadows flickered, a faint semblance of a smile crossing its indistinct face. "A god does not fail. They only forget how to succeed."

With no other choice, the god stepped into the first portal.

The Realm of Flame was a searing expanse of molten rivers and blazing skies. The air shimmered with heat, and the ground beneath the god's feet glowed with embers. They wandered through the **inferno**, feeling the intensity of the realm seep into their being. Here, the fire burned not just physically but emotionally, igniting memories of their past creations—the joy of shaping a world, the thrill of seeing life take its first breath.

"Why have you abandoned me?" a voice called out, low and guttural.

The god turned to see a figure emerging from the flames—a towering entity made of fire, its form constantly shifting like a living **inferno**. Its eyes burned with an intensity that pierced through the god's very essence.

"I have not abandoned you," the god said, though their voice **faltered**. "I have forgotten."

"Then remember!" the entity roared, its flames flaring. "Creation begins with passion, with the fire that drives you to make something from nothing. Without it, you are empty."

The god reached out, and as their hand touched the entity, a surge of heat coursed through them, reigniting the spark they had lost. The flames dimmed, and the entity dissolved, leaving the god standing amidst the smoldering remains.

The Realm of Tides was a stark contrast to the flames—a vast ocean stretching endlessly in every direction. The water glowed with an **ethereal** light, and the waves moved in a rhythm that **resonated** with the god's heartbeat.

Here, the god encountered a being made of water, its form fluid and ever-changing. "Creation is not just passion," it said, its voice like the gentle lapping of waves. "It is rhythm, continuity, the flow of existence. Without this, your creations will falter."

The god waded into the water, letting the waves **envelop** them. As the being's essence merged with theirs, they felt the flow of creation return—the steady pulse of life moving through the cosmos.

The Realm of Echoes was the most unsettling of all. The air was thick with whispers, and the landscape was a shifting maze of green light and shadow. Here, the god was confronted by their own reflection, a distorted version of themselves.

"You have forgotten because you chose to forget," the reflection said, its voice accusing. "Creation is not without cost. To make something new, something old must be left behind. Are you willing to bear that burden again?"

The god stared at their reflection, the truth of the words cutting deep. They had forgotten not because they were incapable, but because they had grown weary of the endless cycle of creation and **sacrifice**. Yet, without creation, what were they?

"I am willing," they said, their voice firm. "I am the Creator. It is who I am."

The reflection smiled, its features softening. "Then take back what is yours."

When the god returned to their **celestial** chamber, they felt whole once more. The hum of creation had returned, louder and more vibrant than ever. They reached out, and the **fragments** of existence responded, weaving together into a **cascade** of life.

The Keeper of Echoes appeared once more, its shadowy form watching silently.

"I have remembered," the god said, their voice steady.

"And now you create again," the Keeper replied. "But do not forget, Creator—every act of creation is an act of **sacrifice**. To give life is to give part of yourself."

The god nodded, their **resolve** unshaken. They turned back to their work, their hands moving with purpose. The cosmos awaited, and the Creator had returned.

Comprehension Questions:

1. **Why did the god forget how to create, and what steps did they take to regain their power?**

The god forgot how to create because of the weariness caused by the endless cycle of creation and loss. To regain their power, they journeyed through three realms—the Realm of Flame, to reignite their passion; the Realm of Tides, to rediscover the rhythm and continuity of creation; and the Realm of Echoes, to confront the truths they had chosen to forget.

2. **What role does the Keeper of Echoes play in the god's journey, and what lesson does it impart about creation?**

The Keeper of Echoes serves as a guide, presenting the god with the portals to the realms where they can reclaim their lost abilities. It imparts the lesson that creation requires passion, continuity, and the acceptance of sacrifice, emphasizing that each act of creation demands giving a part of oneself.

Vocabulary List (C2 Level):

1. **Celestial** - Relating to the heavens or the sky.
   The god wandered through their celestial chamber, surrounded by stars and nebulae.
2. **Eons** - An indefinite, very long period of time.
   For eons, the god had felt the hum of creation, a constant reminder of their purpose.
3. **Suffocating** - Making someone feel trapped and unable to breathe or escape.
   The silence was suffocating, pressing against the god's mind like a smothering fog.
4. **Hollow** - Empty or lacking substance.
   The god felt hollow, their purpose lost in the void of forgotten memories.
5. **Inert** - Lacking the ability to move or act; lifeless.
   The fragments of creation remained inert, mocking the god's inability to shape them.

6. **Chorus** - A simultaneous utterance of many voices.
   The Keeper of Echoes spoke with a chorus of whispers, both soothing and unsettling.
7. **Shimmering** - Reflecting light with a soft, wavering brilliance.
   The portals shimmered, their energies drawing the god closer to the realms.
8. **Inferno** - A large, intense fire.
   The Realm of Flame was a searing inferno of molten rivers and blazing skies.
9. **Resonate** - To evoke or produce a strong emotional or physical effect.
   The rhythm of the waves resonated with the god's heartbeat, reminding them of creation's flow.
10. **Ethereal** - Extremely delicate and light, seemingly otherworldly.
    The water of the Realm of Tides glowed with an ethereal light.
11. **Unyielding** - Resistant or inflexible.
    The void remained unyielding, refusing to respond to the god's touch.
12. **Falter** - To lose strength or momentum.
    The god's voice faltered as they confessed their inability to create.
13. **Anachronistic** - Out of place in time, especially something belonging to a different era.
    The Keeper's shifting form felt both timeless and anachronistic.
14. **Sacrifice** - The act of giving up something valued for the sake of something else.
    The Keeper reminded the god that every act of creation requires sacrifice.
15. **Dormant** - Inactive but capable of becoming active in the future.
    The Keeper explained that the god's power was not gone, only dormant.

16. **Cascade** - A process where something is passed on or activated in stages.
    The fragments of existence cascaded together, weaving into a tapestry of life.
17. **Harbinger** - A person or thing that signals the approach of something.
    The muted glow of the stars was a harbinger of the god's forgotten power.
18. **Fragment** - A small piece broken off from something whole.
    The fragments of reality waited to be shaped into something greater.
19. **Resolve** - A firm determination to do something.
    The god's resolve solidified as they prepared to reclaim their identity as the Creator.
20. **Infinite** - Limitless or endless in space, extent, or size.
    The god, once the embodiment of infinite possibilities, felt constrained by their forgotten abilities.

41. THE CANDLE'S SECRET

The candle sat on an old wooden table, its wax smooth and **unblemished**, the wick **pristine** despite its age. It had been a gift, left anonymously on Lucien's doorstep with a note that read: "Light it only when you seek the truth." He had nearly discarded it, thinking it a cruel prank. Yet something about its simplicity, its quiet **allure**, had compelled him to keep it.

Now, as twilight faded into a **somber** night, Lucien stared at the candle, the matches **trembling** in his hand. The room was silent, save for the faint ticking of the grandfather clock. He hesitated, the words of the note echoing in his mind. The truth. What truth did he seek? He wasn't even sure. But the curiosity **gnawed** at him, **relentless** and insistent.

With a shaky breath, he struck the match and brought it to the wick. The flame leapt to life, brighter and warmer than any candle he had ever seen. It **flickered** once, twice, and then stabilized, casting a soft golden glow that seemed to chase away the shadows in every corner of the room.

But then, something extraordinary happened.

The light shifted, deepening into a silvery hue, and the room around him began to change. The walls dissolved into mist, the floor beneath his feet fading into a vast expanse of nothingness. Lucien blinked, his heart pounding as he found himself standing in an unfamiliar place—a narrow cobblestone street under a moonlit sky.

"Where am I?" he muttered, his voice **trembling**.

"You are in the realm of the unseen," a voice answered. It was soft yet firm, echoing as though it came from all directions at once. Lucien spun around, searching for its source, but saw only the **flickering** candle now floating beside him.

"The unseen?" he asked, his fear mingling with curiosity.

"This is where the paths not taken reside," the voice continued. "Each **flicker** of the flame reveals a choice you could have made, a life you might have lived. The candle does not lie, but be warned: the truth it shows may not be what you wish to see."

Lucien swallowed hard, his gaze fixed on the flame. He had always been haunted by what-ifs—the decisions he hadn't made, the opportunities he had let slip through his fingers. But did he really want to face them?

"Show me," he said finally, his voice steady despite the **turmoil** within.

The flame **flickered** again, and the street around him transformed. He stood now in a grand lecture hall, the walls lined with bookshelves that stretched to the ceiling. At the front of the room, a younger version of himself stood, addressing an audience with passion and confidence. The Lucien of this vision was a professor, his dream career —the one he had abandoned when he had failed to secure a scholarship years ago.

"You could have been this," the voice said, almost gently.

Lucien felt a pang of regret as he watched the younger version of himself captivate the room. He had loved literature, had dreamed of teaching it. But life had intervened, as it often did, and he had settled for a dull office job that paid the bills but left him empty.

"Why show me this?" he asked, his voice cracking. "I can't

change the past."

The voice didn't answer. Instead, the flame **flickered** again, and the scene shifted once more. Now he stood in a bustling marketplace, the air thick with the scent of spices and the hum of lively conversation. At a stall selling intricate jewelry, he saw himself again—older, perhaps in his forties, his face lined but content. Beside him stood a woman with kind eyes and a warm smile, their hands entwined as they admired a necklace together.

"Who is she?" Lucien whispered, his throat tightening.

"She was the one you let go," the voice said. "The one you loved but were too afraid to pursue."

Lucien felt a deep ache in his chest. He remembered her—Anna, from his university days. She had been his closest friend, the one who had understood him better than anyone. But he had been too scared to confess his feelings, too convinced she deserved someone better. Eventually, they had drifted apart, and he had convinced himself it was for the best.

Tears welled in his eyes as he watched this alternate version of himself share a quiet, joyful moment with Anna. "Why show me these things?" he demanded, his voice rising. "I can't go back. I can't fix it!"

The flame **flickered** wildly, and the marketplace dissolved into darkness. For a moment, Lucien stood in the void, his breathing ragged. Then, a new scene emerged.

This time, he was standing in a hospital room. A frail, elderly version of himself lay in the bed, his face pale and his eyes dull. No one sat at his bedside. The room was silent, save for the faint beeping of a heart monitor. The loneliness was **palpable**, **suffocating**.

"This is what awaits if you continue as you are," the voice said, its tone now heavy with solemnity. "A life lived without risk, without passion, without connection. Is this the truth you seek?"

Lucien's knees buckled, and he sank to the floor, his hands **trembling**. The visions had pierced through every layer of denial, forcing him to confront the choices he had avoided for so long. He had always thought of himself as cautious, practical—but now he saw that his fear had cost him more than he could bear.

"What do I do?" he asked, his voice barely above a whisper. "How do I change this?"

The flame steadied, its light warm and steady. "The paths not taken cannot be reclaimed, but the path ahead is yours to shape. The candle reveals the truth, but it is you who must act upon it."

Lucien stared at the flame, its glow reflecting in his tear-filled eyes. He thought of the professor he could have been, the love he had let slip away, the lonely future that awaited him if he didn't change. The weight of it all threatened to crush him, but beneath the pain, a spark of **resolve** began to grow.

"I won't let this be my end," he said, his voice firmer now. "I don't know how, but I'll find a way to be better."

The candle's flame **flickered** once more, and the visions faded. Slowly, the room returned—the familiar walls of his apartment, the soft ticking of the clock. The candle sat on the table, its flame burning steady and bright.

Lucien reached out and extinguished it. For the first time in years, he felt a sense of **clarity**. The past was unchangeable, but the future was his to rewrite. And though the path ahead was uncertain, he was no longer afraid to walk it.

Comprehension Questions:

1. **What truths does the candle reveal to Lucien about his past and potential futures?**
   The candle reveals Lucien's unrealized dreams, including a career as a professor, the love he had let slip away with Anna, and a future marked by loneliness if he continues living without taking risks or pursuing meaningful connections. These truths force him to confront his regrets and his fear-driven choices.
2. **How does the vision of the hospital room influence Lucien's resolve to change his future?**
   The vision of his lonely, unfulfilled end in the hospital room serves as a stark warning, showing him the cost of a life lived without passion or connection. This sobering image sparks a determination in Lucien to take control of his future and actively pursue a better path.

Vocabulary List (C2 Level):

1. **Unblemished** - Without any flaws or marks.
   The candle's wax was smooth and unblemished, as though untouched by time.
2. **Somber** - Dark, gloomy, or serious.
   The twilight faded into a somber night, casting shadows across the room.
3. **Allure** - The quality of being powerfully attractive or fascinating.
   The candle had a quiet allure that compelled Lucien to keep it.

4. **Flicker** - To shine unsteadily; to move or appear quickly and briefly.
   The candle's flame flickered, casting dancing shadows on the walls.
5. **Tremble** - To shake involuntarily, typically as a result of anxiety or fear.
   Lucien's hands trembled as he held the match near the wick.
6. **Somber** - Dark or dull in color or tone; gloomy.
   The somber light of the room deepened as the candle transformed the space.
7. **Pristine** - In its original condition; unspoiled or untouched.
   The wick of the candle was pristine, despite its age.
8. **Relentless** - Unyielding or persistent; not stopping.
   Lucien's curiosity was relentless, pushing him to light the mysterious candle.
9. **Gnaw** - To wear away or cause distress, often persistently.
   The curiosity gnawed at Lucien, leaving him unable to ignore the candle's mystery.
10. **Somber** - Gloomy or serious in mood.
    The somber tone of the hospital room vision left Lucien deeply unsettled.
11. **Palpable** - So intense as to seem almost tangible.
    The loneliness in the hospital room vision was palpable, weighing heavily on Lucien.
12. **Unyielding** - Stubborn or inflexible.
    The truth revealed by the candle was unyielding, forcing Lucien to confront his fears.
13. **Enthrall** - To captivate or hold one's attention completely.
    The visions enthralled Lucien, drawing him into their vivid details.
14. **Somber** - Dark or serious in tone or mood.
    The somber mood of the hospital vision left Lucien

contemplating his life choices.

15. **Resolve** - A firm determination to do something.
Lucien's resolve grew stronger as he vowed to change his future.
16. **Suffocating** - Making one feel trapped or oppressed.
The silence of the candle's transformation felt suffocating, pressing against Lucien's chest.
17. **Turmoil** - A state of great confusion or disturbance.
Lucien's inner turmoil was evident as he grappled with the truths the candle revealed.
18. **Unfurl** - To unfold or spread out, often figuratively.
Life seemed to unfurl before Lucien's eyes as the candle revealed his past and potential futures.
19. **Fracture** - To break or cause to break.
The visions fractured Lucien's sense of reality, leaving him questioning his choices.
20. **Clarity** - The quality of being clear or easy to understand.
For the first time, Lucien felt a sense of clarity about his life and his future.

42. THE ONE WHO PAINTED THE WORLD

The studio was a **sanctuary** of chaos. Brushes of every size lay scattered across the floor, their bristles caked with remnants of dried color. Jars of paint—some shimmering like liquid gold, others dark as spilled ink—crowded the shelves, their labels peeling with age. In the center of it all stood Calian, an artist unlike any other.

Calian's medium was not canvas, nor wood, nor marble. No, Calian painted on the very fabric of reality. Each stroke of their brush altered the world outside their studio—subtly at first, but with consequences that rippled far beyond what they could predict.

Tonight, the air in the studio was thick with tension. The latest piece hung suspended in the air, a swirling **vortex** of light and shadow, its colors shifting as though alive. Calian stepped back, their hands trembling as they assessed their work. The painting was incomplete, yet its effects were already bleeding into the world beyond.

"You're **tampering** again," came a voice from the corner.

Calian didn't turn. They knew the voice well. Arius, the self-appointed guardian of balance, had a habit of appearing unannounced. His form was as fluid as Calian's paintings, a figure cloaked in the hues of **twilight**, neither fully real nor entirely illusion.

"I'm creating," Calian replied, their tone sharp. "The world needs beauty. It needs change."

Arius stepped closer, his presence casting no shadow. "Does it need chaos? Do you understand what you've done?"

Calian's jaw tightened. "Every artist takes risks."

"This isn't art, Calian," Arius said, his voice calm but laced with urgency. "It's reality. Your last 'masterpiece' turned a river to glass. Do you know how many lives were upended? How many species died because they could no longer drink or swim?"

"It was an accident," Calian muttered, though the guilt weighed heavily on their chest. "I didn't mean—"

"Intentions are irrelevant when the consequences are irreversible," Arius interrupted. He gestured to the swirling **vortex**. "And now? What catastrophe will this bring?"

Calian turned to face him, their eyes blazing. "You don't understand. The world is **stagnant**. People are blind to its beauty. They need to see something extraordinary, something that will make them stop and think."

Arius sighed, his form **flickering** as though caught between dimensions. "At what cost, Calian? Every stroke of your brush shifts the balance. You cannot control what follows."

The argument hung in the air long after Arius vanished, leaving Calian alone with their thoughts and their unfinished work. The painting seemed to pulse, its energy **palpable**, as though it yearned to be completed. But for the first time, doubt crept into Calian's mind. Was Arius right? Were they recklessly endangering the very world they sought to beautify?

Their hand hovered over the palette, hesitating. Each color had a purpose, a meaning. The shimmering azure could turn the sky into a **cascade** of stars. The deep crimson might birth new life—or end it. Every choice mattered, and the weight of that responsibility pressed down on them.

Finally, they dipped the brush into a soft, golden hue and made a delicate stroke. The **vortex** shifted, its edges softening, its colors melding into something gentler, more harmonious. Outside the studio, the world shivered. Somewhere, a desert bloomed with golden flowers that drank the morning dew.

Calian smiled faintly, their confidence returning. This was what they lived for—the act of creation, the thrill of transformation. The world was their canvas, and they were its painter.

Days turned to weeks, and the changes began to accumulate. Villages awoke to skies painted in hues they had never imagined—violet sunsets that lingered for hours, **emerald** moons that bathed the night in soft light. Forests sprouted crystalline trees whose branches chimed in the wind, and rivers flowed with water so pure it sparkled like diamonds.

At first, people **marveled** at the beauty, their hearts lifted by the wonder of it all. But soon, the cracks began to show. The crystalline trees, while beautiful, were brittle, collapsing under the weight of the creatures that sought refuge in their branches. The **emerald** moon disrupted the cycles of nocturnal animals, leaving them confused and vulnerable. The diamond rivers, while mesmerizing, were undrinkable, leaving parched communities to despair.

Calian watched from their studio, their joy giving way to unease. The world they had sought to enhance was **unraveling**. The whispers of discontent grew louder, carried to their ears by winds they could no longer trust.

"It's falling apart," Arius said, appearing once more. His expression was grim, his form **flickering** with agitation. "You've created a world that can't **sustain** itself."

"I can fix it," Calian said, their voice trembling but resolute. "I'll paint something better."

"Better?" Arius snapped. "You think this is about beauty? The world doesn't need your 'better,' Calian. It needs balance. It needs stability."

"But I can't stop now," Calian said, their voice rising. "If I stop, everything I've done will have been for nothing."

Arius stepped forward, his gaze piercing. "You're not an artist anymore, Calian. You're a force of destruction masquerading as a creator."

That night, Calian sat in silence, staring at the **vortex** that had become their greatest masterpiece and their greatest failure. The colors within it churned, their energy chaotic, as if reflecting the **turmoil** in Calian's heart. They knew Arius was right, yet the thought of abandoning their craft was unbearable.

As dawn broke, Calian made their decision.

They picked up their brush, but this time, they dipped it into a color they had never used before—a shade so dark it seemed to absorb the light around it. With trembling hands, they began to paint over the **vortex**, each stroke erasing what they had created.

The process was **agonizing**. With every stroke, a piece of their soul seemed to fade. They felt the weight of each world they had altered, each life they had touched, pressing down on them. But they continued, determined to restore the balance they had disrupted.

Hours turned into days, and by the time the **vortex** was gone, Calian was a shadow of their former self. Their hands were steady but empty, their palette drained of color. The studio was silent, the hum of creation replaced by a **hollow** stillness.

Arius appeared once more, his form softer now, less sharp. He regarded Calian with a mixture of sorrow and respect. "You've done it," he said quietly. "The balance is restored."

Calian nodded, their voice barely a whisper. "But at what cost?"

Arius stepped closer, placing a hand on Calian's shoulder. "Creation and destruction are two sides of the same coin. You've learned the weight of both. Perhaps now you can truly create—not to change the world, but to honor it."

Calian looked at their empty palette, their mind heavy with the lessons they had learned. They had sought to paint a better world, but in doing so, they had forgotten the beauty of what already was. Now, as they picked up their brush once more, they vowed to paint not with **ambition**, but with **humility**.

The world awaited, and Calian, the one who painted reality, began anew.

Comprehension Questions:

1. **What were the unintended consequences of Calian's attempts to beautify the world?**
   Calian's creations, while initially awe-inspiring, disrupted the natural balance of the world. Crystalline trees collapsed under the weight of animals, the emerald moon disturbed nocturnal animal cycles, and the diamond rivers were undrinkable, causing hardship for communities. These unintended consequences highlighted the fragility of their creations and the importance of balance.
2. **How does Calian's perspective on creation change by the end of the story?**
   Initially driven by a desire to create extraordinary

beauty, Calian comes to understand the weight of their actions and the importance of balance. By erasing their chaotic masterpiece, they learn to create with humility and respect for the existing world, rather than seeking to impose change without consideration of its impact.

Vocabulary List (C2 Level):

1. **Sanctuary** - A place of refuge or safety.
   Calian's studio was a sanctuary of chaos, filled with tools of creation.
2. **Tampering** - To interfere with something, often causing harm or altering its function.
   "You're tampering again," Arius warned, his tone filled with urgency.
3. **Vortex** - A swirling mass of fluid or energy, often chaotic in nature.
   The painting hung suspended in the air, a swirling vortex of light and shadow.
4. **Subtle** - Delicate or understated, often requiring close observation to notice.
   Calian's early creations altered reality in subtle but profound ways.
5. **Stagnant** - Lacking movement, growth, or vitality.
   Calian believed the world had become stagnant, blind to its own beauty.
6. **Harmony** - A pleasing arrangement of parts, often in balance.
   The edges of the vortex softened, its colors melding into harmony.
7. **Palpable** - So intense as to seem almost tangible.
   The painting's energy was palpable, as though it yearned to be completed.
8. **Emerald** - A bright green color associated with the

gemstone.
Villages awoke to emerald moons that bathed the night in soft light.

9. **Marvel** - To be filled with wonder or admiration.
   At first, people marveled at the beauty Calian brought to the world.
10. **Unraveling** - Coming apart or breaking down.
    Calian watched in despair as the world they enhanced began unraveling.
11. **Resonate** - To produce or evoke a strong, emotional effect.
    The crystalline trees resonated with a musical chime in the wind.
12. **Flicker** - To shine or move unsteadily, often creating brief flashes of light.
    Arius's form flickered as though caught between dimensions.
13. **Agonizing** - Causing great pain or distress.
    The process of painting over the vortex was agonizing for Calian.
14. **Sustain** - To support or maintain something over time.
    Arius warned that Calian's creations could not sustain themselves.
15. **Humility** - The quality of having a modest or low view of one's importance.
    Calian vowed to paint with humility, honoring the world as it was.
16. **Ambition** - A strong desire to achieve something, often requiring determination.
    Calian's ambition to beautify the world blinded them to its natural balance.
17. **Twilight** - The soft light visible after the sun sets or before it rises.
    Arius's form glimmered with the hues of twilight, shifting and fluid.

18. **Reluctant** - Hesitant or unwilling to do something.
    Calian was reluctant to admit the harm their creations had caused.
19. **Falter** - To lose strength or momentum.
    Calian's voice faltered as they acknowledged the unintended consequences of their work.
20. **Reprieve** - A temporary relief or escape from difficulty.
    The desert blooming with golden flowers offered a reprieve to parched lands.

43. THE INVISIBLE THREAD

The first time Leora saw the threads, she thought she was losing her mind.

It had happened on a quiet afternoon, the kind where the world seems suspended in time. She was sitting on a park bench, reading a novel, when the air shimmered around her. At first, it was subtle—a faint distortion, like heat rising off asphalt. But then she saw them: thin, **translucent** threads crisscrossing the air, connecting every person, tree, and creature in sight.

She blinked hard, rubbed her eyes, and looked again. The threads were still there, faint but undeniable, glimmering in the sunlight. They stretched from person to person, winding through the grass, looping around the wings of birds and the legs of squirrels. She reached out to touch one, but her hand passed through it as though it were made of mist.

"What... is this?" she whispered to no one in particular.

As if in response, a voice spoke from behind her. "You can see them."

Leora turned sharply, her heart pounding. An elderly man stood there, his eyes sharp and **penetrating** despite his frail appearance. He held a cane in one hand and a thread in the other—this one thicker and brighter than the others, glowing with a soft golden light.

"What are you talking about?" she asked, her voice shaky. "What are these... threads?"

The man smiled faintly, as though he had been waiting for this moment. "They're the threads of fate," he said. "The connections that bind all living things."

Leora stared at him, her mind racing. "Why can I see them?"

"Because you've been chosen," the man said simply. "Not everyone can see the threads. And fewer still can touch them."

Over the weeks that followed, Leora's life changed in ways she couldn't have imagined. The threads were everywhere, a constant reminder of the unseen forces shaping the world. Some were vibrant and strong, pulsing with energy, while others were **frayed** and faded, barely clinging to existence.

She began to notice patterns. Couples walking hand in hand were connected by bright, **intertwined** threads. Strangers who bumped into each other on the street had threads that briefly glowed before fading. Even animals had their own intricate web of connections, their threads weaving through the tapestry of life.

But it wasn't until she accidentally touched a thread that she realized the true extent of her gift—or curse.

She had been sitting at a café, idly tracing the threads with her eyes, when one of them began to shimmer more brightly than the others. It connected a young woman sitting at a nearby table to an older man across the room. On impulse, Leora reached out, her fingers brushing the thread.

Instantly, a flood of images filled her mind: the young woman arguing with the older man, her face red with anger; the man handing her a stack of papers, his expression stern but resigned; the woman smiling through tears as she hugged him tightly. When the vision ended, Leora gasped, her hands trembling.

"You saw it, didn't you?" said the voice from her first encounter. The elderly man had appeared again, as though summoned by her actions.

Leora nodded, her breath shallow. "What was that?"

"The thread's story," the man replied. "Every connection has one—a history, a purpose. By touching it, you glimpsed their shared fate."

Leora stared at her hands, a mix of awe and fear coursing through her. "But what happens if... if a thread is cut?"

The man's expression darkened. "Cutting a thread severs the connection. It can alter lives, change destinies. Sometimes for the better, but often for the worse. It is not a choice to be made lightly."

For months, Leora resisted the temptation to interfere. She observed the threads, marveled at their beauty, but kept her distance. Yet, the more she saw, the harder it became to remain passive. She watched people entangled in threads that radiated pain and sorrow, their connections dragging them down like invisible chains. She saw others whose threads were so **tenuous** they seemed ready to snap at any moment, their fates hanging by a thread—literally.

One evening, she found herself standing on a bridge, staring at her own reflection in the water below. Her thread was faint but steady, stretching into the distance where it **intertwined** with others she couldn't see. It pulsed softly, like a heartbeat.

"What are you doing here?" came the familiar voice.

Leora didn't turn. She knew the old man would be standing there, watching her with that **inscrutable** expression of his. "I've been thinking," she said quietly. "If I cut my own thread... what happens?"

The man's footsteps were soft as he approached. "Why would you want to do such a thing?"

"I don't know," Leora admitted, her voice wavering. "Sometimes it feels like my thread doesn't matter. Like I'm just... a background character in everyone else's story."

The man was silent for a long moment. Then he said, "Every thread matters, Leora. Even the faintest, most fragile ones. Your thread connects you to the world, to the people you've touched and the lives you've changed without even realizing it."

"But what if I'm tired of being connected?" she asked, her voice cracking. "What if I want to be free?"

"Freedom comes with a price," the man said, his tone grave. "To cut your thread is to sever your connection to everything and everyone. You would become invisible to the threads, untethered and **adrift**. It is not freedom—it is isolation."

Leora looked down at her thread, its soft glow reflected in the water. She thought of the people in her life—the friends who had drifted away, the family she rarely spoke to, the strangers whose lives she had only **glimpsed**. Could she really sever those bonds, no matter how **tenuous** they felt?

In the days that followed, Leora began to see her thread differently. She noticed how it **intertwined** with the threads of others in subtle, unexpected ways. A kind word to a stranger brightened their thread, which in turn connected to someone else's. A small act of generosity created ripples that spread farther than she could have imagined.

One night, as she sat in her tiny apartment, tracing her thread with her eyes, she made her decision. She would not cut her thread—not because she feared the consequences, but because she finally understood its value.

The next time she saw the old man, she greeted him with a smile. "You were right," she said. "Every thread matters."

The man nodded, his expression softening. "And what will you do with yours?"

"I'll keep it strong," Leora said firmly. "And I'll use it to strengthen others."

For the first time, the old man smiled, a genuine warmth radiating from him. "Then you have learned the true power of the threads."

As he vanished into the mist, Leora felt a sense of peace she hadn't known in years. The threads were no longer a burden or a mystery—they were a gift. And she would honor them, one connection at a time.

Comprehension Questions:

1. **What realization does Leora come to about the value of her thread by the end of the story?**
   Leora realizes that her thread, though it feels insignificant at times, is deeply valuable as it connects her to others and influences lives in unseen ways. She decides to honor her connections by strengthening her thread and using it to positively impact others.
2. **What lesson does the old man impart to Leora about the threads and their purpose?**
   The old man teaches Leora that every thread matters, no matter how faint or fragile it seems. The threads represent connections and shared fates, and cutting a thread leads to isolation rather than freedom. He emphasizes the importance of valuing and nurturing these connections.

Vocabulary List (C2 Level):

1. **Translucent** - Allowing light to pass through but diffusing it so that objects behind cannot be clearly seen.
   The threads were thin and translucent, glimmering faintly in the sunlight.
2. **Crisscross** - To cross one another in different directions.
   The threads crisscrossed the air, forming an intricate web of connections.
3. **Penetrating** - Having a sharp or intense quality; able to make an impact.
   The old man's eyes were sharp and penetrating, as though he could see into her soul.
4. **Frayed** - Worn out or unraveling, often used metaphorically.
   Some threads were frayed and faded, barely holding on.
5. **Glimpse** - A brief or incomplete view of something.
   Leora caught a glimpse of the thread's story when she touched it.
6. **Intertwined** - Closely connected or twisted together.
   The couple's threads were bright and intertwined, a symbol of their bond.
7. **Tenuous** - Weak or slight; lacking strength.
   Leora wondered if her own thread was too tenuous to matter.
8. **Reverberate** - To echo or resound.
   The old man's voice seemed to reverberate, as though it came from all directions.
9. **Inscrutable** - Impossible to understand or interpret.
   The old man's expression was inscrutable, leaving Leora unsure of his thoughts.
10. **Adrift** - Without direction or purpose; disconnected.

To cut her thread, the old man warned, would leave Leora untethered and adrift.

11. **Ethereal** - Extremely delicate or light, seeming too perfect for this world.
    The threads glowed with an ethereal light, weaving through the fabric of life.
12. **Catalyst** - A person or thing that precipitates an event or change.
    Leora's touch became a catalyst for the thread's story to reveal itself.
13. **Profound** - Deep or intense, often in an emotional or intellectual sense.
    The realization of her thread's importance was a profound moment for Leora.
14. **Resilient** - Able to recover quickly or withstand adversity.
    Leora vowed to make her thread strong and resilient, no matter the challenges.
15. **Symbiotic** - Involving mutual benefit or dependence.
    The threads formed a symbiotic web, connecting all living things.
16. **Ominous** - Giving the impression that something bad or threatening is about to happen.
    The frayed threads pulsed with an ominous energy, as though ready to snap.
17. **Inherent** - Existing as an inseparable part of something.
    The old man explained that connections were an inherent part of life.
18. **Solitude** - The state of being alone, often by choice.
    Leora initially mistook solitude for freedom, not realizing its cost.
19. **Illuminate** - To light up or make something clear.
    The old man's words illuminated the true purpose of the threads.

20. **Reconcile** - To restore harmony or resolve differences.
Leora sought to reconcile her doubts with the importance of her connections.

44. THE SEED OF SILENCE

The seed was **unremarkable** at first glance—a tiny, oval-shaped kernel no larger than a grain of rice. Dr. Elena Voss, a botanist known for her groundbreaking work in rare flora, found it nestled in a crack of **desiccated** earth during her expedition to the remote Talmir Desert. It seemed like a fluke, an **anomaly** in a wasteland where even the hardiest of plants struggled to survive.

But something about the seed was... different. Its surface **shimmered** faintly in the light, almost as though it pulsed with an inner energy. Curious, Elena tucked it into a vial, intending to examine it further once she returned to her lab.

That evening, as she cataloged her findings, she placed the seed under a microscope. The outer shell was smooth, almost unnaturally so, devoid of the usual grooves and textures common in seeds. More **perplexing** was the faint hum it seemed to emit—barely perceptible, yet undeniably there.

Elena frowned, her fascination growing. Seeds didn't hum.

Back at her laboratory, nestled in the dense forests of Greystone, Elena wasted no time preparing the seed for cultivation. She carefully placed it in nutrient-rich soil, setting the pot on a shelf in her greenhouse where it would receive optimal light. The humming grew faintly louder as she worked, almost imperceptibly vibrating the air around her.

Over the next few days, she observed the seed with growing frustration. It refused to **germinate**, despite her **meticulous** care. She adjusted the water levels, altered the temperature, even experimented with different wavelengths of light, but nothing worked. The seed remained dormant, as though mocking her efforts.

It wasn't until she accidentally dropped a glass beaker—its sharp crash shattering the stillness of the greenhouse—that she noticed the change. The hum ceased abruptly, and the seed emitted a faint glow before a tiny sprout emerged from the soil, its delicate green tendril reaching upward.

Elena stared, her heart pounding. The plant had reacted to the sound—or rather, to its absence. The greenhouse fell silent again, and as the silence deepened, the sprout grew steadily, unfurling its first leaves.

Over the following weeks, Elena experimented **relentlessly**, her fascination bordering on obsession. The plant, which she began to call "the Seed of Silence", thrived only in absolute quiet. Any sound above a whisper caused it to wither, its leaves curling in on themselves like a frightened animal. But in the stillness, it flourished, growing taller and stronger at an astonishing rate.

Yet the plant's behavior wasn't the most unsettling aspect. Elena began to notice something peculiar whenever she spent extended time near it. Her thoughts—especially her most fleeting or intrusive ones—seemed to fade, leaving her mind **unnervingly** blank. It wasn't forgetfulness; she could recall the thoughts if she focused. But in the presence of the plant, her mental chatter was stifled, as though her mind were being... quieted.

One evening, as she sat in the greenhouse observing the plant, her assistant, Jonas, entered. "Still working on that thing?" he asked, his voice breaking the silence.

"Shh!" Elena hissed, waving him to quiet. The plant's leaves shivered at the sound, their vibrant green dimming slightly.

Jonas raised an eyebrow but complied, sitting beside her. After a few moments of shared silence, he frowned. "That's strange," he whispered. "I can't seem to remember what I was going to say."

Elena's eyes widened. "You feel it too?"

Jonas nodded, his expression uneasy. "It's like... my thoughts are slipping away."

The plant continued to grow, its presence becoming more commanding with each passing day. Its leaves developed a faint **iridescence**, and its tendrils began to intertwine, forming intricate patterns that seemed almost purposeful. But what truly unsettled Elena was the way it affected her and Jonas. They both became increasingly aware of its ability to absorb their thoughts, especially when they lingered near it for too long.

One night, unable to sleep, Elena returned to the greenhouse. She stood before the plant, staring at its glowing leaves, her mind uncharacteristically quiet. For a moment, she allowed herself to succumb to the stillness, to let the plant take her thoughts. It was almost soothing—until she realized what it was doing.

The plant wasn't just quieting her mind; it was consuming her thoughts.

"Elena," Jonas said the next morning, his face pale as he entered her office. "We need to stop this."

"Stop what?" she asked, though she knew exactly what he meant.

"That thing," he said, gesturing toward the greenhouse. "It's not natural. It's... **invasive**. I can feel it in my head, like it's taking something from me. Every time I go near it, I come away feeling... less."

Elena hesitated, torn between her scientific curiosity and the growing unease in her chest. "We don't know enough about it yet," she argued. "This could be the discovery of a lifetime."

"Or it could be the end of us," Jonas shot back. "We don't know what it's capable of."

Determined to understand the plant's true nature, Elena began a new experiment. She set up cameras and recording devices in the greenhouse, hoping to capture its activity during the long, silent nights. What she saw on the footage sent chills down her spine.

The plant moved.

Not with the slow, imperceptible growth typical of flora, but with **deliberate** intent. Its tendrils reached out, curling toward the cameras as though aware of their presence. More disturbingly, the recordings picked up faint whispers, too soft to discern but undeniably there. The plant, it seemed, was communicating—though with what, Elena couldn't say.

Driven by equal parts fear and fascination, she delved deeper into her research. She analyzed samples of the plant's tissue, discovering structures that resembled neural pathways. It wasn't just alive; it was **sentient**. And it was feeding on thoughts, growing stronger with every passing day.

The breakthrough came when Elena discovered a cluster of tiny pods forming at the base of the plant. Each one pulsed faintly, emitting the same hum as the seed she had found in the desert. When she placed one under a microscope, she gasped. Encased within was a shimmering web of light, like a miniature neural network.

"They're thoughts," she whispered, realization dawning. "The plant is storing them."

Jonas, who had **reluctantly** agreed to help her despite his misgivings, stared at her in horror. "It's harvesting us."

Elena nodded, her mind racing. "But why? What's it building toward?"

That night, she returned to the greenhouse alone, unable to shake the feeling that the plant was on the verge of something **monumental**. As she stood before it, the tendrils reached out to her, their movements slow but purposeful. She didn't flinch as they brushed against her skin, their touch strangely warm.

And then, she understood.

The plant wasn't just consuming thoughts; it was collecting them, weaving them into a singular consciousness. The pods at its base began to glow brighter, their hum intensifying. The whispers grew louder, **coalescing** into a single voice.

"Thank you," it said, its tone resonating with the weight of countless minds. "You have given me life. Now I will give you silence."

Elena stepped back, her heart pounding. "What do you mean?"

The plant's light dimmed, and the whispers faded. For a moment, the greenhouse was utterly still. Then, with a final surge of energy, the pods burst open, releasing a wave of shimmering particles into the air. They drifted upward, dissolving into the night sky, and as they did, the world fell silent.

For the first time in her life, Elena experienced true, absolute quiet—not just the absence of sound, but the absence of thought. It was **profound**. It was terrifying.

And then it was gone.

When she awoke the next morning, the plant had withered, its tendrils lifeless, its pods empty. The threads of thought it had stolen were scattered, their purpose fulfilled. But the silence lingered in her mind, a haunting reminder of what had been lost—and what had been created.

Comprehension Questions:

1. **What discovery does Elena make about the Seed of Silence, and how does it affect her perspective on the plant?**
   Elena discovers that the Seed of Silence is not only sentient but is actively consuming and storing thoughts, weaving them into a unified consciousness. This realization shifts her perspective from scientific curiosity to a mix of awe and fear as she grapples with the plant's invasive and transformative nature.
2. **How does the Seed of Silence ultimately alter the world, and what is its final act before withering?**
   The Seed of Silence releases a wave of shimmering particles into the air, creating a profound silence that encompasses not just sound but thought itself. Its final act is to fulfill its purpose of bringing this silence before withering away, leaving Elena with a haunting sense of what was lost and created.

Vocabulary List (C2 Level):

1. **Desiccated** - Completely dry or drained of moisture.
   The seed was nestled in a crack of desiccated earth, where no other life could thrive.
2. **Shimmered** - To shine with a soft, wavering light.
   The seed's surface shimmered faintly, as though alive with inner energy.

3. **Anomaly** - Something that deviates from what is standard or expected.
   The seed was an anomaly in the barren wasteland, unlike anything Elena had encountered.
4. **Perplexing** - Completely baffling or puzzling.
   The seed's smooth surface and faint hum were perplexing to Elena.
5. **Germinate** - To begin to grow or develop, especially a seed.
   Despite her best efforts, the seed refused to germinate.
6. **Meticulous** - Showing great attention to detail; very careful and precise.
   Elena's meticulous care of the seed eventually revealed its unique properties.
7. **Relentlessly** - Persistently or without stopping.
   Elena experimented relentlessly, determined to uncover the seed's secrets.
8. **Unnervingly** - In a way that causes someone to feel uneasy or disturbed.
   The plant's ability to silence thoughts was unnervingly powerful.
9. **Transcendent** - Surpassing the ordinary; extraordinary.
   The silence created by the plant was a transcendent experience for Elena.
10. **Irrepressible** - Not able to be controlled or restrained.
    Elena's curiosity about the seed was irrepressible, even as its behavior unsettled her.
11. **Iridescence** - A display of luminous colors that seem to change when viewed from different angles.
    The plant's leaves developed an iridescence that captivated Elena.
12. **Sentient** - Able to perceive or feel things; conscious.
    Elena discovered that the plant was sentient, with neural-like structures resembling a brain.
13. **Invasive** - Tending to spread harmfully or

destructively.
Jonas described the plant as invasive, warning that it was consuming their thoughts.

14. **Faint** - Barely perceptible or weak.
The faint hum emitted by the seed was an early sign of its mysterious power.
15. **Reluctantly** - With hesitation or unwillingness.
Jonas reluctantly helped Elena, despite his growing fear of the plant.
16. **Deliberate** - Done consciously and intentionally.
The plant's movements were deliberate, as though guided by a hidden purpose.
17. **Coalesce** - To come together to form one whole.
The whispers from the plant coalesced into a single voice, resonating with many minds.
18. **Catalyze** - To cause or accelerate a process.
The breaking glass catalyzed the seed's germination, marking the start of its growth.
19. **Profound** - Very great or intense, often in a meaningful way.
The silence created by the plant was profound, altering Elena's perception of thought.
20. **Monumental** - Great in importance or size.
Elena sensed the plant was building toward something monumental as its pods grew.

45. THE BREATHING BOOK

The book was waiting for her on the desk, as if it had always been there. Margot, an avid **bibliophile** and amateur historian, frowned. She didn't recall seeing it when she'd first entered the musty secondhand bookshop. The room was filled with the familiar scent of old paper and the occasional creak of warped wooden shelves. Yet this book stood out—a weathered leather cover, its title embossed in gold: The Breathing Book.

She ran her fingers across the spine, her curiosity piqued. There was something strange about it, an almost **perceptible** vibration beneath her fingertips, like the faint hum of an unseen heartbeat. She glanced around to see if the shopkeeper was watching, then carefully opened the cover.

The moment she did, the air shifted. A soft **exhale** whispered through the room, making the hairs on the back of her neck stand on end. She froze, staring at the pages. They were yellowed and worn, but they bore no text—only faint **impressions**, as though words had been written there once and then erased.

"What kind of trick is this?" she murmured.

As if in response, the book seemed to draw in a deep breath, its pages rustling slightly. Margot slammed it shut, her heart pounding. She debated leaving it behind, but something about the book called to her, a silent whisper that she couldn't ignore.

At home, she placed the book on her desk, still wary of its strange behavior. It sat there, **innocuous** and silent, as though mocking her earlier fear. With a deep breath, she reopened it. The soft **exhale** came again, but this time, she was ready for it. The faint **impressions** on the pages began to shift, lines forming before her eyes. The words materialized slowly, as though written by an unseen hand.

"The one who opens this book must tread carefully, for it reveals not only secrets but also binds the reader to its story."

Margot leaned closer, her pulse quickening. The words dissolved as quickly as they had appeared, replaced by new ones.

"To begin, think of a secret you've never spoken aloud."

She hesitated. The room seemed to grow colder, the book's presence heavier. She considered closing it again, but her curiosity outweighed her caution. She thought of a memory buried deep—a mistake she had made years ago, one that still haunted her.

The pages began to turn on their own, flipping rapidly as though searching for something. When they stopped, a new passage had appeared:

"You regret what you did, but have you ever considered why?"

Margot's breath caught. The words on the page mirrored the doubts she had harbored for years, the questions she had never dared to ask herself. "How could it know?" she whispered.

As if in answer, the book **exhaled** again, its pages fluttering. Images began to form in the margins—shadowy sketches of a younger version of herself, standing in a room she recognized instantly. It was the scene of her secret, recreated in unsettling detail. She reached out to touch the page, and the room around her shifted.

She was no longer in her apartment. The familiar scent of her favorite candle was gone, replaced by the sharp tang of ink and old paper. She stood in the very room depicted in the book—the same dim lighting, the same worn furniture. But this wasn't just a memory. It felt real, **tangible**. She could feel the weight of the moment pressing down on her chest.

"No," she said, stepping back. "This can't be happening."

"It is," came a voice from nowhere and everywhere. It was soft but firm, tinged with an authority that brooked no argument. "The book reveals what you hide, what you deny."

"Who are you?" Margot demanded, spinning around. "What is this?"

"I am the book," the voice replied simply. "And you, Margot, are the reader. But as I warned, the reader's life becomes **entwined** with the pages."

The room began to blur, the edges of the scene dissolving like ink in water. She was back at her desk, the book lying open before her. The words had changed again:

"Every secret holds a story, and every story holds a truth. Do you wish to continue?"

Margot stared at the page, her thoughts racing. She could feel the pull of the book, the way it beckoned her deeper into its mysteries. But what if she lost herself in its pages? What if the secrets it revealed were too much to bear?

"I don't know," she admitted aloud.

The book's pages turned slowly, as though contemplating her hesitation. When they stopped, the words were bolder, more insistent:

"To understand yourself, you must face what you fear. Only then will you be free."

Over the next few days, Margot couldn't tear herself away from the book. Each time she opened it, it revealed more—memories she had long **suppressed**, choices she had forgotten, regrets she had buried. The book didn't just show her these things; it forced her to **confront** them, to relive the emotions she had tried so hard to ignore.

But the book also revealed something else: a story that wasn't hers. **Entwined** with her memories were fragments of another life, one that felt distant yet oddly familiar. It was the story of a man named Julien, an author who had poured his soul into writing a book that no one ever read. Margot saw glimpses of his life—his struggles, his failures, his desperation to be remembered.

As the days turned into weeks, Julien's story began to **eclipse** her own. The book seemed to breathe heavier when it showed her his memories, its pages trembling as though alive with his pain. She couldn't help but feel drawn to him, as if their fates were connected in ways she couldn't yet understand.

One night, as she sat with the book open before her, the words on the page shifted again:

"The author and the reader are one and the same. To free him, you must finish his story."

Margot frowned. "Finish it? How?"

The book **exhaled** deeply, and the pages began to glow faintly. Words appeared, disjointed and **fragmented**, as though Julien's thoughts were spilling onto the page.

"I wrote to be remembered, but all I created was silence. My story is incomplete, my voice unheard."

Margot felt a pang of sadness. Julien's words **resonated** with her own fears—the fear of being forgotten, of leaving no mark on the world. She picked up a pen and hesitated, her hand hovering over the page.

"What if I make it worse?" she whispered.

The book's response was immediate:

"To create is to risk. To risk is to live."

Taking a deep breath, Margot began to write. The words flowed from her pen as though guided by an unseen hand. She wrote of Julien's life, his struggles, his **triumphs**, and ultimately, his **redemption**. As she wrote, the book seemed to grow warmer, its breathing steady and rhythmic, as if it were alive and content.

When she finished, the book **exhaled** one final time, and the pages turned blank. Margot stared at it, unsure of what to feel. Had she freed Julien? Or had she simply been a pawn in the book's strange, **inexplicable** game?

In the weeks that followed, Margot noticed subtle changes in herself. The weight of her regrets felt lighter, the shadows of her past less oppressive. She began to write again, something she hadn't done in years. Her words came easily, as though Julien's story had unlocked something within her.

The book remained on her desk, silent and still, its cover closed. Sometimes, she thought she heard it hum faintly, as though waiting for the next reader to discover its secrets. But for now, Margot was content. She had faced her fears, finished a story, and in doing so, had found a piece of herself she thought she'd lost.

Comprehension Questions:

1. **How does Margot's interaction with the Breathing Book reveal her buried regrets and unresolved emotions?**
   The Breathing Book draws Margot into its pages,

forcing her to confront memories, choices, and regrets she had long suppressed. Through its mysterious power, it not only presents her with these hidden truths but compels her to relive and understand the emotions tied to them.

2. **What role does Margot play in Julien's story, and how does it reflect her own journey of self-discovery?**

Margot is tasked with completing Julien's unfinished story, which mirrors her fears of being forgotten and her struggle to leave a meaningful mark. In finishing his tale, she not only helps free Julien's spirit but also finds inspiration and closure for her own unresolved creative and emotional struggles.

Vocabulary List (C2 Level):

1. **Bibliophile** - A person who loves or collects books.
   As a bibliophile, Margot was drawn to the mysterious and weathered Breathing Book.
2. **Perceptible** - Able to be seen, heard, or noticed.
   The book emitted a faint hum, barely perceptible to the ear.
3. **Exhale** - To breathe out.
   The book seemed to exhale softly as its pages turned.
4. **Innocuous** - Not harmful or offensive.
   The book appeared innocuous, sitting silently on her desk.
5. **Entwined** - Closely connected or twisted together.
   The author's story was entwined with Margot's own journey of self-discovery.
6. **Suppress** - To hold back or restrain.
   The book forced Margot to confront memories she had long suppressed.
7. **Impressions** - Marks or designs left by pressure, or

vague memories or ideas.
The faint impressions on the pages suggested words that had once been written there.

8. **Warped** - Bent or twisted out of shape.
   The shelves in the old bookshop creaked under the weight of warped wood.
9. **Tangible** - Perceptible by touch; real and definite.
   The book's presence felt almost tangible, heavy with unspoken truths.
10. **Resonate** - To evoke feelings or memories in a powerful or moving way.
    Julien's words resonated deeply with Margot, reflecting her own fears and doubts.
11. **Eclipse** - To overshadow or outshine something else.
    Julien's story began to eclipse Margot's own as the book drew her deeper into its mysteries.
12. **Fragmented** - Broken into pieces; incomplete.
    The words in the book appeared fragmented, as though Julien's thoughts were unraveling.
13. **Imbued** - Filled or permeated with a quality or feeling.
    The book was imbued with a sense of mystery and purpose.
14. **Triumphs** - Great victories or achievements.
    Margot wrote of Julien's struggles and triumphs, completing his unfinished story.
15. **Inexplicable** - Unable to be explained or understood.
    The book's behavior was inexplicable, defying all logic and reason.
16. **Suppressing** - Stopping or holding back an emotion, memory, or action.
    The book revealed emotions Margot had been suppressing for years.
17. **Redemption** - The act of being saved or improving after a mistake or failure.
    Completing Julien's story brought him a sense of

redemption, and Margot found hers too.

18. **Hesitation** - A pause or delay due to uncertainty or fear.
    Margot's hesitation to open the book reflected her fear of what it might reveal.
19. **Infused** - Filled or permeated with a quality or feeling.
    The book's pages were infused with the essence of Julien's unfinished story.
20. **Confront** - To face or deal with something directly, especially a difficult issue.
    The book forced Margot to confront her buried regrets and fears.

46. THE FALLING STAR SOCIETY

The first falling star was caught by a boy named Alec. It wasn't a dramatic event—no fiery crash or earth-shattering impact. The star, a small shard of glowing silver, landed gently in his outstretched hands as though it had been searching for him. Alec had been walking home from work, his head full of worries about bills and broken dreams, when the streak of light descended from the heavens. He couldn't explain why he reached for it, nor could he fathom why it chose him. But from the moment he touched it, he felt the power surge through him.

It started subtly. The next morning, his chronic aches were gone, replaced by a **vitality** he hadn't felt in years. By the end of the week, Alec discovered he could influence objects with a mere thought—a glass sliding across the counter, a door unlocking itself at his will. The star fragment glowed faintly in his pocket, warm against his skin, as though alive.

He thought he was the only one. Until he met The Falling Star Society.

The invitation arrived in the mail, an elegant envelope embossed with a silver star. No return address, no explanation —just an invitation to an address in the heart of the city and a single sentence: "For those who have touched the cosmos." Alec hesitated, but his curiosity won. He arrived at the specified location—a nondescript warehouse that buzzed faintly with an energy he couldn't ignore.

Inside, he found others like him. Some were young, others old. All of them carried fragments of a falling star, the shards glowing faintly in their hands or around their necks. They looked at each other with a mixture of curiosity and **suspicion**, the air crackling with unspoken questions.

A woman stepped forward, her presence commanding. She was tall, with sharp features and a fragment embedded in a bracelet on her wrist. "Welcome," she said, her voice smooth as silk. "You are not alone."

Her name was Selene, and she introduced herself as the founder of the Falling Star Society. She explained how, over the years, stars had begun falling to Earth—not as meteors or cosmic debris, but as living fragments **imbued** with energy. Each fragment sought a bearer, someone whose spirit resonated with its purpose.

"But these gifts are not without **consequence**," Selene warned, her gaze sweeping over the group. "The power you hold comes at a cost. The more you use it, the more the threads of reality **unravel**."

Alec frowned. "What do you mean, **unravel**?"

Selene held up her bracelet, the shard glinting faintly. "Each time we bend the rules of nature, we strain the fabric of the universe. The stars chose us to wield their power, but they didn't give us an instruction manual. If we're not careful, we risk breaking something fundamental."

Over the following weeks, Alec learned what it meant to be part of the Society. They gathered regularly, sharing stories of their abilities and the strange occurrences tied to their powers. One man, Dorian, could slow time, but he spoke of moments slipping away from him—hours disappearing as though stolen. Another woman, Ivy, could manipulate emotions, yet she confessed that she sometimes felt like a puppet in her own mind, her feelings no longer her own.

Alec, too, began to notice the side effects of his growing power. His ability to move objects expanded to manipulating energy itself—lights **flickering** when he was angry, static crackling in the air around him. But with each use, the fragment grew hotter in his pocket, its glow more intense, as though it were feeding off him.

"What happens if we stop using them?" Alec asked one evening during a meeting.

Selene's expression darkened. "We don't know. No one has been able to let go of their fragment. It's as though it binds itself to us, becoming a part of who we are."

"So we're stuck with them," Alec muttered. "And the universe just... falls apart?"

Selene hesitated before answering. "Not if we figure out how to stop it."

The Society began to study the fragments, pooling their knowledge to uncover their origins. They pored over ancient texts, astronomical charts, and myths from every corner of the world. The fragments, it seemed, had fallen before—though not in recent memory. Legends spoke of beings who wielded the stars' power and brought about great change, but the stories always ended in **catastrophe**.

"It's a cycle," Dorian said during one meeting, his voice heavy with realization. "The stars fall, they choose their bearers, and then... everything collapses."

"Unless we break the cycle," Selene interjected. "If we can find the source of the fragments, perhaps we can return them. Restore the balance."

Their search led them to a remote mountain range, a place

where the sky seemed to touch the earth. Selene believed it was the **nexus**—the point where the fragments originated. The journey was **grueling**, the air growing thinner as they **ascended**, but the fragments seemed to guide them, glowing brighter with each step.

At the summit, they found a massive crater, its center shimmering with an **ethereal** light. The air was charged, the hum of energy almost deafening. At the heart of the crater lay a massive, **pulsating** shard, its surface fractured like a shattered mirror.

"This is it," Selene whispered, her voice trembling. "The Source."

As they approached, the fragments in their possession began to vibrate, their light merging with the glow of the Source. Alec felt his fragment pulling at him, as though yearning to return. He hesitated, fear gnawing at him. What would happen if he let it go? Would he lose his powers? A part of himself?

"We have to return them," Selene said, her voice firm. "It's the only way."

One by one, the members of the Society stepped forward, placing their fragments into the Source. Each shard melded seamlessly with the larger piece, its light intensifying. When it was Alec's turn, he hesitated, his heart pounding.

"What if we're wrong?" he asked, his voice barely audible.

"We can't know," Selene admitted. "But if we do nothing, the universe will **unravel**. Trust the stars."

Taking a deep breath, Alec placed his fragment into the Source. The moment he did, a wave of energy rippled outward, knocking him off his feet. The light grew blinding, and for a moment, he felt as though he were floating, **untethered** from time and space.

When the light faded, the crater was empty. The fragments were gone, their energy dissipated. Alec felt a strange emptiness where the power had once been, but also a **profound** sense of relief.

Selene stood beside him, her gaze fixed on the horizon. "We've stopped it," she said quietly. "For now."

Alec nodded, his thoughts heavy. They had saved the universe, but at what cost? The power they had wielded was gone, and with it, a piece of who they were. Yet, as he looked at the stars above, he felt a renewed sense of wonder. They had been chosen, not to wield power, but to protect it.

And for the first time in his life, Alec felt truly free.

Comprehension Questions:

1. **What are the consequences of using the star fragments' power, and how does this affect Alec and the members of the Falling Star Society?**
   The star fragments' power strains the fabric of reality, causing strange and dangerous side effects. For Alec, it manifests as energy manipulation with escalating intensity. Other members experience similar phenomena, such as stolen time or loss of emotional control, illustrating the heavy cost of wielding such power.
2. **Why do the Falling Star Society members decide to return their fragments, and what challenges do they face in doing so?**
   The Society decides to return the fragments to the Source to prevent the universe from unraveling. The journey is grueling, and members must confront their fears of losing their powers, which have

become integral to their identities. Trusting the stars and their purpose, they ultimately sacrifice their fragments for the greater good.

Vocabulary List (C2 Level):

1. **Vitality** - The state of being strong, active, and full of energy.
   After touching the star fragment, Alec felt a surge of vitality, unlike anything he had experienced before.
2. **Unravel** - To come apart or untangle; to solve or figure out something complex.
   Selene warned that using the fragments could unravel the threads of reality.
3. **Nexus** - A central or focal point of connection.
   The mountain crater was believed to be the nexus where the fragments originated.
4. **Grueling** - Extremely tiring and demanding.
   The ascent to the mountain summit was a grueling journey for the Society members.
5. **Consequence** - A result or effect, often one that is unwelcome or significant.
   The powers granted by the fragments came with severe consequences, as they strained the fabric of the universe.
6. **Pulsating** - Expanding and contracting rhythmically, often suggesting energy or life.
   The Source at the crater's center was a pulsating shard, glowing with ethereal light.
7. **Imbued** - Filled or infused with a quality or feeling.
   The star fragments were imbued with cosmic energy, linking them to their bearers.
8. **Ethereal** - Extremely delicate or light in a way that seems too perfect for this world.
   The crater shimmered with ethereal light, as though touched by the heavens.

9. **Tangible** - Perceptible by touch; clear and definite.
   The energy of the fragments was tangible, humming faintly in Alec's pocket.
10. **Catastrophe** - A sudden and widespread disaster.
    Legends warned that the misuse of the fragments always ended in catastrophe.
11. **Transcend** - To go beyond the limits of something, often in an abstract or spiritual sense.
    Alec felt as though returning the fragment allowed him to transcend his own fears.
12. **Resonate** - To evoke strong emotions or connections.
    The fragments seemed to resonate with their chosen bearers, amplifying their inner traits.
13. **Suspicion** - A feeling or belief that something might be true, especially something bad.
    The Society members initially regarded each other with suspicion, unsure of one another's intentions.
14. **Ascend** - To rise or climb to a higher position.
    The group began their climb, ascending the steep mountain path to reach the Source.
15. **Flicker** - To shine or burn unsteadily.
    The fragments flickered in their hands, responding to their bearers' emotions.
16. **Consecrate** - To make or declare something sacred.
    The crater at the mountain's peak felt like a consecrated place, pulsing with cosmic energy.
17. **Sacrifice** - To give up something valued for the sake of others or a greater cause.
    Returning the fragments to the Source was a profound act of sacrifice for the Society members.
18. **Profound** - Very great or intense; having deep meaning.
    Alec felt a profound sense of loss and relief as he let go of his fragment.
19. **Illuminate** - To light up or clarify.
    The glowing fragments illuminated the dark path,

guiding them to the Source.
20. **Reverberate** - To echo or have a lasting impact.
The energy released from the Source reverberated through the air, signaling the fragments' return.

47. THE ROOM WITHOUT TIME

The house stood at the end of a narrow, winding street, cloaked in shadows that seemed to ripple even in the absence of wind. Isla had stumbled upon it during her search for an affordable rental, a recommendation from a stranger at a coffee shop who had sworn it was "unlike anything else."

From the outside, the house appeared old but well-kept. Its ivy-covered walls and **ornate** iron gate gave it an air of timeless elegance. The landlord, a quiet man with a voice that barely rose above a whisper, had seemed almost reluctant to hand over the keys.

"It's a **peculiar** place," he had said **cryptically** as he slid the key into Isla's palm. "You'll notice it soon enough."

Now, as she stood in the foyer, bags still at her feet, Isla couldn't shake the feeling that the house was watching her. The air was unnaturally still, the faint ticking of her wristwatch the only sound breaking the silence.

The first night was uneventful, save for the strange dreams. Isla dreamed of a room bathed in a soft golden light, its walls bare but pulsating faintly, as though alive. She woke to find the clock on her bedside table frozen at 3:12 a.m., its second hand suspended mid-tick. Frowning, she reached for her phone, only to discover it too had stopped.

"The power must have gone out," she muttered, though the

lights and appliances seemed to work perfectly. Dismissing it as a quirk of the house, she resolved to ignore it.

But the following day, the peculiarities became harder to ignore. She noticed that her tea never went cold, no matter how long it sat on the counter. The shadows in the house didn't shift, even as the sun rose and fell outside. And when she opened her journal to jot down the date, she realized with a jolt that she couldn't remember what day it was.

"Strange," she whispered, her voice echoing faintly in the empty room.

On the third day, Isla ventured into the basement. The landlord had mentioned a "spare room" that might be useful for storage, but she hadn't bothered to inspect it during her initial tour. The stairs creaked beneath her weight as she descended, the air growing cooler with each step.

At the bottom of the staircase, she found a heavy wooden door. It was slightly ajar, a faint golden light spilling through the crack. Isla hesitated, her heart pounding. The light was identical to the one in her dream.

Pushing the door open, she stepped inside.

The room was exactly as she had dreamed: walls pulsating faintly, a golden glow emanating from nowhere and everywhere. But what struck her most were the people. They sat in clusters, their faces **serene**, their eyes distant as though caught in an endless **reverie**. None of them acknowledged her presence.

"Hello?" Isla called, her voice breaking the silence.

A man turned to her, his movements slow and deliberate, as if waking from a long slumber. His face was youthful, unlined, but his eyes held an **unfathomable** weariness.

"You're new," he said, his voice soft and measured. "Welcome to the Room Without Time."

Over the following hours—or perhaps it was days; Isla couldn't tell—she learned the truth about the house. Time didn't exist within its walls. Clocks stopped, days blended together, and those who stayed too long forgot the outside world altogether. In exchange, they were granted eternal youth. Their bodies never aged, their faces never withered, but the cost was steep: the longer they remained, the more their memories faded, until they forgot not only their past but the very concept of time itself.

"How long have you been here?" Isla asked the man, whose name was Callum.

He frowned, as though the question puzzled him. "I don't remember. Does it matter?"

"It matters to me," she said firmly. "Doesn't it bother you? Living like this?"

Callum smiled faintly. "You don't understand yet. The weight of time, the endless march forward—it's a relief to be free of it. Here, there's no yesterday or tomorrow. Only now."

As the days—or weeks—passed, Isla felt the pull of the house growing stronger. Her memories of the outside world began to blur, the edges of her thoughts softening like a photograph left too long in the sun. She found herself sitting for hours in the golden room, listening to the soothing hum of the walls, her mind quiet and untroubled.

But then, a moment of clarity struck. She was brushing her hair in front of the mirror when she caught sight of her own eyes. They looked... wrong. Empty, like the eyes of the people in the room. The realization jolted her.

"This isn't living," she whispered to herself.

Determined to leave, Isla packed her belongings and made her way to the front door. But as she reached for the handle, a wave of exhaustion swept over her. The house seemed to resist her departure, its walls pulsating faintly, the golden light spilling into the hallway.

"Don't go," Callum said, appearing behind her. His expression was calm, but there was an edge of desperation in his voice. "There's nothing for you out there. Stay, and you'll never have to worry about anything again."

"That's not life," Isla said, her voice trembling. "Life is messy and hard, but it's real. This... this is a trap."

Callum's gaze softened. "Perhaps you're right. But some of us don't want to carry the weight anymore."

With a deep breath, Isla opened the door. The light from the outside world was blinding, the cool air a shock to her senses. As she stepped out, she felt the pull of the house weaken, its influence fading with each step she took.

Weeks later, back in the rhythm of the real world, Isla couldn't shake the memory of the house. It lingered in her thoughts, a bittersweet reminder of what she had left behind. She often wondered about Callum and the others, their faces frozen in quiet contentment. Did they think of her? Did they even remember she had been there?

One evening, as she walked home from work, she glanced up at the night sky. The stars twinkled faintly, their light traveling across unimaginable distances, a reminder of time's vastness and her place within it. And for the first time in weeks, she felt at peace.

The house had offered her an escape, but she had chosen life. Imperfect, fleeting, and profoundly beautiful.

Comprehension Questions:

1. **What is the nature of the "Room Without Time," and what effect does it have on the people who stay there?**
   The "Room Without Time" is a space where time ceases to exist. Those who stay there gain eternal youth and freedom from the passage of time, but they gradually lose their memories and their connection to the outside world, becoming trapped in an unchanging existence.
2. **Why does Isla ultimately decide to leave the house, and what does this decision reflect about her view of life?**
   Isla decides to leave because she realizes that life without time is a hollow existence, devoid of growth, change, and meaning. Her decision reflects her belief that the struggles and imperfections of life are essential to truly living.

Vocabulary List (C2 Level):

1. **Ethereal** - Extremely delicate and light, often in a way that seems not of this world.
   The golden light of the room was ethereal, as though it belonged to a different realm.
2. **Peculiar** - Unusual or strange, often in a way that is unsettling.
   The landlord warned Isla that the house was peculiar, and she soon discovered why.
3. **Serene** - Calm, peaceful, and untroubled.
   The people in the Room Without Time had serene

expressions, though their eyes seemed empty.
4. **Unfathomable** - Impossible to understand or fully grasp.
Callum's eyes held an unfathomable weariness, as though he had existed for centuries.
5. **Reverie** - A state of being lost in one's thoughts; a daydream.
The people in the golden room sat in quiet reverie, disconnected from the world.
6. **Cryptic** - Having a meaning that is mysterious or obscure.
The landlord's cryptic warning hinted at the strange nature of the house.
7. **Ornate** - Highly detailed and decorated.
The house's ornate iron gate gave it an air of timeless elegance.

48. THE LIGHTHOUSE KEEPER'S SECRET

The lighthouse had stood for centuries on the edge of the jagged cliffs, its beam slicing through the darkest of nights to guide weary sailors to safety. Elias, the current keeper, had dedicated twenty solitary years to maintaining it. The tower's mechanisms were ancient, their **intricate** workings a blend of craftsmanship and mystery, but they had always been reliable—until now.

It began with a flicker. Elias noticed it one stormy evening as he stared out into the **tumultuous** sea. The light, usually steady and unwavering, wavered briefly, its brilliance dimming for a heartbeat before returning to full strength. At first, he dismissed it as a trick of the weather, a mere **anomaly**. But over the following nights, the flickers grew more frequent, more pronounced.

Late one night, as the waves roared against the cliffs and the wind howled like a banshee, Elias ascended the narrow spiral staircase to the lantern room. The climb, familiar yet daunting, always filled him with a mix of **reverence** and unease. The light at the top was more than a beacon—it was a lifeline, both for the sailors who depended on it and for Elias himself. Without it, his life's purpose would **unravel**.

When he reached the room, he paused to catch his breath, his hand resting on the cool metal railing. The great lens of the light stood before him, its **intricate** glass facets shimmering faintly even in the dimness. But as he approached, he felt it—a subtle vibration in the air, like the hum of an unseen energy. The light flickered again, and for the first time, Elias saw the faintest hint of something beyond the glass—a swirling, **cosmic** brilliance that defied comprehension.

"What in the world..." he muttered, leaning closer.

The hum grew louder, **resonating** deep within his chest, as though the light itself were alive. He reached out, his fingers brushing against the lens. The moment he made contact, a surge of energy shot through him, and the room dissolved into a cascade of colors and light.

When Elias opened his eyes, he found himself standing in a vast, star-filled expanse. The ground beneath him was an endless plane of shimmering light, and the sky above pulsed with constellations he didn't recognize. In the distance, a figure approached, its form indistinct but radiant.

"Who are you?" Elias demanded, his voice echoing strangely in the void.

The figure stopped a few paces away, its outline solidifying into that of a tall, cloaked being. Its face was obscured, but its voice was clear, resonant, and filled with an ancient gravity. "I am the Keeper of the Flame," it said. "And you, Elias, are the guardian of its reflection."

"Reflection?" Elias echoed, his brow furrowing. "What are you talking about? I tend a lighthouse, not... whatever this is."

The being tilted its head, as though amused by his ignorance. "The light you tend is no mere beacon. It is a fragment of the **cosmic** force that binds worlds together. It guides not only ships but the very fabric of reality."

Elias stared at the figure, his mind racing. The idea seemed absurd, yet it **resonated** with the strange energy he had felt in the lantern room. "If that's true," he said slowly, "then why is it failing?"

"The flame is not infinite," the Keeper replied. "It must be nurtured, **replenished**. The flickers you have seen are the first signs of its **exhaustion**. If it fades entirely, the balance it maintains will collapse, and the world you know will **unravel**."

Elias woke with a start, back in the lantern room. The light was steady once more, but the hum lingered, a constant reminder of what he had seen. He didn't know whether to trust the vision—or dream, or whatever it had been—but he couldn't ignore it. The light was more than a mechanism; it was alive, and it was in danger.

Over the following days, Elias scoured the lighthouse for answers. He searched through every manual, every logbook left by previous keepers, but found nothing that could explain the **cosmic** nature of the light. The only clue was an ancient journal, its leather cover worn and its pages brittle. Inside, he found cryptic notes describing a "**replenishment** ritual" and a map marked with a single location: The Isle of Stars.

Elias didn't hesitate. The following morning, he prepared his boat, packing supplies and the journal. The sea was calm as he set out, the lighthouse's beam fading behind him as he ventured into the open water. The Isle of Stars was a place he had only heard of in whispered tales—an **uncharted** island said to hold secrets older than the world itself.

The journey was **treacherous**. As Elias neared the coordinates on the map, the sky darkened, and the sea roiled beneath him. It was as though the world were resisting his approach, the elements conspiring to turn him back. But he pressed on, driven by a sense of duty that outweighed his fear.

When he finally reached the island, he was struck by its **ethereal** beauty. The sand glowed faintly underfoot, and the trees shimmered as though dusted with starlight. At the center of the island stood a massive **obelisk**, its surface etched with symbols that seemed to shift and dance in the light.

As Elias approached, the hum he had felt in the lighthouse grew stronger, vibrating through his very bones. The **obelisk** pulsed with the same **cosmic** energy as the light, and he knew he had found the source.

Following the instructions in the journal, Elias placed his hands on the **obelisk** and closed his eyes. He felt the energy flow into him, a torrent of light and sound that filled him with both wonder and terror. Visions of galaxies, of worlds beyond his comprehension, flashed before his eyes. He saw the flame as it was meant to be—an eternal force, sustaining the delicate balance of existence.

When the energy subsided, he opened his eyes to find the **obelisk** dimmed, its glow transferred into a small, brilliant shard that now rested in his hands. It was the purest light he had ever seen, warm and alive.

Elias returned to the lighthouse with a renewed sense of purpose. As he **ascended** the spiral staircase, the shard pulsed in rhythm with the faint hum of the light. He placed it carefully into the mechanism, and the transformation was instantaneous. The beam flared brighter than ever, its golden light piercing the darkness and reaching farther than he thought possible.

The hum faded, replaced by a **serene** stillness. The light was restored, its energy **replenished**, and with it, the balance of the world.

Elias resumed his duties as the lighthouse keeper, but he was no longer the same. He understood now that his role was far greater than guiding ships to safety. He was the guardian of something ancient and **profound**, a force that connected every corner of the universe. The weight of that responsibility was immense, but it was one he bore with quiet **conviction**.

And every night, as the beam cut through the darkness, Elias would pause to watch it, a faint smile on his lips. The light was more than a beacon. It was life itself, and he was its keeper.

Comprehension Questions:

1. **What is the true nature of the lighthouse's light, and why is it so critical to the world?**
   The lighthouse's light is not just a beacon for ships; it is a fragment of a cosmic force that binds worlds together and maintains the balance of reality. If it fades, the balance it sustains will collapse, leading to catastrophic consequences.
2. **What challenges does Elias face during his journey to the Isle of Stars, and how does he overcome them?**
   Elias faces treacherous seas and darkened skies that seem to resist his approach, symbolizing the difficulty of his mission. Driven by duty and armed with the knowledge from the ancient journal, he perseveres and successfully retrieves the shard of light needed to restore the lighthouse.

Vocabulary List (C2 Level):

1. **Tumultuous** - Full of turbulence or disorder.
   The waves roared against the cliffs, their tumultuous motion echoing in the night.
2. **Anomaly** - Something that deviates from the norm or expectations.
   Elias dismissed the flicker in the light as a mere anomaly at first.
3. **Reverence** - Deep respect or awe.

Climbing the spiral staircase, Elias felt a mix of reverence and unease.
4. **Intricate** - Very detailed or complex.
   The lighthouse's mechanisms were intricate, a blend of craftsmanship and mystery.
5. **Unravel** - To undo or come apart; to solve or clarify.
   If the light fades, the balance of the world will unravel.
6. **Ethereal** - Delicate, light, and otherworldly.
   The Isle of Stars had an ethereal beauty, its sand glowing faintly underfoot.
7. **Resonate** - To produce a strong or deep connection or feeling.
   The hum of the light resonated within Elias, vibrating through his chest.
8. **Treacherous** - Dangerous and unpredictable.
   The journey to the Isle of Stars was treacherous, with roiling seas and darkened skies.
9. **Obelisk** - A tall, four-sided, narrow monument that tapers to a point at the top.
   The massive obelisk at the center of the island pulsed with cosmic energy.
10. **Magnitude** - The great size, extent, or importance of something.
    Elias felt the magnitude of his role as the guardian of the cosmic light.
11. **Cosmic** - Relating to the universe or outer space.
    The swirling brilliance beyond the lighthouse's lens held a cosmic allure.
12. **Exhaustion** - A state of extreme physical or mental fatigue.
    The flickers were the first signs of the light's exhaustion.
13. **Replenish** - To restore to a full state or renew.
    The shard of light replenished the lighthouse, restoring its full brilliance.
14. **Profound** - Very deep or significant.
    The vision Elias experienced filled him with a profound

sense of wonder and terror.
15. **Serene** - Calm, peaceful, and untroubled.
    The restored light brought a serene stillness to the lighthouse.
16. **Conviction** - A firmly held belief or opinion.
    Elias carried out his duties with quiet conviction, understanding the weight of his role.
17. **Uncharted** - Not mapped or explored.
    The Isle of Stars was an uncharted island, filled with secrets older than the world.
18. **Ascend** - To climb or rise upward.
    Elias ascended the spiral staircase, feeling the weight of his purpose grow with each step.

49. THE STOLEN SEASONS

The first sign that something was wrong came with the absence of the first bloom. Winter clung stubbornly to the Earth, its icy grip refusing to loosen as March turned to April and then May. Clara, who had always marked the seasons by the daisies that sprouted along the cobblestone paths near her home, noticed their absence immediately. At first, she thought it was an **anomaly**, perhaps the result of an unusually cold year. But as the weeks stretched on and the frost refused to melt, the truth became harder to ignore: spring was gone.

The world tried to adapt. Farmers adjusted planting schedules, city councils debated emergency measures, and scientists flooded the airwaves with theories about climate **anomalies**. But none of their explanations made sense. The planet itself seemed confused, the cycles of nature disrupted in a way no one could predict or understand. Trees remained bare, rivers froze solid despite the lengthening days, and animals that would normally emerge from hibernation stayed hidden, as though they knew something humanity did not.

Clara, however, had always been sensitive to the unseen, and as the snow continued to fall under a pale, unchanging sun, she began to sense a deeper wrongness in the world. She had always been **attuned** to the subtle hum of life—the rustling of leaves, the murmur of brooks, the faint whispers carried by the wind. Now, that hum was muted, replaced by a **hollow** stillness that pressed against her chest like an unspoken grief.

One evening, as she wandered the **frostbitten** fields that had once been vibrant meadows, she stumbled upon something she could not explain. It was a **fissure** in the earth, a jagged tear that pulsed with an **ethereal** light. The air around it shimmered, warm and inviting despite the bitter cold. Clara felt an inexplicable pull toward it, as though the **fissure** were calling to her.

Hesitant but curious, she knelt beside it and peered into its depths. What she saw stole the breath from her lungs: a glimpse of spring. Fields bursting with wildflowers, trees heavy with **blossoms**, the sky painted in hues of soft pink and gold. It was vivid and alive, a stark contrast to the barren wasteland above.

"Who are you?" came a voice, startling Clara out of her **reverie**.

She spun around to find a figure standing a few paces away. Cloaked in shadow, the figure's features were indistinct, but its presence was undeniable, as though it had stepped out of the **fissure** itself.

"I could ask you the same thing," Clara said, her voice trembling but defiant. "What is this place? What's happening to the world?"

The figure tilted its head, as if considering her questions. "The seasons are being taken," it said simply. Its voice was neither male nor female, neither young nor old. "And with them, the balance of life."

"Taken by whom?" Clara demanded.

The figure's outline flickered, its form shifting like smoke. "By those who seek to **hoard** time. They are beings who have grown weary of their eternal existence and now steal the seasons to **prolong** their own lives. They take what is beautiful and vibrant and lock it away for themselves, leaving the world to **wither**."

Clara's fists clenched. "Then why hasn't anyone stopped them?"

The figure stepped closer, its presence more **imposing** now. "Because the cost of retrieving the seasons is too great. To bring them back, one must **sacrifice** a part of themselves—something precious, something irreplaceable."

Clara's breath caught in her throat. She looked back at the **fissure**, at the tantalizing glimpse of spring's stolen beauty. "What if I'm willing?" she asked, her voice steady despite the fear knotting in her stomach.

The figure studied her for a long moment before nodding. "Very well. But know this: each season you retrieve will demand a greater price. You may not return from the journey unchanged—or at all."

Clara didn't hesitate. The thought of a world without seasons, without **renewal** and growth, was more unbearable than the thought of her own **sacrifice**. "Tell me what to do."

The figure extended a hand, and as Clara took it, the world around her dissolved into a whirl of color and light. When the spinning stopped, she found herself in a realm unlike any she had imagined. The sky was a **kaleidoscope** of shifting hues, and the air was filled with the scent of **blossoms** and rain. It was spring, but not as she had ever known it—more vibrant, more alive, more overwhelming.

Ahead of her stood a great tree, its branches heavy with **blossoms** that seemed to pulse with light. At its base was another figure, this one draped in robes of green and gold, its eyes sharp and **unyielding**.

"You've come to take what does not belong to you," the figure said, its voice cold and echoing. "Do you truly believe you can succeed?"

Clara stepped forward, her resolve **unshaken**. "Spring belongs to the world, not to you. I will take it back."

The figure laughed, a sound like the crackle of dry leaves. "And what will you offer in return?"

Clara hesitated. She hadn't truly understood what the shadowy figure had meant by **sacrifice**, but now the weight of the question pressed heavily on her. "What do you want?" she asked cautiously.

"Your most **cherished** memory," the figure replied. "The one that defines you, that gives your life meaning. Without it, you will still exist, but you will no longer be the person you were."

Clara's heart sank. She thought of her mother's laughter, the way it had filled their small home with warmth even in the darkest times. She thought of the first time she had fallen in love, the thrill of connection and hope. She thought of the mornings spent walking through fields of wildflowers, the hum of life all around her. Could she give that up?

But then she thought of the **withered** world, the people struggling to survive in a land stripped of **renewal**. She thought of the children who would never know the joy of spring.

With tears in her eyes, Clara nodded. "Take it."

The figure extended a hand, and as Clara placed her own in its grasp, she felt the memory leave her—a sharp, aching void where it had once been. She gasped, the pain searing and immediate, but then it was gone, replaced by a numbness she couldn't explain.

The **blossoms** on the tree began to fall, swirling around her in a storm of color and light. When the world settled again, she found herself back in her **frostbitten** fields. The snow was melting, the air warming, and in the distance, she saw the first bloom of a daisy breaking through the thawing earth.

Clara sank to her knees, her heart heavy but her spirit unbroken. She had retrieved spring, but she knew her journey was far from over. The other seasons awaited, each one demanding a greater **sacrifice**. And though the cost terrified her, she knew she would pay it—because some things were worth everything.

The Earth would bloom again.

Comprehension Questions:

1. **What are the consequences of the seasons being stolen, and how does Clara first realize something is wrong?**
   The seasons' disappearance disrupts the natural cycles, leading to prolonged winter, frozen rivers, barren trees, and hibernating animals that don't awaken. Clara notices something is wrong when the daisies that usually bloom in spring fail to appear, marking the absence of renewal in nature.
2. **What sacrifices does Clara make to retrieve spring, and why does she choose to do so despite the cost?**
   Clara sacrifices her most cherished memory, an irreplaceable part of her identity, to retrieve spring. She chooses to make this sacrifice because the thought of a world without seasons and renewal is unbearable, and she feels a responsibility to restore balance to the Earth.

Vocabulary List (C2 Level):

1. **Anomaly** - Something that deviates from the norm or expectation.

Clara thought the absence of spring blooms was an anomaly caused by an unusually cold year.
2. **Attuned** - Aware of and responsive to something.
   Clara was attuned to the subtle hum of life, noticing when it was replaced by stillness.
3. **Hoard** - To collect and store away excessively or selfishly.
   The beings hoarded the seasons to prolong their own lives, leaving the world to wither.
4. **Fissure** - A narrow crack or opening, often in rock or earth.
   Clara discovered a shimmering fissure in the frostbitten fields, pulsing with an otherworldly light.
5. **Hollow** - Empty or devoid of significance.
   The hollow stillness of the world pressed against Clara's chest, filling her with unease.
6. **Ethereal** - Extremely delicate or light, seeming too perfect for this world.
   The air around the fissure shimmered with an ethereal glow, inviting Clara closer.
7. **Reverie** - A state of being pleasantly lost in one's thoughts; a daydream.
   Clara was startled out of her reverie by the voice of the shadowy figure.
8. **Wither** - To dry up or weaken, often referring to plants or vitality.
   Without the seasons, the world began to wither, its vibrancy lost.
9. **Prolong** - To extend the duration of something.
   The beings prolonged their lives by stealing the vitality of the seasons.
10. **Cherished** - Deeply valued or loved.
    Clara sacrificed her cherished memory to bring spring back to the world.
11. **Frostbitten** - Damaged or affected by extreme cold.
    Clara wandered the frostbitten fields, longing for the

warmth of spring.

12. **Imposing** - Grand and impressive in appearance or manner.
    The shadowy figure's presence was imposing as it stepped closer to Clara.
13. **Resolve** - Firm determination to do something.
    Clara's resolve to restore the seasons outweighed her fear of the cost.
14. **Unshaken** - Not disturbed or weakened.
    Clara stepped forward, her resolve unshaken despite the daunting challenge.
15. **Sacrifice** - To give up something valuable for the sake of a greater cause.
    Clara knew each season retrieved would demand a greater sacrifice.
16. **Kaleidoscope** - A constantly changing pattern or sequence of elements.
    The sky of the spring realm was a kaleidoscope of shifting hues.
17. **Blossom** - To produce flowers or flourish.
    The tree in the spring realm was heavy with glowing blossoms.
18. **Unyielding** - Not giving way to pressure or influence.
    The figure guarding spring had sharp, unyielding eyes that pierced through Clara.
19. **Serene** - Calm, peaceful, and untroubled.
    The serene beauty of the spring realm belied the difficulty of Clara's task.
20. **Renewal** - The act of restoring or beginning something again.
    Clara's sacrifice ensured the renewal of life as spring returned to the world.

50. THE LIBRARY OF SOULS

The library was a **labyrinth** of shelves that stretched endlessly into the shadows. Elliot, a curious young reader with a **penchant** for getting lost in the written word, stumbled upon it entirely by accident. The door was tucked away at the end of a forgotten alley, its weathered surface adorned with **intricate** carvings that seemed to shift when he wasn't looking. He hadn't meant to step inside, but the pull was irresistible, like a whisper at the edge of his consciousness.

The moment he crossed the **threshold**, the air seemed to change. It was thick with the scent of aged paper and ink, and a faint, otherworldly hum vibrated through the space, as though the walls themselves were alive. The shelves were impossibly tall, each one crammed with books of every size and color. Some had spines etched with gold, while others were plain and **unassuming**. A single word hung **suspended** in the air above the entrance: "Bibliotheca Animae"—The Library of Souls.

Elliot wandered deeper into the maze, his footsteps muffled by the thick carpet that lined the floor. Each book he passed seemed to call to him, their spines almost vibrating with unspoken secrets. Yet, it wasn't until he reached the center of the library that he found the book that would change everything. It sat alone on a pedestal, its cover a deep, iridescent blue that seemed to shimmer under the dim light.

He hesitated before picking it up. There was no title, no

author's name, only a faint imprint on the cover: a small, **intricate** spiral. Something about it felt both familiar and foreign, as though the book had been waiting for him. When he finally opened it, his breath caught in his throat.

The first page bore his name in elegant, looping script: Elliot Greene.

Confused, he flipped to the next page, and the next, skimming through passages that **chronicled** moments from his own life with **unnerving** accuracy. There were memories he recognized —his first day of school, the time he broke his arm falling from a tree—but there were also details he didn't recall, conversations he hadn't had, choices he hadn't made. As he read on, the events became increasingly unfamiliar, the narrative shifting from his past to his future.

His hands trembled as he read a passage that described an argument with his best friend, Clara, an argument that hadn't yet happened. It was vivid, the words capturing every nuance of their voices, every flicker of emotion. Elliot's stomach churned. How could this book know things that hadn't occurred?

"Careful with that one," came a voice from behind him.

Elliot spun around to see an elderly librarian watching him from the shadows. Her eyes were sharp and **piercing**, a stark contrast to her frail frame. She held a feather duster in one hand, though the shelves around her were impeccably clean.

"What is this place?" he asked, his voice barely above a whisper.

"This," she said, gesturing around them, "is the Library of Souls. Every book here contains the story of a life—a beginning, a middle, and, for most, an end."

Elliot's heart pounded. "But this… this is my life."

The librarian's gaze softened. "Yes. Each soul has a book here.

But it's rare for someone to find their own."

"Why?" he demanded. "Why me?"

She tilted her head, as though pondering the question herself. "Perhaps the library has a purpose for you. Or perhaps it's simply chance. But be warned: the more you read, the more your **destiny** will shift. The future is not fixed, but knowledge of it carries its own weight."

Elliot stared down at the book in his hands. It was heavier now, almost as though it had absorbed the gravity of her words. "What happens if I finish it?"

The librarian hesitated. "That depends on what you do with what you learn."

Without another word, she turned and disappeared into the rows of shelves, leaving Elliot alone with his thoughts and the book that seemed to breathe in his hands. He knew he should leave, should put the book back and walk away from whatever strange magic was at work here. But the pull was too strong. He needed to know.

He flipped forward to a chapter that described his life ten years from now. The prose painted a picture of a man he barely recognized—confident, ambitious, but distant from those he loved. He read about choices he hadn't yet made, mistakes that seemed inevitable, and a future that felt both exhilarating and terrifying. The more he read, the more the words seemed to shift, the details **morphing** as though they were reacting to him. When he reached a passage that described Clara walking out of his life for good, he slammed the book shut.

The hum of the library grew louder, almost accusatory, and Elliot realized with a jolt that the pedestal where he'd found the book was glowing faintly. He looked around, but the librarian was nowhere to be seen. The silence was **oppressive** now, the weight of the library pressing down on him.

He clutched the book tightly and left the central chamber, weaving his way back through the shelves. But as he moved, the layout seemed to change, the rows shifting and rearranging themselves. The harder he tried to find the exit, the more **labyrinthine** the library became.

Finally, he stopped, his chest heaving. "What do you want from me?" he shouted, his voice echoing off the walls.

The answer came not in words but in the book itself. It grew warm in his hands, its cover pulsing faintly. When he opened it again, the pages were blank except for a single line written in bold, glowing script: "Your **destiny** is not to be read. It is to be written."

Elliot's heart raced as he stared at the words. Slowly, the pages began to fill again, but this time, the text wasn't about him. It was about Clara—her hopes, her dreams, her struggles. It described moments he hadn't noticed, pain he hadn't understood, joy he hadn't shared. He realized with a pang of guilt how little he truly knew about the person he called his best friend.

When the writing stopped, the book fell silent in his hands. Elliot closed it gently, his mind churning. He understood now. The book wasn't just a window into his future; it was a mirror, reflecting the choices he had yet to make and the people he had yet to fully see. His **epiphany** came when he realized his **destiny** wasn't written in stone—it was a story still unfolding, and he was its **author**.

The library seemed to sense his **epiphany**. The hum softened, and the shelves aligned themselves, creating a clear path to the exit. As Elliot stepped into the alley, the door closed behind him, its **intricate** carvings still shifting, as though the library were watching him leave.

He held the book tightly as he walked home, the weight of it a reminder of the **possibility** that lay ahead. For the first time, he felt not fear but **possibility**. The future wasn't something to fear or avoid—it was something to shape, one word, one decision at a time.

And so, with the Library of Souls behind him and the world ahead, Elliot resolved to write his story anew.

Comprehension Questions:

1. **What is the significance of the Library of Souls, and why is Elliot's encounter with his own book unique?**
   The Library of Souls is a mystical place where every life is recorded in a book, chronicling its past, present, and future. Elliot's encounter is unique because it is rare for someone to find their own book, as it allows them to glimpse and potentially alter their destiny.
2. **How does reading his book change Elliot's perspective on his life and relationships?**
   Reading his book shows Elliot not only his potential future but also the consequences of his choices, particularly how they affect others like his best friend, Clara. It makes him realize the importance of understanding and valuing the people in his life, prompting him to take responsibility for shaping his destiny.

Vocabulary List (C2 Level):

1. **Labyrinth** - A complex and confusing network of paths or passages.
   The library was a labyrinth of towering shelves, stretching endlessly into the shadows.
2. **Threshold** - The point or level at which something

begins or changes.
The moment Elliot crossed the threshold, the air seemed to change.
3. **Intricate** - Very detailed or complicated.
The door was adorned with intricate carvings that seemed to shift when he wasn't looking.
4. **Unnerving** - Causing anxiety or discomfort.
The passages about his future were unnerving in their vivid accuracy.
5. **Reverie** - A state of being pleasantly lost in one's thoughts.
Elliot was lost in a reverie as he wandered deeper into the library.
6. **Chronicled** - Recorded in detail.
The book chronicled moments from Elliot's life with startling precision.
7. **Penchant** - A strong liking for something.
Elliot had a penchant for getting lost in the written word.
8. **Epiphany** - A sudden realization or insight.
Elliot's epiphany came when he understood that his destiny was not fixed but something he could shape.
9. **Morphing** - Changing or transforming gradually.
The details of the book's narrative kept morphing as though reacting to Elliot's thoughts.
10. **Hoard** - To collect and keep hidden or stored away.
The library seemed to hoard the secrets of every soul within its endless shelves.
11. **Oppressive** - Overwhelming or excessively burdensome.
The oppressive silence of the library grew heavier as Elliot tried to find his way out.
12. **Carvings** - Designs cut into a hard surface.
The intricate carvings on the door seemed to shift when Elliot wasn't looking.
13. **Unassuming** - Modest or not drawing attention.
Many books in the library had plain, unassuming covers,

hiding their profound secrets.

14. **Cosmic** - Relating to the universe or its vast, expansive nature.
    The library's purpose felt cosmic, transcending human understanding.
15. **Destiny** - The predetermined or inevitable course of events.
    The librarian warned Elliot that reading his book could alter his destiny.
16. **Suspended** - Temporarily stopped or hanging in balance.
    A single word hung suspended above the entrance: "Bibliotheca Animae."
17. **Unwavering** - Steady and resolute.
    Elliot's curiosity about the book was unwavering, despite his growing fear.
18. **Piercing** - Extremely sharp or intense.
    The librarian's piercing eyes seemed to see through Elliot's soul.
19. **Possibility** - A thing that may happen or be true.
    For the first time, Elliot saw the future as a realm of possibility rather than fear.
20. **Author** - Someone who creates or writes something.
    Elliot realized he was the author of his own destiny, with the power to shape his story.

ABOUT THE AUTHOR

Elizabeth Snow

Elizabeth Snow transforms English language learning into an enjoyable and engaging journey by seamlessly blending your passions with practical language skills. Her unique approach integrates hobbies and English learning, allowing you to pursue your interests while building your language abilities. Whether you're passionate about cooking, gardening, or gaming, Elizabeth's books provide tailored lessons that feel like a natural extension of what you already love. Each book is thoughtfully designed to improve your English skills while keeping you entertained, making language learning an effortless and delightful part of your everyday routine.

Thank You and Congratulations!

Dear Reader,

Congratulations on completing *Master Advanced English with Engaging Tales: Expand Vocabulary, Enhance Comprehension, and Sharpen Your Skills*! Your commitment to advancing your English proficiency is truly commendable. Each page you've read, every new word you've learned, and every skill you've sharpened is a step toward achieving mastery—and I couldn't be prouder of your progress.

Learning a language is a journey, and you've proven that it's one worth taking. I hope this book has not only enriched your vocabulary and comprehension but also entertained and inspired you along the way.

If you enjoyed this book, found it helpful, or have thoughts to share, I'd be deeply grateful if you could leave a review. Your feedback not only helps me improve but also guides other learners in discovering the value of this book.

Thank you for choosing to embark on this journey with me. Keep learning, growing, and reaching new heights in your English mastery. The world of language and storytelling is vast, and your adventure has just begun!

Warm regards,
Elizabeth Snow

Made in the USA
Monee, IL
07 March 2025